THE
BONSAI
WORKSHOP

Herb L. Gustafson

 Sterling Publishing Co., Inc. New York

Library of Congress Cataloging-in-Publication Data

Gustafson, Herb L.
    The bonsai workshop / by Herb L. Gustafson ; photography by the author ; drawings by Sally A. Markos.
       p.   cm.
    Includes bibliographical references (p.   ) and index.
    ISBN 0-8069-0556-5
    1. Bonsai. 2. Bonsai—Pictorial works. I. Title.
    SB433.5.G87   1994
    635.9'772—dc20   93–43460
                                                CIP

Book Design by Judy Morgan
Edited by R.P. Neumann

10 9 8 7 6 5 4 3 2 1

Published by Sterling Publishing Company, Inc.
387 Park Avenue South, New York, N.Y. 10016
© 1994 by Herb L. Gustafson
Distributed in Canada by Sterling Publishing
℅ Canadian Manda Group, P.O. Box 920, Station U
Toronto, Ontario, Canada M8Z 5P9
Distributed in Great Britain and Europe by Cassell PLC
Villiers House, 41/47 Strand, London WC2N 5JE, England
Distributed in Australia by Capricorn Link (Australia) Pty Ltd.
P.O. Box 6651, Baulkham Hills, Business Centre, NSW 2153, Australia
Printed in Hong Kong
All rights reserved

Sterling ISBN 0-8069-0556-5

Acknowledgments

This book is dedicated to my wife, Susan Y. Gustafson. Not only did she provide the initial stimulus necessary for me to embark on a work of this magnitude, but without her continued support with the manuscript, this project would not have been possible.

Special thanks to my friends and professional colleagues: Percy Hampton, Ray and Myra Willard, J. Branson Smith, Laksar Geer, Diane Lund, and Bob Boltzer.

It is my sincere wish to recognize my professors and mentors: John Naka, Saburo Kato, Tom Yamamoto, Tai Ichi Katayama, Toshio Saburomaru, Toshio Kawamoto, Kenji Murata, Zeko Nakamura, and Wu Yee-Sun.

I appreciate the use of Jim Payne's root-over-rock trident maple for illustrating that style. With that one exception, all bonsai shown are from the author's collection. All of the photographs were taken by the author. Thanks go out to Prof. Kathy Hoy for her brush paintings which adorn Chapter Two. The wonderful drawings were rendered by Sally A. Markos from crude illustrations that I used in a workshop manual for my students at Lane Community College in Eugene, Oregon. The input I received from the Fall Term 1992 advanced class contributed greatly to the success of this manuscript. Thank you for your support of this project.

Finally, a very special thank-you to my father for all the support he has given me in spite of myself. It has not gone unnoticed or unappreciated. Thanks.

Contents

Preface

Many people have told me, "I have read several books on bonsai, yet I feel that I still don't have the necessary skills to create bonsai. I'm just not confident that once I purchase a bonsai, I can keep it alive!" I designed this book with the beginner to intermediate bonsai enthusiast in mind. I attempt to outline, in a clear and understandable format, some of the rudiments of the care, creation, and display of trees in miniature.

Most of the currently available books and magazines cover a particular aspect of bonsai training in great detail—only to lose relevancy because some particular species is not readily available in the reader's local area. Some literature is so bound by the correct "rule" for good bonsai that many beginners are simply intimidated from attempting to prune an ungainly gathered spruce or pine.

The recent burgeoning interest in bonsai in the Western world has encouraged the genesis of fairly radical design ideals as compared to the traditional Japanese approach that is so often read about in the existing bonsai literature. I particularly try to address these new ideas in this book.

Japanese literature, to be fair, loses much in translation to the English. Nothing is quite as pure as the Japanese language describing its nature, its seasons, or its art; however, I believe the untrained bonsai beginner could use just a bit more detail and guidance in the early stages. Weather differences from Japan to other parts of the world, in particular the West, significantly alter the choices of plant material for creating a bonsai. Basic bonsai care changes considerably throughout the four seasons and regional advice is necessary.

I think it is crucial to instill in the beginner the importance of just learning how to keep a tree alive. Just like other art forms, it is imperative that the artist first learn how to observe, "mix paints," "do rough sketches," experiment, and fail a few times; then, finally, savor the satisfaction of their first "still life" or pastoral scene.

Through the past 30 years of working with bonsai, I have found that most beginners have similar questions. There are probably only about 100 basic questions. This book is intended to answer those questions and to enable the bonsai student to firmly grasp the basics of bonsai culture. Once the horticulture of bonsai is understood, the mind is freed up to concentrate on the finer aspects of this unique hobby—that of original design and creation.

Unfortunately, to most Western ears the word *Banzai* from World War II and the word *Bonsai* are so similar that they get pronounced the same more often than not. I believe it is the premier task of the beginning student to note that these two words have different meanings and pronunciations. The "o" in *bon* sounds like "bone" and the "s" in *sai* sounds like "sigh." And further, as a favor to all bonsai lovers, bring the correct pronunciation to the attention of friends and acquaintances.

Herb L. Gustafson

1

BONSAI DEFINED

THE WORD BONSAI IS MADE UP OF TWO JAPA-nese characters or word phrases, *bon* and *sai*. The "bon" is the pot, tray, or container, and the "sai" is the tree, shrub, or planting. Various literal translations might be "tray tree," "potted planting," or the like. Note that these translations make no reference to aspects normally attributed to bonsai. There is no mention of size, species, or environment, for example. The word bonsai could equally apply to indoor and outdoor plants. Bonsai defined in this way allows the free use of annuals, perennials, bulbs, tubers, vegetables, mosses, grains, etc. The dwarfing properties of the container itself apply to all living plants.

The original word *bonsai* comes from the Chinese word *P'en Tsai*. It sounds similar to bonsai and has nearly the same meaning.

THE ART OF BONSAI

Trees have their good and their bad qualities, characteristics, or tendencies. I like to think of bonsai material as bonsai in the "rough." Rarely does the artist "add" to a tree. Rather, by selectively pruning and moving branches around with wire, the tree is actually simplified. The artist reduces the unpleasant aspects and enhances finer qualities. Japanese visual art epitomizes the desire to reduce an artistic statement to the least number of elements necessary. With this way of seeing, if the strongest statement in a painting is the wren balancing on a wisteria branch, then why clutter the picture with all kinds of garden background? Similarly, if a landscape can be uncluttered and reduced to its strongest element, that remaining element is even further enhanced.

I believe that the ultimate challenge for the bonsai designer is to expose the essence of the tree. A few well-placed branches express to the viewer the mountain cliff, seashore, canyon, desert, or deep woods landscape. The tree conveys its environment—its sun, wind, rain, and soil. More obvious, it will indicate the seasons.

The art of bonsai is telling a story through living illusion. The two trees in **1–1 and 1–2** are the same height; however, it is instantly obvious that if you shaped your bonsai like the one in **1–2**, it would "look" older, and in a pot it would, therefore, look taller.

When someone asks you how old your bonsai is, try to find out how old the viewer thinks it is first. If they guess too high, it is a good indication that you are successful in

1–1

1–2

your illusion. Actually, it is not polite to ask the age of a bonsai.

One difficult aspect of bonsai is the development of style. I have found it easier at first to copy known successful designs because of their three important points. As a general rule of thumb, these are represented by the three points of a scalene triangle—a three-sided figure which has no two sides of equal length (see **1–3**). Examine these three points carefully on your new design. They should be obvious to the viewer.

1–3

Perhaps the most difficult aspect of practising bonsai is trying to develop aesthetic judgment. I suggest to those who find themselves struggling in trying to shape an unruly tree to try a couple of helpful shortcuts. First, draw your bonsai material in pencil. Make sure that all major branches are represented and are reasonably in proportion to the rest of the drawing. Then, you can "prune" your tree—with an eraser.

You will also notice right away that you have been forced to find the front of the tree and are now treating your bonsai as a two-dimensional subject. Always try to improve your tree. Remove inconsistencies and unnecessary clutter. Bring out the essence.

Certainly, good bonsai art is not random. We do not abuse our trees in order to achieve ruggedness. I believe that good art should reflect its environment. Dead wood remaining on a bonsai should not look as though it

needs to be pruned off. Exposed roots should not look careless.

The artist strives to find avenues for personal expression within the confines of good horticultural practice. Bonsai exists because it is a pleasant mix of form, thought, and suggestion in a miniature world, and like all good art, it endures.

THE HORTICULTURE OF BONSAI

Bonsai, above all, are living plants and need proper care for survival. Even if the style you have chosen suggests a barren, windswept ravine, you do not need to grow it under those conditions! Keep your bonsai healthy and alive, or you will have defeated the whole purpose of the art.

Let's compare the naturally dwarfed tree and its habitat with an uninhibited full-size tree; then we can make some suggestions on how to use this natural dwarfing phenomenon to our best advantage.

1. Air. In air are the essential gases for respiratory exchange. Air movement is simply wind. Trees grow smaller in windy areas because air movement removes moisture, and only a smaller, more compact plant can manage to conserve moisture. Close to the ground an air current finds it much more difficult to move because of its own turbulence. Plants in windy areas take advantage of this "friction" phenomenon and hug close to the surface. Each year, the plant will send out tentative new growth in all directions into the wind. If the air is too dehydrating, these new shoots do not survive, but are simply pruned back by nature. The plant will supply energy to its inner successful shoots and will form new buds closer to the ground.

Plants that cascade close to vertical rock walls are subject to this same stress. By keeping your bonsai pinched back and trimmed well each year, particularly in spring, you can achieve windswept results without wind—and also without large amounts of pruning which might leave scars.

The windswept tree's branches are not actually bent by the wind, as it may appear. Over time those new buds that face the wind, or which project out into the strong wind currents, die. The successful buds out of the wind eventually make up the large branches (see **1–4**).

The passage of air over a plant has some beneficial effects as well. Improved circulation reduces the

1–4

chances of fungus, rot, and mildew. For this reason, it is good horticultural practice to water bonsai on a slightly windy day. Excess moisture is removed quickly, avoiding damage that can result from dampness. In addition, dead wood left intentionally on the tree will hold its beautiful silver color instead of rotting away.

2. Water. Trees in nature that have to struggle for water are considerably more dwarfed than the same varieties of trees next to a stream or spring. In drought conditions, it is simply impossible for a tree to become large and expose all that surface area to the sun. In response to this extreme dehydration, it can only survive as a small and compact tree. The tree's efforts to grow up and out simply die from dehydration.

Restricting water on bonsai is an effective way to reduce the size of its general outline. Smaller leaves result, and the distances between leaves, or internodes, become shorter, thereby giving the tree an attractive lacy appearance. This effect is particularly desirable on deciduous trees as displayed in winter. On evergreens, shortening the internodes allows more branches to form along the trunk line.

Water carries nutrients. On bonsai that do not get much water, nutrition is also reduced, and, therefore, growth is restricted. The large drain holes in the bottom of bonsai pots help dwarf the tree because any excess moisture is quickly removed. Air is sucked down from the soil surface as it follows water through the soil. Excess moisture under the pot quickly evaporates due to the raised legs on the pot.

3. Soil. Stunted trees in nature are commonly found growing in coarse, decomposed rock inside a rock crevice. Bonsai, similarly, can duplicate this condition by using a coarse, well-drained soil that contains mostly inorganic particles. Also, the bonsai pot restrains the roots just as the rock crevice does in nature. Every year the freezing and thawing of the rocks around the moist tree create more naturally decomposed rock for the roots to grow in. Bonsai, similarly, should be allowed to feel as much of the seasonal heat and cold as they can stand and still survive. A bonsai grower has to learn how to keep a tree somewhat pot-bound, but not to the detriment of the health of the bonsai.

With careful attention to particle size in your soil, you can essentially recreate the conditions that are present in a mountain rock crevice. In preparing the soil, all very small particles, such as dust and silt, are discarded. They are useless to the plant because particles that small will clog the soil and not allow good air circulation. (Refer to the discussion of soils in Chapter 5 on potting.) High amounts of organic material are appropriate for potting plants that thrive on organic matter on the forest floor, such as the rhododendron. But growing a juniper in that much rotted humus is unhealthy. High desert plants are adapted to highly inorganic soils. This type of soil provides proper drainage, minerals, and pH for these specialized plants.

4. Sun. Ultraviolet light dwarfs leaves. Plants that grow in a great deal of sun have greatly reduced leaf size. The cactus will only expose a few leaves to the sun during its spurt of growth when water is readily available. High desert plants tend to have small leaves. Rain forests have luxurious growth and favor plants with large leaves. The natural occurrence of small-leafed and broadleafed plants also relates to regional amounts of rainfall, but two identical azaleas, planted in the yard under different light conditions, will exhibit a variance in leaf size immediately on their new growth.

Bonsai grown in as much sun as they can stand will dwarf better than if grown under low light. Be aware of the individual plant's needs, and give it almost too much light. The key word here is "almost." Too much light and the plant will sunburn, dry up, and be damaged.

6. Nutrients. Visualize the bristlecone pine growing on its rocky precipice. From where does it get nutrients? What little it receives is from various sources, such as nitrogen-fixing bacteria in the soil, or the fungal mycorrhizae attached to its roots, or possibly an occasional bird dropping. Residue from the pine itself, mixed with other decaying organic material from adjacent plants, can provide some nutrients. In any case, nutrients are few and far between. Imagine now, your bonsai on such a restricted diet. Growth would be almost slowed down to a standstill. New buds, when they do appear, are small and carefully located along selected compact branches. Needles are smaller, lighter in color, and, again, the internodes would be compact. Fertilizers should be applied to bonsai only in small balanced amounts at regular intervals to promote the dwarfed growth we desire rather than the large, lush growth that looks out of character on a windswept pine.

6. Cold. All plants grow healthiest when subject to their native light/dark and hot/cold seasonal cycles. If a bonsai is not allowed to get cold in the winter, the spring growth will be weak. Most bonsai seem to thrive from being exposed to near-freezing weather for a few days. Make sure that the pot is not too wet or it might crack. If you place the bonsai in the ground and cover the pot under a light layer of natural mulch, it will be fine.

7. Altitude. Trees near the timberline are among the most spectacular naturally dwarfed plants. The thinner air and ultraviolet light contribute to the dwarfing process. Temperature extremes from day to day are more pronounced in this setting. Do not pamper your bonsai. Within the context of good horticultural practice, give your bonsai as much natural fluctuation as it can tolerate and still remain healthy.

Toughen up your trees. Restrict water. Give them exercise by gently moving the branches around with your hands. This toughens up the bark, gives character to the limbs, and increases their girth to assist the illusion of age. Give your plants all they need to stay healthy—but not to excess—or your bonsai may take on the appearance of a spoiled, greenhouse tropical plant.

THE BONSAI GROWER'S COMMITMENT

Most beginners, or students, share the same fear: they are afraid of killing their bonsai. A wise old master once told me, "You have to prune a lot, you have to pot a lot, you have to water a lot, you have to kill a lot." I like to think that the killing part is perhaps optional with good training, but the point is well taken. The hard part is in being able to control the degree of stress that a plant will take and still remain healthy. The word "stress" is used

not in a psychological sense, but in reference to the horticultural practice of just knowing how much is too much and how much is too little. The same principle applies to all aspects of bonsai culture: water, air, soil, pot, pruning, etc. The commitment is, then, the willingness to learn, to experiment, and most of all, to accept the results of these efforts.

Another commitment is time. The student must understand that the growth process takes time. There are no shortcuts. Thinking in terms of a growing year is the usual yardstick by which success is measured. When you wire a branch, it is with the understanding that the wire will come off within a year. When that year has nearly passed and you find yourself taking off the wire, you will or should experience a deep sense of satisfaction. In essence, you both have one more annual ring.

It is all too easy to forget these important reflections as you work on your trees. Time: there is no replacement; it is always forward and constant. Use it to your advantage. I believe that the quality of the time spent on everyday tasks at home or at work pales by comparison to that spent with your trees. Study bonsai and you will learn more than bonsai.

MATERIALS NEEDED

A Plant. Take your time when selecting what you would like to work on, and pay close attention to the needs of the plant. Is your specimen an indoor or outdoor plant? Does it grow best in shade or full sun? How large is the plant? Familiarize yourself with the natural characteristics of the plant before attempting to dwarf it. Keep in mind that the foliage will only dwarf to a certain degree (see **1–5**).

1–5

1–6

Wire Cutter. Proper bonsai wire cutters have the cutting location at the very tip of the tool (see **1–8**). Avoid types of pliers that have a notch next to the hinge or swivel point designed for cutting wire.

It is very important that wire be removed from the branch by cutting it off, thus the need for cutting at the tip of the tool. Do not unwind it! You are in danger of stripping the bark and killing or permanently injuring the branch or trunk being wired. Make sure that your wire cutter is sufficiently strong to handle 4, 6, and 8 gauge wire.

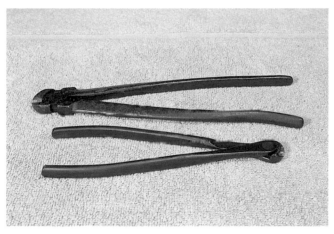

1–8

A Pot. Remember that the *bon* in bonsai is the pot or container. Half of your bonsai presentation is the pot. It should balance the tree, look esthetically pleasing and horticulturally acceptable (see **1–6**).

Wire. The best wire is soft copper wire; it has the most desirable qualities. Copper, when heated to a cherry-red color, then quenched quickly in water, becomes soft and pliable, perfect for forming around tender and sensitive tree branches (see **1–7**). Contrast this with iron, for example, or a number of other metals. The heating and quenching process that softens copper actually does the reverse for most other metals. After placement, copper wire will harden over time—gently but firmly—holding branches in the desired position. The thickness of the branch determines the thickness of the wire that is appropriate to use.

Soil. The beginner must above all thoroughly understand soil (see **1–9**). See Chapter 5 for details on how to prepare bonsai soil. With good soil it is hard to overwater or underwater your tree. The soil provides the plant with the ability to resist disease. Good soil protects against winter die back and a host of other problems. Your long-term success depends on your soil and your understanding of soils.

1–7

1–9

Books. I encourage the beginner always to advance his or her knowledge of the subject. So many times I am asked what may seem to be the simplest of questions about bonsai, and I resist the urge to respond with "How much time do you have?" My intention is to stimulate the beginner's interest so that the student seeks out other authors and learns from other sources such as meetings, shows, clubs, and conventions. One of the greatest joys of learning as an adult is embracing the concept that increasing your knowledge of the subject in the face of so much to learn should be pleasurable.

Work Space. My early bonsai experiences come to mind whenever I think of this topic. I was getting mud all over the kitchen table, tracking it into the house on my shoes, using tools from the garage, and leaving them dull, dirty, and rusty. My bedroom had pots all lined up on the windowsill, and, therefore, there were water stains down the front of the panelling below. It wasn't until I took lessons in Japan that I realized the importance of a work space. Studying in Japan I felt honored to use the stool I was given to sit on. I had a large turntable in front of me. Drawers full of tools, bins full of rocks, and containers of prescreened bonsai soil complete with scoops were set out ready and waiting. Wire on large spools was within easy reach—wire of all sizes! What an experience!

Back to reality at home, I realized that I had been making it inconvenient to be creative. I highly recommend having a small area dedicated just to bonsai and organizing your tools into a box or drawer.

Turntable. Nothing is quite as frustrating as trying to prune, wire, or assemble a bonsai without benefit of a turntable. Bonsai are three-dimensional sculptures that must be worked on from front to back and both sides, and then from the front again (see **1–10**). Commercially

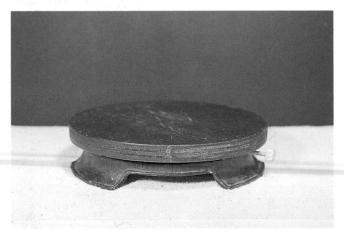

1–10

made Japanese turntable are available from most bonsai nurseries. Turntables are also fairly easy to make in the woodshop for those who care to create their own design. Perhaps least expensive is a plastic tray designed for storage purposes in a kitchen cabinet. I have come across other devices that work reasonably well, including the ever popular lazy Susan-type of hors d'oeuvre tray and an old-fashioned piano stool.

1–11

Wedges. Visualizing a new position for a tree usually requires the viewer to step back a bit from the work and take some time looking at the new angle. Three wooden wedges of the size shown in **1–11** are inexpensive and useful tools that will never wear out and will be used practically every time you prune, pot, or repot. I recommend three, because you can use them to obtain a tripod effect for a pot or rock that needs to be raised.

Chopsticks. For potting purposes, a chopstick driven into fresh bonsai soil is wiggled about with a simultaneous thrusting and vibrating motion. The vibrations and pushing motions of the chopsticks help eliminate air pockets in the soil during potting or repotting. Any similarly shaped device will work; fingers are too clumsy for this.

Root Hook. A useful commercially available tool, the root hook is an inexpensive purchase you will use countless times (see **1–12**). You can make one, if you are so inclined, from a large bent spike or oversized nail embedded in a wooden handle. This tool assists during potting and repotting by combing out tough and entangled roots for pruning. It also loosens tough clay deposits found in the roots of field-grown nursery stock.

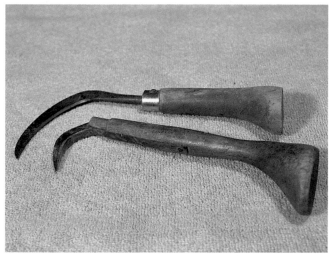

1–12

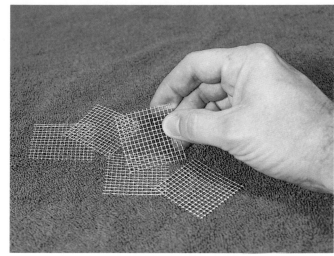

1–14

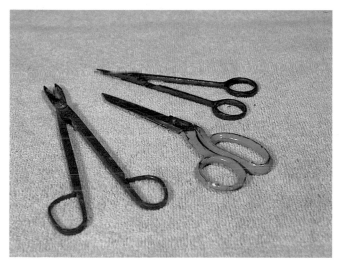

1–13

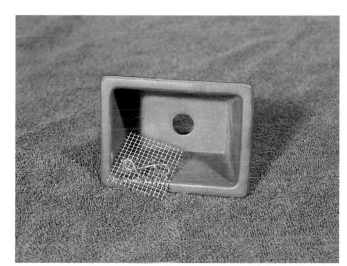

1–15

Scissors. Simple, everyday, multipurpose scissors are useful for cutting string, twine, nylon thread, fishing line, and identification tags (see **1–13**). Keep them handy.

Screen. Since bonsai soil is prescreened to discard all particles smaller than one-sixteenth of an inch, ordinary window screen is a perfect cover for the drain holes of your bonsai pot (see **1–14**). I recommend cutting a small square about one inch larger than the drainage hole you are covering. Place this square over the top of the hole, and secure it by making a small staple from copper wire as shown in **1–15 and 1–16**. Metal or plastic screen seem to be better than fibreglass. Steel or iron screens are not my first choices, but they are acceptable since they still support the soil and keep out pests until the need to repot.

1–16

1–17

Screen Cutter. Never cut screen material with your scissors or bonsai trimmers; they will be ruined. Instead, an old pair of scissors, sheet metal shears, or poultry (kitchen) shears are more suitable (see **1–17**). Screen squares can be cut out and kept with your bonsai tools—then they will be readily available for potting.

Gloves. Many people are not fully aware which plants they are allergic to; some may find the pricking of a pine needle tip quite irritating, whereas others may develop a rash from handling juniper. Take whatever precautions are necessary to enjoy working on bonsai (see **1–18**). For those who cannot stand working with gloves, a bit of moisturizer or other hand cream offers some protection. It also facilitates the removal of pitch from your hands after working.

1–18

Apron. Some soils, wound sealers, and plant residues will stain clothing. I also find it convenient to use an apron pocket for holding frequently used tools.

Wound Sealers. The best wound sealer is one that is mixed in advance of pruning. It is simple to prepare your own. Find some clay or mud and mix it with shoe polish of an appropriate color to match the color of the

bark. Wounds treated in this manner have some protection from insects and disease and look inconspicuous as well.

Saws. There are any number of pruning saws available at garden centers. There are also saws specifically designed for bonsai use. Bonsai saws have small, narrow blades that cut on the pull stroke (see **1–19**). Cutting with a pruning saw that has teeth that cut only on the push stroke can be dangerous to the tree and to the person doing the sawing.

1–19

1–20

Pliers. A common set of pliers has a number of uses pertaining to bonsai (see **1–20**). I recommend needle-nosed pliers for bending and manipulating wire, blunt-nosed pliers for stripping bark, and adjustable channel lock or vise-grips for bending and shaping large dead branches.

Tamping Trowel. This is a useful, although not required, tool for tamping down loose soil after transplanting. I don't know of any gardening trowel that is small enough for bonsai work other than a Japanese bonsai trowel, although a palette knife makes an adequate substitute.

Soil Scoops. The traditional Japanese soil scoop is shaped nicely at the tip so that bonsai soil is not crushed as it is picked up out of the storage bin. It is also delivered to the exact spot where soil is needed. One of the nicest features, however, is that the spoon or storage part of the scoop is missing its floor and is replaced by screen (see **1–21**). As soil is moved from storage to pot by the scoop, the soil can be screened once more.

Brushes. The fingers are also too clumsy for finishing the soil surface after potting or repotting. A large artist's brush or a small trim brush about one inch wide really does the trick (see **1–22**). The brush contours the surface, removes excess soil from exposed roots, wipes away debris from rocks and moss, and cleans the rim of the pot. Smaller brushes, such as small artist's brushes (see **1–23**), become useful applicators for lime sulfur on driftwood areas or to apply alcohol or detergents to scale and sucking insects of all kinds. The entire tree does not have to be sprayed everytime a pest is discovered. Merely remove it, or treat the infected areas directly.

Tweezers. Another handy bug snatcher, a tweezer will fit into crevices where fingers can't go (see **1–24**). Use them for weeding or to remove unsightly liverwort or bracket fungus. I like to use them with a small cotton ball full of insecticide to deliver a dose of pesticide to scale insects.

Can Cutter. With the advent of plastic nursery containers, can cutters have become an almost prehistoric instrument, but occasionally . . .

Oil. Use a quality tool oil on your tools after cleaning and after sharpening (see **1–25**). Tools will last a lifetime with proper care. In addition, clear mineral oil will suffocate most soft-bodied insects and even some tougher ones, too. Also, cleaning your pots with clear mineral oil will remove mineral salts and polish the pots for show.

Epoxy. Various forms of glue and paste are useful for bonsai as sealers or to repair bark. Epoxy, although inconvenient to mix, still seems to have more practical applications for bonsai than all the others. Use it to repair pots and tools, secure rocks and wire, mend broken branches, fasten string to a rock, or a myriad other uses.

Lead Sinkers. Attach a large fishing sinker to the end of a branch for a weeping appearance. Smaller, round weights, sometimes known as split shot, are great for securing wire or string to rocks. Simply thread string, wire, or fishing line through the sinker, and squeeze the weight closed. Then hammer the lead weight into a rock crevice and the wire or line will be held firmly in place.

1–21

1–22

1–23

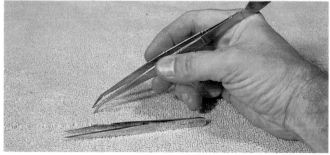

1–24

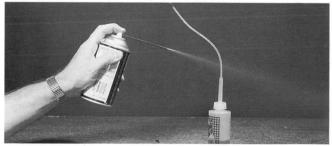

1–25

2

THE HISTORY OF BONSAI

ANYTHING MORE THAN THE BRIEFEST IN-
troduction to the history of bonsai I feel would be inappropriate for the beginning bonsai enthusiast. I review
some of the important historical milestones and refer
the beginner to three other sources which can satisfy an
interest in further study. My focus in this book is to
address the practical problems and frustrations encountered by beginning students, but I encourage you
to consult other books and available literature on any
question or area of interest. Specifically for the history
of bonsai, I refer you to the venerable *Man Lung Artistic
Pot Plants* by Wu Yee-Sun, a pioneer work on Chinese
P'en Tsai; second, *Bonsai, Its Art, Science, History and
Philosophy* by Deborah Koreshoff; third, *The History of
Bonsai* by Kawasumi Masakuni, which appears in the
issues of "Bonsai International Magazine."

The First Bonsai. When was bonsai first discovered?
Bonsai cultivation probably is a natural extension of a
general knowledge of potted plant material. I think it
has been invented many times. As a nine-year-old boy,
being poor at athletics I took an interest in the wildflowers in the outfield of the playground. There were
purple ones, white bell-like ones, and some that seemed
edible. I carefully dug up some of the best ones and
potted them in acorn shells, thimbles, walnut husks, and
small containers I found around the house. Soon I had a
collection of perennial miniatures and some fungus on
my windowsill. I discovered through trial and error how
to pot, transplant, water, fertilize, prune, and care for
these small potted plants. I had begun to shape and
control their growth. Successive generations by my efforts were becoming dwarfed—leaves, flowers, seeds,
nuts, and berries. It wasn't until a few years later that a
friend gave me my first bonsai book. I devoured every
bit of information from that book, but mostly it seemed
odd to me that other people had been doing for centuries what I had generated spontaneously. So you can
understand why I suspect that the "first bonsai" has
been invented many times in many different places.
Here are a few historical examples of what I mean.

Egypt. On the walls of ancient tombs dating back
4000 years, there are excellently preserved carvings
and paintings of potted plants, both indoor and outdoor. The question is, did anyone from this period in
Egypt or surrounding countries ever shape a tree for
artistic purposes? Probably, if not certainly. Did anyone
in the same period of time notice that the pot tended to
keep the tree small? Well, I would hope so.

India. Physicians of ancient India (circa 1000 B.C.)
depended on potted trees for fresh sources of naturally

occurring medicinal herbs and extracts. The ancient
Hindu doctors found it necessary to keep these trees
small (dwarf them) for ease of transporting door to
door. Did anyone from this area of the world, eastern
Europe to Mongolia and south to the Indian Ocean,
ever prune off leaves and branches to maintain a natural tree shape? Probably. Did anyone ever cultivate
these dwarf trees for the purpose of display? Apparently so. These trees were displayed, it is thought, as a
symbol of office, as prominently as a barber's pole.

China. By the year 200 A.D., established styles of
dwarf trees were associated with all the major cantons
or provinces of China. They had colorful names such as
the "Earthworm" style of Szechuan, the "Dancing
Dragon" style of Anhwe, and the "Three Winding" style
of the North. As mentioned in Chapter 1, the Chinese
word for artistic potted plant is *P'en Tsai*, meaning pot
and planting, respectively. There is evidence that *P'en
Tsai* was already well developed before 2000 B.C. It was
certainly a precursor to modern bonsai.

Japan. In all fairness to Japan, the art of bonsai has flourished there as it has in no other country. Bonsai appeared in Japan circa 1300 A.D., and appealed to many cultural and artistic characteristics of the Japanese. Japanese art has historically been saturated with symbolism and cultural significance. All Japan's art forms are methodically reduced to their essence for clarification and study. Landscape paintings contain just a few well-placed brush strokes, poetry flourished as the diminutive Haiku, and flower arrangers worked to accomplish simplicity. Japan has contributed more to bonsai than all other sources combined. From Japan we get our present-day styles, tools, pots, horticultural knowledge, inspiration, and standards of excellence.

Europe. The first major bonsai exhibition in Europe was at the Paris World Fair Exposition in 1889, the same year as the building of the Eiffel Tower. In 1909, a large bonsai collection went on display in London. In both cases, however, the bonsai failed to thrive under the care of Westerners. Rumors started of "Japanese magic" and "Oriental secrets" necessary for bonsai to survive outside Japan.

United States. There are bonsai nurseries in most major cities. The import market for bonsai-related products is strong. There are thousands of clubs, associations, and societies in all 50 states. Continuing education courses on bonsai are common. Shops in malls sell bonsai pots, and every bookstore carries a half dozen bonsai books and is willing to take special orders for other titles. The latter half of the twentieth century has seen bonsai steadily increasing in popularity in the United States and throughout the world.

Who invented bonsai? Certainly the Japanese refined and perfected the art as only they could. But if whoever invented the first bonsai had not, someone else would have and probably did. It is not hard to imagine many individuals discovering the dwarfing of trees in many times and many places, whether a plant tender in Egypt, a Hindu doctor in India, a gardener in ancient China, a fourteenth-century Buddhist monk in Japan, or an athletically inept nine-year-old boy in the United States in the twentieth century.

Cascading alpine fir.

Elevated shelf that provides summer display of plants and, when covered with clear plastic sheeting, serves as winter protection.

Bunjin-*style alpine fir.*

Landscape created with three rhodo-dendrons, Satsuki azaleas, rocks, gravel, and moss.

Windswept, driftwood-style Juniper Shimpaku.

Trident maple in its fall color.

Slanting and weeping style cypress in a drum pot.

The deciduous rhododendron "Pioneer" in its fall color.

Fall color of Acer campestre.

Broom-style English oak, Quercus robur, *just starting to show its fall color.*

3
STYLES

I HAVE SEEN BONSAI STUDENTS FACING THEIR first tree with the same blank expression that I must have had when with great anticipation I enrolled some years ago in a college painting course, buying all of the best equipment, only to find my ideas evaporate as I faced my first white, and very blank, canvas. Similarly, the bonsai students have assembled, all around them, the tools and equipment necessary for success, yet everything remains at a standstill. This is when the student has a fine opportunity to apply rules. Rules for proceeding—rules to help the student get from the tenuous stage into the activity of inspiration.

RULES—WHERE THEY COME FROM

Rules help to simplify tasks, breaking them into digestible pieces. Rules help the beginner and advanced student alike. They come from the masters. When old and established bonsai are scrutinized carefully, many common measurements, proportions, and relationships can be observed. For example, let's study the relationship between the height of the pot and the diameter of the trunk. Measurements taken from these masterpieces of bonsai reveal that the height of the pot averages 1.28 times the diameter of the trunk at its widest point. What does this mean? With this "rule" as a guide, the student has information on which to base the choice of a pot as opposed to having no idea whatsoever of what to buy.

In the experience with my blank canvas recounted above, I was helped out of my difficulty by the "rules" of visualization—the concept that ideas could be projected from the mind onto the canvas much as a slide projector might. The rough outline could be quickly sketched in with a pencil. I could then use these bold shapes as references for filling in, shaping, changing, and highlighting the remaining details. Bonsai benefits from a similar process of visualization; the larger, more important aspects of style are roughed in first, then the finer aspects of detail and finishing complete the design.

Discard the rules when you feel confident that they no longer serve you. Go back to relying on their insight when you are faced with design difficulties. Once you know the rules, then you can bend or break them when necessary. If the rule says a branch must be located at such and such a place and your tree, for instance, does not have a branch there, what do you do? You compensate. It is far better to know that a key design element is missing and compensate, than to have the feeling something is wrong yet not be able to put your finger on it.

One rule states that the Number Two branch should be on the opposite side of the trunk from the Number One branch. What if it isn't? You remember the rule, but the Number Two branch, perhaps, cannot be made to be opposite the Number One branch. You decide to compensate for this potential defect and convert a problem into a solution. How? Possibly you rotate the tree to reveal a little more of a back branch and slightly alter other branches to minimize visual gaps. Perhaps, you add a larger rock to draw the viewer's eye from the open space. The point is, you compensate for the defect by a number of subtle adjustments to create a satisfying and complete design. This is why I recommend learning the rules first, so that you can break them—with intelligence and confidence.

Here follows a list of instances when bending or breaking the rules is appropriate.

1. Horticultural Practice. Unusual shapes, rare varieties, extremely odd specimens, and group plantings do not favor strict adherence to classic bonsai rules. Many style changes have to be completed in steps. If a branch cannot be bent into the proper shape on the first day, don't despair. Take your time; the tree will appreciate the care and effort. Keep in mind the basic needs of the plant. Do you really want a cascading *arborvitae* . . . !? If so, plan on going through some intermediate steps along the way. How about a windswept wisteria? Driftwood-style African violets? Perhaps not.

2. Stage of Development. Most advanced hobbyists and professionals will pot only about 10 percent of their collection. They are assuming, unconsciously perhaps, that when potting time comes around, the trees that are chosen for the bonsai pot are about 90 percent complete. Please reread the foregoing sentence over many times to understand its significance.

Much of what happens to a bonsai in training does not conform to the rules of show. There is a whole new set of rules designed to accomplish maximum benefit during training, especially training in oversized pots and growing in the ground. For example, additional branches are allowed to remain below the Number One branch for the purpose of fattening the trunk. The owner knows these branches will be removed eventually as the design develops. Similarly, if you are growing from seed, there is no purpose in subjecting the first few sprouts to the rules of show. Training always takes into consideration the ultimate goal, but this goal may be five years and twenty pruning sessions away.

3. Trees That Refuse to Cooperate. Don't throw them away. Some very nice free-form trees are simply mavericks to the rules. Get a second or third opinion, and then go with your instincts. The shape, form, and texture of its branches may suggest an unusual landscape. The errant tree may do better as a two- or three-tree grouping—or, perhaps, an unusual pot will turn your strange tree into a real eye-catcher. Be bold and persevere.

4. When You Don't Feel Like Following Any Rules at All! Historically speaking, this honor was reserved for the masters. After dedicating a lifetime to following the rules, a wise old master was allowed to establish a personal style, a signature of sorts. Trees were trained to make a statement of individuality and heightened enlightenment. *Bunjinji* style was such a result. But if you are inclined, you won't be breaking the law; go ahead.

3–1

SINGLE PLANTING STYLES

Formal Upright—Chokkan

The beginner always learns the most on his or her first tree; so I think it is appropriate that this discussion of the first style, the formal upright, be the most complete and detailed. Many of these rules are equally applicable to all the other styles that follow.

The formal upright tree is characterized by its strong vertical trunk (see **3–1**). The trunk may be tall or short, but it never waves to and fro. This style is the calmest, most restful style because of the shape of the tree trunk. The top, or apex, is always found directly over the rootage, and the natural symmetry of the planting suggests a lack of wind, stress, and slope to the adjoining terrain. *Chokkan* represents the epitome of a grand old tree deep in the forest primeval.

This style, as is true with all styles, should be either taller than wide or wider than tall. A tree that is exactly as wide as it is tall, curiously enough, looks immature.

About one third of the way up the trunk, coming from one side, appears the Number One branch. This branch should point towards one front corner of the pot. The trunk is located in the pot so that the front edge of the trunk—at the base—is at the halfway point between the front and rear of the pot. The outside edge of the trunk is one third of the way from that same side of the pot.

If the trunk is planted to the left, the Number One branch points towards the right front corner of the pot.

If the tree is planted to the right, the Number One branch points towards the left front corner of the pot. When I mention "corner" of the pot, please remember that all pots will have this corner regardless of shape. It is actually the tree, itself, and where the first significant branch is located that determines where the tree is positioned in the pot.

Obviously, at this point you need to determine the front of the tree. This is established by three factors, and all three must be present in order to have a convincing front to your tree.

First, there must be a rootage spread, called a root buttress, at the base of the trunk (see **3–2**). Rootage provides visual stability for the trunk of the tree.

Second, there must be a Number One branch that points towards one of the front corners of the pot (see **3–3**).

Third, there must be an apex that is directly over the midline of the pot.

After locating the front of the tree, you can now locate the Number Two branch. This branch will be located a bit higher on the trunk and will point towards the opposite front corner of the pot.

The three most important points of your tree—the apex, the Number One branch tip, and the Number

3–2

3–3

have the largest number of branchlets, and be the lowest branch on the trunk. If the Number One branch is slightly curved, so must all other branches. This one branch determines the relative size and shape of all other branches, so choose it carefully. Do not select a weak or spindly branch or a branch almost as big as the trunk. Use the general rule of one third the size of the trunk for the best results.

3. The Number Two Branch Tip. This branch completes the foliage triangle. Visually check this triangle to see that all foliage is contained within this area. The Number Two branch tip points towards the opposite front corner of the pot from the Number One branch. The angle formed by the Number Two branch and the trunk is the same as the angle formed by the Number One branch. The Number Two branch should look like a slightly smaller version of the Number One branch. It should be smaller in diameter, length, width, foliage, branchlets, and general outline. It should come out of the trunk in the bottom third of the foliage triangle, and that junction should be clearly visible to the viewer. Thereafter, all other branches sprout from the trunk in a pinwheel fashion (see **3–4**).

Two branch tip—make up the foliage triangle described briefly in Chapter One. Let's review these points, because they are quite important.

1. The Apex. The apex is the tallest point on the tree. It must be visible, well developed, and well defined. There cannot be two or three competing possibilities. If so, let the pruning tool clearly favor one over the others. It is not necessary to see the trunk at the apex, since most foliage will obliterate the trunk in the top one third of the foliage triangle.

2. The Number One Branch Tip. This tip points towards one corner of the pot when viewed from above. Depending on the angle of the Number One Branch, this tip may be higher or lower than the bulk of the branch itself. In any case, the angle of the Number One branch to the trunk determines the angles of all the other branches on the tree.

The Number One branch is the thickest branch on the tree and the longest. It must contain the most foliage,

3–4

Please note that branches do not overlap each other, and that branch size becomes smaller towards the apex. No branches should be shaded out; they should all receive beneficial sunlight.

As you approach the apex, the branches should become shorter and more numerous, a normal growth pattern. Try to crowd as many branches as you can in the top one third of your foliage triangle without shading any out. The viewer will sense that the top is younger than the bottom third. On trees growing naturally this is what occurs over time.

3–5

3–6

A photograph does not impart any sense of scale to itself without a reference point of some kind. The Scotch pine, *Pinus sylvestris*, is shown in **3–5** with a normal-sized two-year-old Scotch pine seedling in a gallon plastic pot. The bonsai needles are one tenth as long as the seedling! By the end of the summer, the seedling will be taller than the thirty-year-old bonsai next to it.

Informal Upright—Moyogi or Tachiki

Basically the same rules apply to this style as with the formal upright. With all the styles that follow, try to use what you have learned from the formal upright rules together with the new information and additional rules.

The trunk curves in the informal upright style, sometimes gently, sometimes severely (see **3–6**). In any case, the apex remains directly above the base of the trunk. Normally, the branches in this style will curve or undulate as well. If the presence of strong wind, avalanche, cold, or other environmental conditions twisted the trunk of the tree, it certainly would affect the branches. Allow a bit more curvature in the rootage since this will make a more consistent tree. Pay close attention to detail in your Number One branch, allowing the rest of the tree to follow that lead.

Usually the twisting motion is directed from side to side, and the larger bends are found towards the apex—although the reverse is sometimes seen. Extreme exaggerated forms are sometimes called the "octopus style" or *Tako Zukuri* (refer to **3–45**).

In all styles where an undulating trunk is found, it is important to adhere to the following principle with

regard to the front of the tree. None of the bends come forward of the apex. If they did, the tree would look as though it were falling backwards.

The Scotch pine, *Pinus sylvestris*, shown in **3–7** was found located in a local nursery disguised as a "poodle" pine. It had been pruned by the wholesaler as a pom-pom-type plant and was about six feet in height with various balls of foliage stuck out at random heights on the tree. On the left side of the tree, starting at the lowest branch and upwards to the next, is a huge scar that marks where the original trunk used to be. Its removal, in fact, accounts for the large amount of taper found on a relatively short tree of only fourteen inches in height.

The Scotch pine, *Pinus sylvestris*, shown in **3–8** is starting to develop a classical *Moyogi* style. This style, characterized by its gently undulating trunk, throws off a branch on the outside of each curve. Its familiar silhouette is well known for providing a backdrop for ritual Noh plays in Japan. The outline shape is called *Matsu-Zukuri* and can be easily adapted to any hardy conifer. Its height is twenty-four inches. The trunk is four inches in diameter, and the brown unglazed Chinese container has a carving of a dragon across the front.

One of the distinct advantages of growing from seed is the tremendous and sometimes unpredictable results one can obtain. The tree shown in **3–9** is a cultivar of dwarf spruce that I came across among seedlings of *Picea abies mucronata* I have named Yujin spruce—the name I have taken for my bonsai workshop. It develops quickly from cuttings and remains true to form. The tree is only four years old and already sports an inch-and-a-half trunk at ten inches in height.

3–9

3–7

3–8

Slanting Style—Shakan

The *Shakan* style is characterized by an apex that terminates at a point not directly above the base of the tree (see **3–10**). The slant, or angle, may be to the right or to the left. A tree that slants just slightly from the vertical is known as a *Sho-Shakan*. A slightly larger degree of lean, between 30 and 45 degrees, is known as a *Chu-Shakan*. Trees that have a great deal of slant, more than 45 degrees, are known as *Dai-Shakan*.

The trunk is usually somewhat straight, but it may be found with slightly undulating curves. If extreme curves are found on the tree, the correct associated style might be windswept or some other more tortuous form.

3–10

Both the branches and the roots must be harmonious in their shape, size, and direction. Strong rootage is especially important on the "upwind" side of the tree. When naturally stunted trees are subject to the additional forces of gravity and wind that would tend to topple them, the roots on the strong, upwind side tend to be pulled to the surface. These enlarge and display strength and stability at the base of the trunk. For a tree that has uneven levels of rootage, the slanting style allows an elegant natural solution for what may at first appear to be a weakness or design flaw. By tipping the tree so that the uneven rootage is flat with respect to the horizontal, visual stability is achieved at the base of the trunk. Remember to wire the branches out so that they look as though they were always growing that way. The slanting aspect of the tree is never towards the front or the back, but inclines to the left or to the right.

Surface rootage, as in all styles, must be well distributed around the trunk. In the slanting, cascade, and windswept styles, this distribution is especially important. The viewer must not think that the planting is unstable.

The Number One branch tip originates one third the distance up the trunk, just as in the formal upright. This branch should be the thickest, longest, lowest, and most significant element of the bonsai design. It should offset the slant of the trunk and point itself in the opposite direction of the slant of the trunk and towards one of the front corners of the pot. The more that the trunk leans, the longer the Number One branch should reach out in the opposite direction to give visual stability to the planting.

Once the angle of the Number One branch has been established, all other branches repeat the same angle with respect to the vertical. Ignore the angle of the trunk itself, and ignore the undulations of the trunk as well. Reference all the branches to the vertical or from the horizontal.

An unusual bonsai subject, the tree shown in **3–11** is a Golden Threadbranch cypress, *Chaemacyparis pisifera filifera aurea*. This plant spent its first fifteen years in a large peat pot until it had grown four feet high, and its roots had to be extricated from the ground below the pot, which had totally decomposed. It is planted in a Japanese drum-style container. The planting is now only fifteen inches high.

The tree shown in **3–12** is another four-year-old Yujin spruce, *Picea abies mucronata*. It is eleven inches high and is planted in an oval brown Japanese container, nine and one half inches long.

3–11

3–12

Semi-Cascade Style—Han Kengai

The definitive aspect of this style is that the foliage of the Number One branch, at its tip, extends below the level of the rim of the pot—but not so far as below the bottom of the pot (see **3–13**). This patch of foliage is off to one side of the pot rather than in front of or in back of the pot. Too much foliage in front tends to block the view of the trunk line, and too much foliage behind tends to make the tree look in danger of falling over backwards.

Also definitive, but to a somewhat lesser degree, is the frontal profile of the container—the shape formed by the pot when viewed on display. A semi-cascade pot has a nearly square profile—the pot is almost as tall as it is wide. Some of the most beautiful pot designs are semi-cascade pots.

The semi-cascade style, on closer inspection, is nothing more than an extended slanting style. The Number One branch extends itself out and down, and, presumably, if the tree were planted on a mound, rock, or mountaintop, the lower foliage would not touch the ground. The pot functions to elevate the tree so that the proper ground clearance is achieved.

The apex may be situated above the container or not—an apex is not a requirement of this style. Sometimes the typical foliage triangle must be modified to utilize the tip of the Number Three branch as the apex, and the starting and ending points of the foliage along the lowest branch make up the bottom two points of the foliage triangle.

This style, as well as the following cascade styles, do best when special attention is given to ensure strong rootage, effortless exaggerated curvature of the trunk, and frugal, but tasteful, branch positioning. In this style, less is better.

Some named variations on this style are *Dai-Kengai*, or extreme vertical cascade, where the branches seem to hang with a great burden of weight. There is the mountaintop cascade, or *Gaito-Kengai*, which is characterized by the illusion that the branches are hugging close to each other and to the rock in order to avoid the harsh winds and winter cold. *Taki-Kengai* is a waterfall cascade named for the multiple, vertical falling branches that suggest the name. The string cascade, of *Ito-Kengai*, is a simpler design using a few thin, light and airy branches that seem to defy gravity. *Takan-Kengai* is a two-trunk cascade typically found where two competing trees are lodged in the same rocky ledge. In order to survive, they must capture their own share of sunlight and nutrients, or perish.

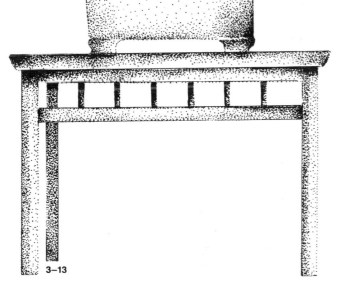

3-13

One doesn't often see a combination semi-cascade and weeping style; however, with the Golden Threadbranch cypress, *Chaemacyparis pisifera filifera aurea*, shown in **3–14**, it seems the best option. This plant was found at the same time as the previously mentioned Golden Threadbranch cypress shown in **3–11**. Together they illustrate the great range of styles that are possible from two basically identical plants.

3–14

Formal Cascade Style—Kengai

The formal cascade style distinguishes itself from the following cascade styles by having a distinct apex (see **3–15**). This does not have to be directly above the pot; it could be slightly to one side.

The cascade pot is much taller than wide. This height allows a considerable drop in elevation by the foliage of the Number One branch, so much so, that in the finished condition the tip of the longest branch actually extends below the bottom of the cascade pot. For display, it is necessary to place the pot on a stand so that the foliage does not touch the table or shelf surface.

For display purposes, the general rule still applies: eye level is halfway up the trunk towards the apex. Since the "cascading" part of this style is in reality an overgrown Number One branch, display of this style need not take this branch's additional height into consideration.

The apex section of the tree—that is, everything above the Number One branch—is best trained and developed as if it were a separate tree. All too often, the importance of the apex area is forgotten; the upright section deserves a careful look. The best cascade styles incorporate a strong apex.

None of the cascading styles use a "weeping" effect to get from up above to down below. If you were to draw the typical cascading curve versus the weeping line, they would differ quite remarkably.

A Mugho pine cascade, *Pinus mugho pumilla*, is shown in **3–16**. The height of the tree is nine inches and the trailing Number One branch is still in training. The dominant pine candle at its outermost extension has been left untrimmed this year to allow for its future growth. Within two years, the cascading branch will be lower than the bottom of the container. This tree is four years old.

The best way to develop a pine cascade in the shortest amount of time is shown in **3–17**. Water the soil in the

3–15

3—16

upright position, but grow the tree down on its side. The apical hormones concentrate in the tip of the cascading branch rather than in the apex, and better back budding will result as well. This technique works especially well for apically dominant plants that are naturally more difficult to train in the cascade style. However, for naturally weeping plants, such as Juniper *procumbens*, this method is not only unnecessary, but actually counterproductive. On the other hand, this is, perhaps, the only way one could achieve a cascading Ginkgo.

Informal Cascade Style—Kengai

Whereas the previous discussions of semi-cascade and formal cascade apply somewhat to this style, it is more apropos to list the exceptions to the rules. Informal cascade implies a lack of dominant apex (see **3—18**). An apex may remain as dead wood at the top—or *jin*. An apex may be present as a raised upper side branch, but often the apex is conspicuously absent. Strong rootage is stressed, and an unusual contortion of the trunk line favored. By keeping the foliage light and well trimmed, long branch reaches can be attained without tipping over the pot. This style sometimes does not extend below the bottom of the pot as in the formal cascade style.

3—17

3—18

3–19

Elongated Style—Goza Kake

An exaggerated Number One branch makes this style special (see **3–20**). Often it is desirable to place such a tree in a matching over-elongate pot to help balance the design. The long branches should not seem overloaded or strained by their own weight, and a general feeling of stillness and stability should exude from the setting. Trees similar to this are placed over water in Japanese gardens as focal points. Sometimes the longest branch is so overextended that it divides vertically into two separate levels similar to what is found in a semi-cascade planting.

Long, straight exposed roots add to the design stability, and varied ground covers communicate to the viewer that this setting is harmonious and long-lived.

The semi-cascade, *Han Kengai*, shown in **3–19** will eventually become a formal cascade as the top and lowermost growing tips increase in length. This is a juniper, *Juniperus communis*, grafted recently with *Shimpaku*. The native juniper's needles are long, pale colored, and very sharp to the touch; so I like to graft this species. The bonsai is about 275 years old and is two feet in height, including the brown Japanese pot.

Weeping Style—Shidare or Zukuri

This style shown in **3–21** is well known because the image of a weeping willow is so familiar. Other trees weep as well and should not be overlooked. Hemlock, birch, wisteria, and laceleaf maple are a few trees that naturally assume this style.

The bottom branches should be bigger than the top, just as in other styles. Also, the young sprouts are trained fairly early. Remember that the large weeping willow will use a thirty-foot arch to achieve its weeping appearance, but a small bonsai is not going to have enough weight at the branch tips to droop the branches sufficiently without assistance. Here is an excellent opportunity to use fishing weights. In general, one of the major drawbacks of weighting branches versus wiring

3–20

branches is that the resulting trained branch curves down much like a fishing pole with a heavy fish on the line. In the weeping style, however, this normally unsightly curve is exactly what you are trying to achieve! Use traditional, copper-wire wrapping techniques for other styles.

Keep your branches well spaced and thinned out. Place your branches well, taking into consideration their style and light requirements. Encourage separate layers.

Please observe that the smaller and higher branches are thin and trickle down inside the larger, more mature lower branches (see **3—22**). It is a common design defect to reverse this condition. The larger branches on a bonsai are going to naturally hang lower because of their weight. The weeping tree will have less, not more, flexibility in its larger, lower branches.

The wisteria shown in **3—23** has come out quite nicely from the previous winter. Purple blooms will start appearing in about a month. The hexagonal container is American. The tree is twenty-two years old and is twenty-two inches high.

3—22

3—21

3—23

The bonsai designs that have been covered so far constitute the most popular designs. Most bonsai material can be influenced into conforming with one of these schemes. Because I feel that it is important to be exposed to some of the more esoteric styles, these others that follow are included for completeness. Since there are so many of them, they are only covered briefly.

The venerable old bonsai shown in **3–25** is one of my favorite trees. I call it "Father Time," not only for its advanced age of 480 years, but because of its shape. One can almost imagine the form of a wizened, ancient human figure shuffling along a faraway garden path. This tree is a native Oregon juniper, *Juniperus communis*, that has been grafted with *Shimpaku*.

3–24

Windswept Style—Fukinagashi

Perhaps another good place to discuss this style, shown in **3–24**, would have been just after the slanting style because they have so much in common (refer to **3–10**).

The trunk does not necessarily have to lean with the wind as do the branches. In many seacoast settings, the trunk leans into the wind and the branches fly away in the opposite direction. The seacliff erodes as the sea encroaches. The tree tries to hang on and slowly leans towards the windward and seaward side. Mountain specimens, however, are usually swept in a consistent direction with the wind.

This is the first style in this chapter that commonly uses *jin* as an element of design, although we already encountered *jin* as an option for the apex of the informal cascade style (refer to **3–18**). *Jin*, in Japanese, means God, and the implication is that when the top of a tree has perished, it was due to some natural event, such as a lightning strike, drought, or fire. The Japanese associate these events quite naturally with a supreme being, and the living tree that displays these scars is truly venerable. In bonsai, a *jin* is a perished and weathered top of a tree. A *shari* is a silvered branch that got "tired" of fighting the wind. When an old tree becomes naturally hollowed out and its driftwood appearance starts to enhance the trunk, it is known as *Saba Miki*.

A good windswept design should have three main design elements that are obvious to the viewer: 1) beach or mountain setting, 2) heavy or light wind, and 3) wind direction.

3–25

Coiled Style—Bankan

The coiled style distinguishes itself by having the trunk wrap around a central space almost as if it were trained around a stake or rock, and, indeed, this is the best way to train a young sapling or whip in this style (see **3–26**). The front is sometimes difficult to locate due to the symmetry "in the round." Its rootage and open branch structure usually help locate a good front presentation. The apex should still terminate with its last little curve coming back towards the viewer.

The coil or spring of the trunk may be quite small and compact or very wide in its sweeps. This style should not be confused with the following twisted-trunk style. In the coiled style, the grain of the wood follows along with the curve of the trunk rather than "barber-pole"-ing along it as in the twisted style (see **3–27**).

Twisted Style—Nejikan

In this style, the trunk may be straight, slanted, slightly curved, or even tortuously undulating, but these characteristics are those of other styles as well. What defines the twisted style is that the trunk itself has grown in a spiral fashion (see **3–28**). Western cedar, Sitka spruce,

3 26

3–27

3–28

and many dry-area junipers naturally have this growth habit. It is particularly obvious on *jin* and *shari* where the weathering of the dead wood tends to exaggerate the hard and soft layers, making this twisting highly visible. Perhaps even more pronounced is the "barber-pole" effect that can be seen in old, rugged specimens of red-barked juniper, where only a narrow strip of live cambium remains to support life among its scattered few branches.

Sometimes a live tree twists around the skeleton of a dead snag. In other instances, a portion of the trunk is dead, initiating the spiral motion. However, there is good evidence that cuttings taken from twisted trees will produce twisted offspring. This supports the idea that the twist is predetermined by its genetic program rather than by environmental stress as we would prefer to believe. Perhaps we prefer environmental stress because it seems so incongruous to imagine the heavily twisted juniper as shown in **3–29** doing the same thing in a calm setting.

3–29

If you have ever seen a nursery grown *Shimpaku*, or, for that matter, any *Shimpaku* grown at lower altitudes, you can appreciate the bonsai shown in **3–30**. This variety of juniper from the Japanese Alps produces most of the world's finest bonsai masterpieces. From a cutting or seedling, the *Shimpaku* can be one of the most frustrating and cantankerous junipers. It grows at a snail's pace, forms funny-looking balls of foliage, and, if not wired extremely early, it will form rigid upright stems that break with the slightest provocation. Fifteen inches high from a cutting, this nongrafted *Shimpaku* is twenty-four years old.

3–30

Knobby-Trunk Style—Kobukan

Some trees have a lot of character when they are contorted, gnarled, or highly textured (see **3–31**). Trees such as apple and quince are improved in style with healed-over scars, *Sabamiki*, and gnarled, exposed rootage. Cork bark varieties of pine, elm, and maple are highly textured with irregular slabs of projecting, exfoliating layers of bark. In addition, some fallen species, such as old birch, alder, and hornbeam, show a great deal of character when sprouts have festered and healed, swelled up, and hardened off over time. Even light attacks of boring insects or galls that have naturally healed can give a tree an especially aged appearance.

All of the trees shown in **3–32**, **3–33**, and **3–34** and the descriptions given above are classified as *Kobukan* trees. They show stress in a practical manner: healed-over scars, victory over pestilence, and distinction in heavy corky layers.

A Japanese cork bark elm is shown in **3–35**. Grown from a cutting only twelve years ago, this tree displays the lower trunk, root, and bark development of a tree twice its age. It was grown in the ground except for the last two years, which probably accounts for its three-inch trunk in that period of time. The bonsai is nineteen inches in height and is planted in a fourteen-inch ivory Japanese oval pot.

3–33

3–31

3–34

3–32

3–35

Hollow-Trunk Style—Sabakan

This style, as the previous one, is associated primarily with certain species (see **3–36**). The *Sabakan* style has a close association with the oaks, especially the golden cup oak, live oak, scrub oak of the high arid regions of the West, and the white oak. Cypress varieties include the bald cypress and Montezuma cypress. Other warm-climate varieties are the baobab, the buttonwood, and wisteria. In colder climates, we see this often in the apple and in softwood conifers such as the larch, pine, cedar, spruce, coast redwood, and giant sequoia. In these latter species, the hollowed-out areas create a pleasing buttress effect in the lower third of the trees. This hollowed effect is especially effective when polished so that the dead wood is smooth, highly textured, and silvery grey (see **3–37**).

Only one branch has been removed from the alpine fir, *Abies lasiocarpa*, shown in **3–38**, since bringing it down from the mountains. The new growth still remains small, indicating that even after several years at this altitude, it is having difficulty adjusting. The second apex seen a few inches below the top will be the eventual top of this tree once it decides to stop "sulking." This fir is 180 years old and twenty inches tall.

3–37

3–36

3–38

3 39

3-40

Peeled Bark Style—Sharikan

The name *Sharikan* is derived from *shari*, or dead wood (see **3–39**). Literally, it is an attack or trauma to the tree. I have seen fine old pine specimens in which the trunk has actually been divided into pie-shaped sections vertically, due to lightning or avalanche. The separate sections grow upwards as new branches grow and thrive. This is not a driftwood style because a live "peeled" section of cambium remains intact throughout the length of the tree and, therefore, provides new branches and apices.

The bonsai shown in **3–40** is a fine example of the Murrayana pine, a variant of the more common Lodgepole pine. Its estimated age is four hundred and twenty five years based on counting annual rings on its roots during repotting. The total height is twenty three inches with a six-inch-diameter trunk. The pot is a signed Japanese piece, five inches tall and twelve inches wide.

Driftwood Style—Sharamiki or Saramiki

This style is easy to spot among a collection of trees (see **3–41**). This tree is largely dead wood, polished by the wind, sand, and sun to a bright silver color. It represents one of the grandest struggles of plant life against the hardships of nature.

3–41

The style is almost synonymous with juniper. Other species are common, such as pine, spruce, hemlock, fir, and cedar. But, I would say that, among the 100 best-known bonsai in the world today, thirty are driftwood-style junipers—largely Sargent juniper from the Japanese Alps.

The driftwood area often comprises over half of the exposed trunk and is carefully carved—if not naturally, then by hand—to blend with the overall design of the tree. This style is typical in high desert areas, timberline, and windswept cliffs overlooking the ocean.

The tree shown in **3–42**, at five hundred eighty years of age, is the oldest in my personal collection. It is a native Oregon juniper found at an altitude of between 4000 and 5000 feet. The native foliage has been completely replaced by grafting on *Shimpaku* juniper. It measures twenty-seven inches in height with a nine-inch-diameter trunk. The container is a heavy grey Japanese pot, five inches high and eighteen inches wide.

3–43

The Split Trunk Style—Sabamiki

Imagine a fine, venerable old tree up on a rocky precipice. One winter the snow load is just too much for the Number One branch, and it is split away from the trunk, but not severed. It remains attached at the base and in the following spring, it begins to grow again.

What develops from such a hypothetical scenario is the *Sabamiki* style (see **3–43**). Looking almost like a two-trunk style, the single tree develops more branches on one side, primarily due to the huge scar on the other side. The smaller trunk is the former Number One branch, and, therefore, not as tall, well developed, or thick. This style is typically bare in spots and quite rugged in appearance. The point of the trauma should be well displayed and should be obvious to the viewer (see **3–44**).

3–42

3–44

3–45

3–46

Octopus Style—Tako Zukuri

If there is such a thing as a "busy" style, this is it (see **3–45**). Over-exaggerated curves, twists, and turns; contorted, well-exposed roots; zigs and zags distort the trunk. All branches echo the tortuous turns, and even the tiny ones are true to form.

The total effect is wonderful to behold (see **3–46**). The tree looks like a scary monster tree out of the nightmares of Ichabod Crane or Hansel and Gretel. The knotholes turn into imaginary eyes and the *Sabamiki* transform into noses and pointed ears.

Root-Over-Rock Style—*Sekijojo or Sekijoju*

When I walk along a primeval forest floor or observe an ancient timberline giant, one striking feature that always impresses me is how the roots of a tree bare against a rock surface (see **3–47**). This is an example of root over rock. The maple tree does this particularly well in young bonsai and is a good species for beginners to use.

The best plantings are accomplished over time by placing a young maple over a picturesque rock and then planting the tree and rock together in a very deep pot made with slatted sides (see **3–48**).

By removing soil slowly from the top surface, over time the roots will penetrate deeper and farther down below the rock. Eventually, as the surface roots get large enough to be exposed to sunlight, a very striking planting will start to reveal itself. In nature, this happens as the result of natural erosion over time and the searching of the roots for nutrients.

3–47

3–48

3–49

3–50

3–51

Exposed-Root Style—Ne Agari

This style differs from the previous one in that there is a great deal of air space where the rock once was (**3–49**). Natural erosion sometimes will expose roots of a tree to the extent that one can walk under some of the more dominant. River banks often will have water-loving border trees with large aerial roots exposed to the elements. Birch, elm, hornbeam, alder, maple, and willow are all good examples. The banyan and fig trees in the tropics will also exhibit this form, but for different reasons. These trees send down from the trunk aerial roots, which, when they reach soil, supply additional nutrition to the tree. Over time, these trees have a large network of roots above the ground exposed to the viewer.

This style is sometimes incorrectly called octopus style (refer to **3–45**). Just having a large number of exposed roots does not necessarily mean it is *Tako Zukuri*. If the trunk and branches are all twisted also, then perhaps it is a candidate (see **3–50**).

The native vine maple, *Acer circinatum*, shown in **3–51** was collected in the Oregon Cascades from a lava flow at an altitude of 3500 feet. Only seventeen inches in height, it sports a five-inch trunk. The container is a Japanese green oval measuring fourteen by three inches. Its estimated age is three hundred years.

3—52

Rock-Grown Style—*Ishizuke, Ishitsuke,* or *Ishitzuke*

One of the more popular Chinese styles, *Ishizuke* can represent an entire ecosystem in a pot (see **3—52**). There are so many styles available to the enthusiast that I feel compelled to mention a few of the subcategories here just to help initiate the beginner to their highly diverse possibilities.

There is the mountain planting, or *Yamagata*, where the single rock represents a mountain with its single tree all weathered and windswept near its crest.

In the island planting, or *Shima Ishi*, the stone is often placed in a *sui ban*, or water tray. The pot is then filled to a shallow level with water and the completed planting looks very much like an isolated island in a calm bay or inland sea.

The cliff planting is called *Dangai Jeppeki Ishi*. Its primary characteristic is the tasteful combination of *Kengai* and *Ishizuke*; a dominant Number One branch plunges down over the rocky precipice and hugs close to the mountain for protection from the wind.

The waterfall rock *Taki Ishi* planting can be one of two approaches; the rock may be the waterfall element or the tree might be. Finding a special rock with a slight quartz or agate vein that looks like running water and placing the tree towards one side can evoke a waterfall scene. In another interpretation, the tree has numerous cascading branches tumbling down the cliff. The branches and foliage suggest whitewater falls and, hence, the name, waterfall style.

Different from *Taki Ishi*, mentioned above, is the mountaintop style, or *Iwayama*. This tree is at the ulti-mate apex of the mountain, and its branches extend downwards on several sides.

The seashore planting, or *Ara Iso*, is characterized by slanted trunks facing the wind, and like the windswept style, the branches facing the wind are either converted into *shari* or bend leeward for relief.

The trunk-style *Ishizuke* is one of the most unique styles in the bonsai repertoire. Known as the *Insho-Gata-Ishi*, the trunk of the tree is the rock. Branches are trained over a trunk-shaped rock, and the effect is un-usual and striking. Done effectively, this style enables the grower to achieve a massive-looking tree in less than ten years, since branch development is the primary concern; the trunk is already formed.

Finally, like the literati, or *bunjinji* forms, discussed at the end of this section on styles, rock plantings are allowed to be free-form or abstract. We might be tempted to call this contemporary were it not for the fact that this is one of the oldest Chinese styles, dating back some eighteen hundred years. This style is called *Chuso-Gata-Ishi* and is characterized by exaggeration, fantasy, and mischief. It is impossible to describe what it looks like; it is easier to list some of the things it isn't. It is not realistic, not to scale, and it is not restful to look upon. The rock is highly contorted and secured at an unstable angle. The plant material may be uncommon—such as mums or tropicals—and the plant is planted in an un-usual place on the rock. The Chinese master Wu Yee-Sun established this as his signature style.

In all of the above styles, the entire tree is growing on the rock; there is no soil in the pot. There is possibly decorative gravel or moss, but the roots are not growing into these elements. In some cases, *Shima-ishi*, the pot is filled with water only.

There are a number of ways to fasten a tree to a rock. I will mention only a few. "Muck" is a mixture of peat, manure, and water. It makes an excellent "sticky" soil to help a tree's roots adhere to the rock right away. Some artists will use string or raffia and wind the tree's roots onto the rock. Then they simply wait for the string to rot away in a year's time, leaving the tree to clasp the rock on its own. Others prefer attaching wire by means of Super Glue, lead fishing weights, or small, inconspicuous screws, and then wiring the tree to the rock for a very strong hold. Whatever the method, strive to be incon-spicuous and make as natural a setting as you can. Make many sketches of your planting beforehand for best results. Try multiple plantings or secondary plantings, such as dwarf azaleas with taller pines, etc. Experiment with various ground covers, such as baby's tears, corsican mint, red creeping thyme, linnaria, and moss. Pay special attention to blending the pot with the rock and the rock with the tree. Notice color, texture, detail, and general shape, and make all elements harmonize.

Some years ago, I hosted a field trip with the Eugene [Oregon] Bonsai Society to collect wild specimens. About thirty members, mostly inexperienced, asked me to give a quick demonstration on how to dig in the rocky terrain. I obliged, and after a few minutes of digging, up popped a rock with a very fat trunked vine maple, *Acer circinatum*, growing on it. Some of the club members still think I staged the event because no one has taken another tree as nice as this one from that area. It is eleven inches high with a seven-inch trunk (see **3—53**) and has been growing on top of this same rock for about five hundred years.

The planting shown in **3—54** begins to approach a grey area between bonsai and *saikei*, or miniature landscape. If the landscape portion of this grove were a bit more dominant, it could be considered a *saikei*. As it is, it is probably more accurately classified as a grove on a rock. The trees are an unusually rare dwarf variety of Alberta spruce known as Waconda spruce. These specimens, only fourteen inches in height, are fifteen years old. The nice flower visible, used as a ground cover, is blue star creeper.

3—54

Broom Style—Hoki Dachi, Hoki Zukuri or Hokidachi

This style has the remote resemblance to a homemade Japanese broom standing on its handle, hence the name. It is a highly twiggy style that is used for deciduous trees almost exclusively (see **3—55**), the notable exceptions being for the Swiss mountain pine, Italian stone pine, and members of the heath or rhododendron families.

3—53

3—55

There is quite a set of elaborate techniques used to achieve the broom style in Japanese elms, maples, and hornbeam, and I will only touch on their principles here. I encourage you to consult advanced Japanese bonsai texts for more information.

First, select a tree that has a suitably large trunk, three inches or more in diameter. Cut off all foliage with a horizontal cut five inches above the root buttress, and then make an asymmetrical notch into the top of the remaining stump. Your tree will now resemble a slightly crooked "M" in profile when viewed from the front. Bind the two "peaks" together lightly with electrician's tape, floral tape, or similar flexible tape. Make sure that the top of the tape does not extend over the top of the cambium layer at either "peak," one of which is slightly higher than the other. The tree will sprout from these two peaks. Allow foliage to grow unchecked until its diameter is at least half as big as the trunk diameter; then repeat the above process, cutting notches always 1½ inches above the old scar. After six years, the beginnings of a broom-style tree are formed.

This is a highly balanced, systematic design with little room for creative expression; but viewed on a winter's day with a fresh blanket of snow on the branchlets, nothing is more striking.

This design may be modified to include the tall, narrow trees or the broad and sweeping pasture tree forms.

The tree shown in **3–56 and 3–57** is unusual for bonsai purposes, but one that I can recommend highly. It is a linden tree, *Tilia cordata*, native to Europe—especially Germany, where romantic popular songs have been written about its stately grandeur and beauty. The tree's leaves dwarf especially well, particularly if defoliated completely in mid-summer. This specimen is only ten years old and sports a 1¼-inch-diameter trunk and is eighteen inches high. The blue glazed container is from Japan.

Shown in **3–58** is a named variety of Japanese maple called *Sango Kaku*, loosely translated as "blood bark" due to its rich red twigginess in winter. The tree comes out quite red in spring, quickly turning to gold and green hues as the foliage hardens off. The bark is actually at its darkest color in the dead of winter. The stone below the tree is a *suiseki*, resembling an ancient Japanese thatched hut.

The *suiseki* is shown close up in **3–59**, focusing on the ground cover at the base of the tree. It is linnaria, *Cymbalaria aequitriloba*, an invasive plant in the ground; it performs well in larger bonsai containers—better than baby's tears or Irish moss.

3–56

3–57

3–58

3–59

Double-Trunk Style—Sokan

This style is, of course, defined by one tree that has two trunks (see **3–60**). This is an excellent option for a tree that has an extremely heavy branch in the lower one quarter of the trunk. This branch may be trained upwards into another trunk, and the total planting treated as *Sokan*. This style looks best when the second trunk is coming from the main trunk quite low—as low as ground level or slightly above. The second trunk should be smaller in diameter than the first, and the apex should be lower than the apex of the main trunk.

Plant the two-trunk style with one trunk slightly forward of the other, otherwise an ugly "slingshot" effect may result. Avoid side branches that cross the other trunk. Short branches and branches in back are preferable. Treat the whole planting like one tree—not two—in placing the Number One branch, Number Two branch, and so on. In other words, the Number Two branch originates on the smaller trunk.

3–60

Triple-Trunk Style—Tosho

This style has much in common with the two-trunk *Sokan* above. The smallest trunk begins higher on the tree than the others and ends at an apex lower than the others (see **3–61**). Again, like the *Sokan*, treat the branches as if the tree trunks were just one trunk. Avoid crossing trunks in front with side branches, and encourage short back branches for depth.

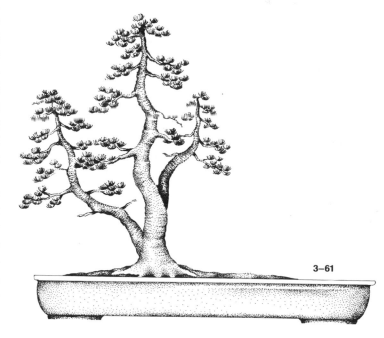

3–61

Place the front of the tree so that no two trunks are equidistant from the viewer. The triangle formed by the tree trunks should have uneven sides.

This style is quite often found in collected conifers. These rugged old trees have a habit of pushing up a new trunk whenever the main trunk is dwarfed by freezing conditions or strong prevailing winds. Sometimes alpine conifers will have numerous unsuccessful attempts at forming a main trunk; consequently, the tree is forced to maintain a shape close to the ground.

An unusual planting of alpine fir, *Abies lasiocarpa*, is shown in **3–62**. It was collected from the western Cascade mountain range in Oregon at an altitude of 4500 feet. Its unorthodox styling largely comes from the respect due a naturally occurring specimen that is approximately half a millennium in age. It has been named "Atlas" because of its spreading upper arms, as if to support the weight of the globe. More recently, the name has been reinforced by the fact that Atlas would be a more likely candidate to move this bonsai around the backyard than I. Its mere two feet in height is deceiving considering this slow-growing conifer makes wood so dense it cannot float. As well, its classification as "four-handed" bonsai does not address the fact that it is unlikely there will be four hands around when it needs to be moved!

Sprout Style—Miyama Kirishima or Kabudachi

This style is often seen in nature when an old stump will sprout again (see **3–63**). Sometimes a fallen section of a tree will spring up with new shoots or a section of a rotten log is still alive and continues to grow against all odds.

Arrange new sprouts as you would arrange flowers in a vase; keep them spread out and very compact. Avoid crossing or highly disfigured branches. Keep the foliage confined to the basic foliage triangle, and show off the oldest and most rugged section or stump.

3–63

3–62

Raft Style—Ikadabuki

Many times in the woods we see a tree that has fallen down, but remained alive. These trunks have branches growing upwards from the fallen trunk that begin to resemble individual trees in their own right. But we know that all originate from the old, fallen, trunk that must still have some viable roots. This phenomenon can be created in a bonsai pot by laying down a tree and making sure that some of the roots remain well planted. We can then train the now upward-facing branches of the tree into a forest style (see **3–64**).

Vary the location of your new branch trunks; avoid lining them up in a row along the original trunk. Work on separating each "tree" by pruning them individually. Do not intertwine branches. Use the tallest "tree" to make a distinctly taller apex than the others. The smaller "trunks" should remain shorter.

Roots-Connected Style—*Netsunari*

Most of us are familiar with the natural growing characteristics of willow, quince, wild cherry, hawthorn, Chinese raintree, and vine maple. What these trees have in common is that they sucker easily from exposed roots. I had three hawthorn trees in the parking strip in front of my house. Their roots would surface two or three feet away from the main trunk and sprout. I mowed them down for a few summers along with the grass, but they kept coming back even stronger. I learned the hard way what root-connected style meant. One thing it means is that if you spray Round-up on one tree, all the trees die.

3–64

3—65

This style differs from the raft style in three ways. First, the roots are definitely roots, not the downed trunk of another tree (see **3–65**). Second, more than one tree can be planted to achieve increased depth, whereas *Ikadabuki* style is always one tree. Third, species are selected that will make the style convincing. The trees named above are the most frequent examples. By contrast, a pine tree in *Ikadabuki* style is not unusual; there are several well-known masterpieces. Attempting to utilize a pine tree in *Netsunari* style creates a conflict by definition. Pine never exhibits this style in nature, and therefore, while one might possibly produce a pine *Netsunari*, it would offend the basic design premise that prefers bonsai to mimic nature.

Bulbs or Perennials—Shitakusa

One of the most effective ways to display your bonsai is in the traditional *tokonoma*. This display area in the entrance hall of a Japanese home provides a plain backdrop for the bonsai and its stand. The stand is often three-tiered and provides extra levels for accompaniment plantings, viewing stones, or miniature figurines called mud figures. An effective combination display consists of the use of all three shelves to portray a complete scene. For example, the highest shelf has a mountaintop viewing stone, the second level is a windswept pine bonsai, and on the lowest shelf is a *Shitakusa*-style meadow of wild iris (see **3–66**). In another exam ple, the top shelf holds an *Ishizuke* rock planting with a mossy fern-filled pot just below it. On the third shelf, two mud figures play chess together under a maple tree.

Keep in mind that the *bon* has a similar dwarfing effect on bulbs, perennials, wildflowers, and annuals; so you can let your imagination run free.

3–67

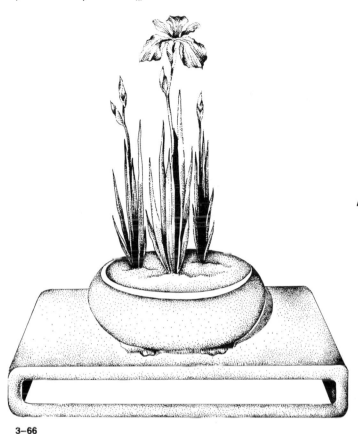

3–66

Grass Plantings—Kusamomo

Similar to *Shitakusa*, grass plantings (see **3–67**) make wonderful scenes when grouped together with bonsai. The nicest bonsai show I have ever attended contained tastefully arranged *Kusamomo* plantings near other larger and more venerable masterpieces. As with the literati school of landscape painting, the mere suggestion of many elements adds up to a stronger visual statement than if each element is reproduced in full.

Remember, bamboo is a grass. Wonderful plantings can be made by taking several root divisions of a dwarf variety of bamboo and placing them in a shallow *saikei* tray. Also try mondo grass, blood grass, or "Buddha's belly" bamboo for an unusual effect.

Bunjin, Literati, and Bunjinji Styles

This is a style that has no style. Literati means "learned man," and this style is associated with the Chinese literati design schools. It has long been thought that the development of individual style is best accomplished through the study of past and present masters. Present-day artists of bonsai still subscribe to this principle. Having learned the basics, the student must progress to the point where personal expression becomes valid. The *Bunjin* style is reserved for those masters who have a desire to create the unexplainable; a freedom to express a personal artistic statement.

Bunjin, therefore, has no rules. I can suggest some common characteristics that the student can study to identify these forms with more understanding.

A *Bunjin* pot is generally round, drum-shaped on edge, and is raised on three legs. The front of the tree tends to be less important than it is in the other styles. The planting is light, airy, sparse, and abstract. The branches are delicately positioned to elevate this ethereal quality. The slender trunk is relatively free of scars or projections. The curves are restrained, not exaggerated. The foliage mass is sparse and compact, and does not usually find itself within a compact foliage triangle. *Saikei* is the most immature bonsai form; *Bunjin* is the highest order.

3–68

3–70

The esoteric design shown in **3–70** has an interesting story behind it. The tree is a Lodgepole pine, *Pinus contorta*, which has spent several years in my backyard until a student challenged me to try to do something with "that." I obliged with this quasi-*Bunjin* style from a five-foot-high questionable bonsai subject. It breaks most of the rules, but judging from the new candles this year, it's going to be a success.

The bonsai pine shown in **3–68** is unusual because it is a long-needled Ponderosa pine, *Pinus ponderosa*, collected from the high desert region of Oregon. You won't find a pruning scar on it because there aren't any. The branches have, of course, been wired into a natural *Bunjinji* style. Estimated to be twenty-five years old, the pine has been in training for only one year. This tree is sixteen inches tall and is in a Japanese container.

The bonsai shown in **3–69** is a fairly obscure pine known as Murrayana pine. It is an alpine subspecies of the better-known Lodgepole pine and, hence, its Latin nomer, *Pinus contorta* "Murrayana." Found in isolated pockets above an altitude of 4000 feet, this type of pine is difficult to transplant, grows slowly, and sports quite small needles. This specimen is twenty-five years old and has never been pruned or wired; a truly natural bonsai.

MULTIPLE PLANTINGS

Two-Tree Style—So-ju or So Ju

Two trees that look good together are a must (see **3–71**). Do not mix varieties. Do not have them too similar in size, nor too different. A good size relationship is to strive to make the smaller tree of the pair not less than one third of the diameter, nor larger than two-thirds of the diameter of the larger tree. If the smaller tree is one half the diameter of the larger, be sure to make it one half the total width, one half the total height, and the lowest branch one half the height of the lowest branch on the larger tree. Keep all relationships proportional.

Plant one tree slightly ahead of the other and slightly off to one side of the pot. Average out the positions of both trees and plant them one third of the way in from one edge of a flat, wide container. Be careful to consider rootage. The taller tree will be planted higher up and will expose more roots.

3–69

3-71

Three-Tree Style—Sambon Yose

Three is an important number to the Japanese and it is always significant in their art. Anyone who has had experience with either Ikebana or Japanese gardening has heard the trio described as representational of the sun, moon, and earth, or heaven, earth, and man, or father, mother, and child.

Place the trees so that no two distances are alike; complete asymmetry is desirable (see **3-72**). Again, the thickest tree is the tallest and widest, is planted the highest, and is the dominant tree in the planting.

Generally the smaller trees are positioned towards the back of the pot so that they contribute to the feeling of depth. The number-three tree in this planting is the

3-72

number-one tree of a second group of trees. For example, if you plant eleven trees, the third-highest tree is planted as the number-one tree of a second group of trees.

The three-tree grove of Alberta spruce, *Picea glauca conica*, shown in **3–73**, is thirty-six inches high. The thirty-year-old tree on the left has four trunks and is clasping a rock. The container is a Korean oval mica pot measuring twenty-four inches across.

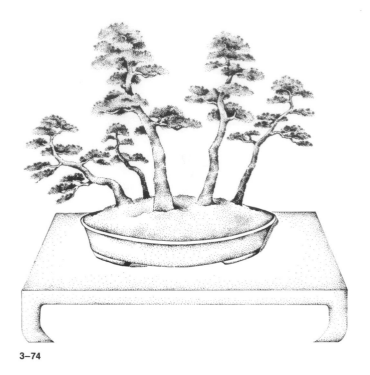

3–74

3–73

Five-Tree Style—Gohon Yose

An example of five-tree-style planting is shown in **3–74**.

Seven-Tree Style—Nanahon Yose

A seven-tree bonsai planting is shown in **3–75**.

The seven-tree grove, *Nanahon Yose*, shown in **3–76** is comprised of maidenhair trees, *Ginkgo biloba*. The tallest tree is twenty-six inches high. The container is an extremely shallow twenty-one-inch oval mica pot from Korea. This is the fourth spring for this grove in this container, and the leaves, which are very difficult to dwarf, are about one third their normal size.

Nine-Tree Style—Kyuhon Yose

A drawing of a *Kyuhon Yose* planting is shown in **3–77**.

The tallest tree in the Japanese larch forest shown in **3–78 and 3–79** spent five years as an individual bonsai; but, after many unsuccessful attempts to stimulate lower branches on the right side, I decided that it would be a better candidate for a tall tree in a grove. The container measures two and one half inches high by twenty-four inches wide and is a mica pot from Korea.

3—75

3—76

3—78

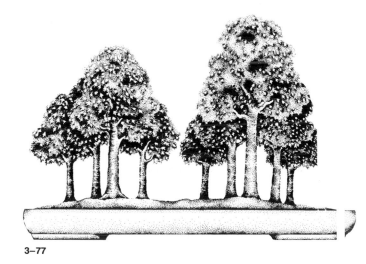

3—77

3—79

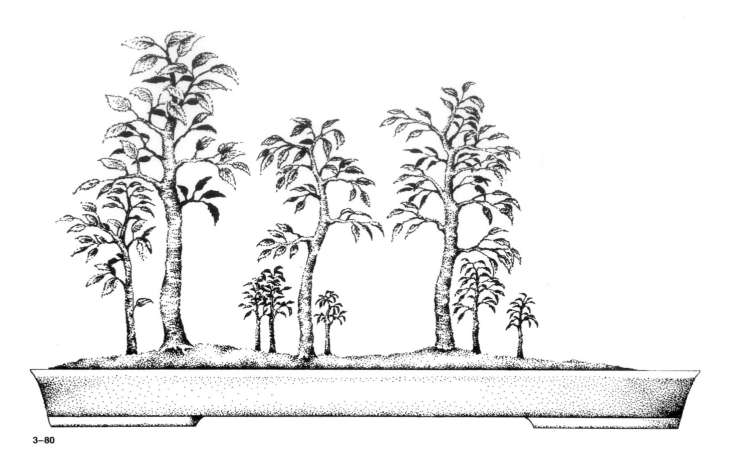

3–80

Group Planting—Yose Uye or Yose Ue

Any forest or group planting containing more than nine trees is a *Yose Uye*. As with any bonsai style, consistency is the key to communicating the scene to the viewer. The wind must be coming from the same direction in all trees. Pay close attention to colors of foliage. Minor irregularities are expected in nature, but not sharp changes in foliage style.

Pay close attention to the total concept of your planting. Is it alpine? Is it on a mound or mountain? Are the smaller trees actually smaller or are they supposed to be farther away? Is the whole scene distant or is it a nearby scene?

You are familiar with the old phrase about not being able to see the forest for the trees. The total effect of more than nine trees should be that of a forest utilizing only a few trees. There should be some large, mature trees as well as small, immature trees.

Small trees can be actually smaller young trees or they can be full-size trees viewed from a distance. The degree of detail determines the difference (see **3–80**).

Make sure that your ground contours make sense. If you have bottom ground, expect to find blueberries or brush. Elm, birch, and willow are found near streams.

Apple and oak need the drainage of a hillside and alpine plants certainly need some rugged peaks. Make the ground level conform to the planting. The soil should show rocks if rocky ground is indicated.

LANDSCAPES

Miniature Landscapes—Saikei

One cannot mention the word *Saikei* without also including its creator, Toshio Kawamoto. After World War II, it was difficult to find new mature plant material to use for bonsai. Mr. Kawamoto promoted the use of immature trees to create miniature landscapes (see **3–81**). It was his idea that later, as the young trees became able to stand on their own, that they could then be promoted to bonsai.

As with all bonsai styles, a complete vision of the scene you are attempting to accomplish is necessary. With *Saikei*, drawings are highly recommended; make a careful detailed sketch showing general outline, location of near ground, middle distance ground, and distant ground. Arrange all rocks and trees so that no two

3–81

elements are the same height. Find a grain in the rock that is common to all and duplicate its presence over and over. Work on developing the feeling of harmony in all elements; a smooth rock does not go well with a contorted pine. Pay close attention to scale and depth.

A *Saikei* pot or tray is a large flat container, preferably oval and eighteen inches long, or more. Larger trays allow the artist to include more detail, such as small bushes, grasses, or ferns.

Saikei may be created with no trees. A windy area in the mountains may have no trees; the ground covers and the rocks speak of high winds and bitter-cold winters. *Saikei* may contain actual or "contrived" water through the use of water trays or dry stream beds. Even the special use of mineral streaks in stone to suggest water is common. All the bonsai styles can be converted to *Saikei* styles by planting the accompanying species rather than including them by suggestion alone.

A complete study of *Saikei* is inappropriate for an introductory bonsai book. I refer you to Toshio Kawamoto's work on *Saikei* for a more in-depth study, or to seek out help from one of his students teaching the subject.

How to Create a Rock-Grown Landscape

The ingredients for this project include many items. The pot is a *Saikei*-type oval container, measuring twenty-three by eighteen inches and one inch in height (see 3–82). The flared edge on this container makes it appear to be more shallow than it actually is. The two dominant rocks are sandstone selected from a variety available at a retail masonry brick and stone shop. Four bags of aquarium gravel are shown: a five-pound bag of inexpensive unwashed gravel and three smaller bags in white, blue, and green for a seacoast effect. The plants are three one-gallon-sized Hinoki cypress, *Chamaecyparis obtusa kosteri*, obtained from a local garden center.

3–82

The flat tray shown in **3-83** has been fitted with small squares of soffit screen secured with copper wire staples and is now ready for the sandstone to be placed over a bed of gravel. Pour about five pounds of coarse gravel into the container (see **3-84**). A turntable helps the work. Smooth out the gravel with a small whisk broom or bonsai brush (see **3-85**). Wash the gravel out with water if necessary. Most aquarium gravel is quite clean.

This batch, as seen in **3-84**, is dusty; so it will receive an additional wash from the garden hose.

The position shown in **3-86** is where the two rocks seem to relate to each other the best. The gap between them provides a nice coastal effect and the sedimentary lines seem to correspond in "geological" time.

The three small trees shown in **3-87** need trimming. We are after a windswept effect that is characteristic of

3-83

3-84

3-85

3-86

3–87

3–89

3–88

3–90

the wind one would find at the beach. The trunks would normally lean slightly towards the beach, but the branches would definitely grow away from the predominant sea breezes.

Take the cypress out of their containers and remove the top layer of soil from their roots (see **3–88**). Locate the tree which has the greatest trunk curve. This is the one that will be closest to the wind. The other two will provide visual support by repetition.

The first tree, shown in **3–89**, has been trimmed. The trunk is leaning towards the shore, but the branches cluster in close towards each other as they attempt to protect themselves from the endless breeze.

The second tree, shown in **3–90**, is trimmed much like the first, except that it is allowed to remain taller, and it retains a lone branch facing the wind because of the protection of the first tree. The same forces affect both trees, so prune them similarly.

The third tree is still slightly taller. It is pruned more upright and will be placed in the most upwind direction of the three. The three trees are shown in **3—91** from left to right: one, two, and three. Place them on the rocks from left to right, starting with tree number one. Cut off only those roots necessary to place the tree in its proper location (see **3—92**). Balance the amount of foliage with the roots that are retained. Keep more roots than necessary, just to make sure the tree survives.

The first tree is shown in place in **3—93**. The other two will be positioned a little higher up on the second rock. There may be some final touch-up pruning to do, but the basic location has been established. The windswept effect, from left to right, is consistent with the shape of the rock.

The three trees, shown in **3—94**, are located on the two rocks. Next, decorative rock is added to enhance the feeling of wave action. For the deep water, add the blue gravel first (see **3—95**). Then follows a layer of green gravel just inside the blue (see **3—96**). The wind is com-

3—91

3—93

3—92

3—94

ing from left to right, so the green is used only where the surf is highly agitated. A final layer of irregular white gravel completes the scene (see **3—97**). For best results, build up concentric circles of gravel around the rocks. It will imitate the secondary waves found around large rocks at the seashore. If you do not like the results, you can always sort out the gravel and start again.

The final scene of creating this rock-grown landscape is shown in **3—98**. This planting is so dependent on the rocks and gravel for its visual impact that it crosses the grey area from bonsai to *Saikei*, or miniature landscape. Moss will eventually cover the soil, and some miniature ground covers will help hold moisture in the tiny root balls remaining under the cypress trees. Lantern wicks can be extended, if desired, from the root masses into waiting water receptacles in back of the rocks. The wicks draw up moisture when it is difficult to regularly water the trees. For show purposes, of course, this device is disconnected and left behind, but reattached after the exhibit.

3—95

3—97

3—96

3—98

Clustered Style—Tsukami Yose

More than just a dense clump of trees, this style is characterized by distinct clusters of certain species (see **3—99**). *Tsukami Yose* style takes into account such species as choke cherry, manzanita, vine maple, red twig dogwood, Arctic willow, Mugho pine, mountain hemlock, and other species that tend to have not only multiple apices, but also grow in clusters in the wild. In contrast to *Yama Yori* (discussed below), where a clump is formed from a single pine cone or seed cluster, this style favors the natural clustering of a parent or dominant tree along with its offspring nearby. Twenty-one or more trees are common to get the desired effect.

3—99

Natural Style—Yoma Yori or Yoma Yose

One year, I was growing some beech from seed; but having no room to promote some of the prolific seedlings into four-inch pots, I had to leave them overwinter in a nursery flat. The following fall through benign neglect I had a group planting that I could no longer separate. But, looked at in another way, I had the makings of a forest planting. What I had created, somewhat by accident, was a *Yoma Yori*: a natural informal grouping of trees that take on the added effect that can only be achieved by total random planting. This effect is lost in the well-ordered and organized *Yose Uye* that was contrived in the section above on how to create a rock-grown landscape.

A natural-style grove, or *Yoma Yori*, is shown in **3—100**. The trunk lines are irregular and random, and the trees have never been pruned. The three trees are Hokkaido elm, *Ulmus parvifolia* "Hokkaido," the smallest leaf size of all the Chinese elm group. These trees are eighteen inches high, and their trunks are still insignificant in diameter in spite of being twelve years old.

3—100

Fallen Cone or Hundred-Tree
Style—Yama Yori

Picture what would happen if the seeds contained in one large pine cone were all to sprout! This doesn't often happen in nature, but sometimes the weather and temperature are just perfect and a great number of successful seedlings all come from one spot on the forest floor. The competition is fierce, because only a few will survive to maturity; but the results are stunning (see **3–101**).

The trunks develop slender and without scars, because there isn't enough light to support branch buds. The many trunks slowly diverge as their respective canopies compete for light and space.

In a bonsai pot, there is nothing quite as dramatic as a birch *Yama Yori*. Imagine a hundred narrow shafts of white bark arising from a single spot. Each tiny tree has a few well-placed leaves to continue the struggle. This is a high-maintenance style, but well worth the effort.

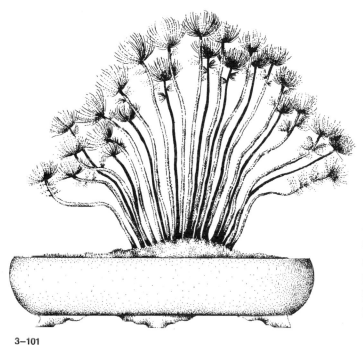

3–101

MICROENVIRONMENTS

Just as Toshio Kawamoto created *Saikei*, Leon Snyder conceived the microenvironment. Mr. Snyder, as a teacher of landscape architecture, has carried the concept of *Saikei* to a new and exciting level. He challenged himself and his students to travel, observe, and finally, to recreate nature's ecosystems in a pot. These works of art are large; three-foot-long pots are a minimum. They are also as accurate a study of nature's forces as can be assembled artificially (see **3–102**). There is a particular emphasis on wind, erosion, geology, varieties, scale, and the interaction of species. Are microenvironments a bonsai art? Probably the definition is being stretched a bit, their execution is well worth it.

3–102

4
PRUNING

PRUNING IS THE REMOVAL OF PLANT TISSUES by mechanical means. We intentionally take away parts of the tree to accomplish a certain shape or to prevent dieback from within the plant. In nature pruning takes place at regular intervals. Each spring, animals eat the new shoots; summer pruning is accomplished by insects; fall pruning is due to frost; and in winter there is natural root and twig dieback.

Consider the alternative: no pruning. Your bonsai branches get longer every year, lose their compact shape, and most important, lose their ability to get back into shape because latent buds will have been covered by thick layers of aging bark. The question then, is not whether to prune, but when, how, and why.

PRINCIPLES OF GROWTH

One characteristic of life is that living things must grow or die—have the capacity and ability to enlarge and multiply. Bonsai must also grow or die. Slow growth still qualifies as growth; however, most healthy bonsai grow quite a bit per year, but their shape is maintained by pruning.

There is a fine line between pruning for style and pruning for the health of the tree. Like other aspects of bonsai care, it is often difficult to distinguish between form and function. When I prune, I am aware that some cuts are for outline shape and not specifically to encourage buds. Good pruning is knowing what you want to accomplish, and making the cut in the manner that will accomplish your goals. A simple example will help.

Suppose your trunk is not well tapered. It starts out nice at the base and then, three inches up, it suddenly gets narrow too fast. By allowing branches in this area to grow untrimmed, the trunk will get bigger. Now comes the critical question: You know that leaf pruning on this species is best done in June, but why would you leaf-prune this tree at all? All you will accomplish is nullifying your efforts to expand your trunk. Develop a conceptual plan for your tree. Ask yourself the critical question: Do I know how to accomplish what I want? What follows is a list to help you establish pruning and growth priorities for your bonsai.

1. Learn how to keep your bonsai alive! This seems obvious, but so many times I have seen a student try to leaf-prune just because it's June; never mind that the tree is barely surviving. If necessary, practise on smaller, easy-to-care-for plants.

2. Learn how to keep your bonsai vigorous and healthy. The necessity to dwarf the foliage and keep the bonsai in a state of partial stress is often emphasized, but it is far better to accomplish the dwarfing in a controlled manner. Why should the struggling plant be pruned at all? It just might be the final insult!

3. Work on trunk development first. Branches and rootage can always come later. The trunk contributes more to the illusion of age than any other design element.

4. Work on developing good rootage. Cover and protect roots that are smaller in diameter than a pencil. Gradually expose larger roots for visual stability.

5. Prune to establish primary and secondary branches, always keeping in mind your style objectives. Prune out problem areas early in the life of your bonsai. Don't wait ten years to finally get rid of an ugly slingshot branch; it is better to have ten years' worth of healing on that big scar.

6. The least important pruning is concern for leaf or needle size. Your bonsai should be 90 percent complete before you consider this aspect of your tree. Work first on the more important defects. You will need maximum photosynthesis to correct trunk defects, and you cannot accomplish this task with reduced leaf size.

As a general rule, whenever you do any pruning, balance your foliage with your rootage. If you remove some roots, it is better to simultaneously reduce the amount of foliage.

For species such as pine and juniper, it is especially important that there not be unutilized roots in the pot or root rot might occur. For example, if you reduce a pine bonsai foliage by half, also prune away some of the roots; not as much as half, but possibly one quarter to one third.

Consider an apple tree in your yard. If you prune it heavily in February, you may be shocked to discover in April that where there were 10 branches last year, now there are 100! What happened? The root base remained intact and the tree tried to replace the foliage surface area it had last year plus new growth it had stored up during the winter. A second pruning in April is necessary to remove these shoots. For bonsai, foliage development is accomplished in the same manner.

Consider the same apple tree, except this time you not only prune the foliage as before, but you dig up the tree and prune the roots as well! You put it back, of course, but now what happens as it buds out? If you cut too many important roots, the tree dies. If you cut some important roots, but not too many, the tree experiences some twig die back and the balance of the branches that live will not fruit. If you cut just as many roots as branches, no shoots will sprout, last year's latent buds will open, and this year's growth will have sparse fruit. If you cut far fewer roots than branches, some latent buds will open in addition to all last year's active buds. The fruit harvest will not be impaired; neither will it be a record-breaking year. Secondary branches may have to be thinned out in April to avoid crowding.

These principles apply to all trees including bonsai. The timing may vary according to climate and species, but the principles are the same.

Another principle of growth is demonstrated by planting identical seeds in different-sized pots. The plants that are in the larger containers sprout a bit earlier—not much, but a bit—and they grow bigger and look healthier than the plants in the smaller containers. (The roots have not yet reached the edges of even the smallest pot!) The plants in the larger containers are greener and start to send out secondary branches sooner. What biological force is at work? A larger container offers the plant more stability than the smaller one; the plant needs watering less often; and the container provides more nourishment as the plant demands it. Now consider the bonsai application; the larger the pot, the easier it is to maintain a tree. There are several lessons to be learned from these examples.

1. Sick trees should be repotted in larger containers or in the ground.

2. If you are still working on trunk development, a large container will help you attain your goal faster.

3. Root development will speed up when the tree is repotted in a larger container.

4. Small pots are inappropriate when utilizing propagation techniques, such as sowing seed, making cuttings, air layering, or grafting.

Growth is regulated by hormones that move about in the vascular system of the tree. An area of growth in a plant is known as a meristem. Hormones can be bud-inducing or bud-inhibiting. When a branch tip is removed by pruning, the bud-inhibitor hormone is carried away with the prunings. The resulting hormonal imbalance stimulates the plant to activate more meristematic areas. Thus, the more you prune, the more you encourage the development of new growth. Some bonsai principles are based on this characteristic of growth.

1. If your plant is leggy, has long internodes, has no foliage inside, but plenty outside, then pinch off the branch tips often during the growing season.

2. If your branches rebranch too far from the trunk, let new growth extend itself for the month of May; then prune back to the point where you desire secondary branching.

3. If you don't have enough branches from your trunk or need additional branches where there are none, allow new growth to extend itself unchecked for two months; then remove all branches, leaving none. Your tree will then have maximum levels of bud-inducing hormone and will be forced to break open adventitious buds that are dormant. Some species, such as Scotch pine, are highly resistant to budding back, but it still works better than anything else you might do. This technique is especially useful on deciduous trees.

There are characteristic hormonal levels for all species. A low-growing azalea will always have greater concentrations of bud inhibitor in the apex areas of the plant than in the side branches. Conversely, the Italian cypress is quite apically dominant, meaning it has a greater concentration of meristematic inhibitors in its side branches than in the strong apex. Because of this natural phenomenon, we must modify our pruning techniques to fit the species.

Now you can understand why the hardest area to develop on an azalea bonsai is the trunk. The solution is to work on developing the trunk first by pinching off all side growth and training a solid, strong leader that will form the trunk. When the full height of the bonsai is attained, pinch off the apex; strong side shoots will spring out in every direction. Remove all the undesirable branches and your general outline will soon be filled out.

For the Italian cypress, the strong apical dominance means that we have to work on developing the branches to their full length. From a well-tapered trunk, encourage a side shoot to grow towards the sun. Pinch off all other growth, especially sprouts along the trunk. Pinch off all upward-facing shoots from the upper surface of the Number One branch, and keep pinching until the desired length is attained. Then start working on the Number Two branch, and so forth. The trunk will develop good taper as you work your way to the top of the tree.

These examples illustrate techniques used to form the traditional pine tree shape, *Matsu Zukuri*, from plant material that resists these shapes. If you would rather create a broom-style azalea or a flame-shaped Italian cypress, these techniques are inappropriate and counterproductive, since the hormone distribution is already in place for forming that shape. Pinching all around is sufficient to maintain its natural outline.

Yet, some plants do better in the *Matsu Zukuri* style than they do in their natural state. Many plants, such as the boxwood, Sawara cypress, juniper, pine, arborvitae, Alberta spruce, etc., drop foliage as soon as it is shaded by new foliage. Look inside a hedge; it's all bare inside! Bonsai will do the same unless the individual branches are spread out horizontally to capture the sun's rays. This is why the broom style is usually reserved for deciduous material rather than broadleaf evergreens or conifers. Nevertheless, larch, metasequoia, bald cypress, tamarack, and ginkgo are comfortable with either broom or pine tree styles. With any style, take into consideration the amount of light necessary for sustaining foliage, and prune back accordingly.

PURPOSE OF PRUNING

One prunes for a variety of reasons. Sometimes only one function is performed; but usually each snip of the pruning tool accomplishes many positive goals. We prune roots so that we may:

1. Get the tree into the pot. By doing so we are allowing the container to partially dwarf the foliage and reduce the internodal spaces. This gives us many more suitable locations for choosing where to prune the foliage.

2. Encourage the roots to divide. Whenever a root is cut, it divides. Rather than have a few large, unproductive roots in the bonsai pot, we can root-prune and force hundreds of new, productive roots to grow.

We prune foliage so that we may:

1. Keep the bonsai small. Even the most crude hedge trimming accomplishes this.

2. Promote more buds. This gives us a greater choice for directing areas of new growth.

3. Shape and style. By keeping the branches trim and the trunk free of suckers, we can add to the illusion of age.

4. Discourage pests and disease. A clean, clear, well-ventilated tree will resist mildew and sucking insects.

5. Create *jin*, *shari*, and *saba miki*. Many pruning tools are designed specifically to create old, dead weatherized areas on bonsai.

6. Allow sunlight to bleach out the trunk, *shari*, *saba miki*, and *jin*.

7. Intentionally create areas of unequal growth. It is just as important to discourage active growth where it is not needed as it is to encourage new shoots in bare areas.

8. Direct growth. By pruning just beyond a new bud that is pointed in the right direction, we avoid the use of wires and add to the delicacy of the branch's secondary and tertiary ramifications.

9. Keep a tree young. If all new growth is cut off repeatedly, the tree weakens and eventually dies. Some new growth must be allowed to ensure the continued health of the plant.

10. Reduce transplanting shock. When doing major potting or repotting work, it is helpful to cut off some of the foliage so that the demand for nutrients from the roots is reduced.

11. Reduce leaf size. Leaf pruning—cutting off all the leaves on a maple tree, for example—makes the new leaves smaller and have a more attractive fall color. The same is true with some conifers.

12. See trunks for potting or shaping. Often deciduous trees are leaf-pruned not only to reduce transplanting shock, but also to help the artist train the branches. When creating group plantings, it is sometimes easier to design or style them with their leaves off. Potting in winter, of course, is best, but sometimes summer potting is necessary.

TOOLS AND THEIR USE

Ask anyone who uses tools to earn a living and he or she will most likely advise you that you should purchase as good a tool as you can afford. I recommend avoiding the really low-cost lines that tool companies produce. In bonsai tools, price does indicate the degree of wearability. On the other hand, it is not necessary for a beginner to purchase a large set of expensive stainless tools with a leather carrying pouch either. A middle ground is best. I am still using some of the tools I bought twenty years ago in Japan.

What follows is a brief list of tools that you should consider for a basic set. I list them in decreasing order of importance; by the time you get to the tenth or twelfth tool, they are clearly optional, and you may add the remaining tools as your personal needs justify.

Concave Cutter.   There is no other tool made in the world for any purpose that duplicates the function of the concave cutter (see **4–1**). Pruning a bonsai without one is cumbersome. There are several varieties made. The best all-around cutter is actually an angled, spherical knob cutter, a minor improvement over the more common concave cutter.

Trimming Shears.   This is any multipurpose trimmer or scissors accurate enough for delicate twigs, yet that can cut smaller roots as well (see **4–2**).

Root Hook.   As mentioned in Chapter One (see **4–3** and refer to **1–12**).

Wire Cutter.   As mentioned in Chapter One, the best kind are the angled bonsai wire cutters (see **4–4** and refer to **1–8**).

Leaf Trimmer.   An inexpensive tool that saves a lot of time (see **4–5**). A fair substitute would be a small pair of scissors suitable for trimming thread while sewing.

Chopsticks.   Bare wood is best (see **4–6 and 4–7**). The kind that are Jacquered are too slippery.

Tweezers and Spatula.   These are found in combination as one tool or available separately (see **4–8**). Many tasks are too clumsy for fingers, such as placing moss, removing insects, picking off leaves or buds, arranging gravel, weeding, etc.

Pliers.   The Japanese *jin*-making pliers have an added feature: a broad, shallow tip on one end of one jaw (see **4–9**). Common adjustable pliers, plus a screwdriver, make an adequate substitution.

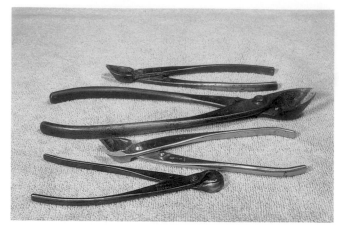

4–1

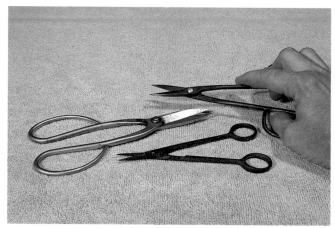

4–2

4–3

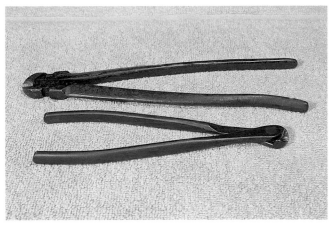

4–4

4–5

4–6

4–7

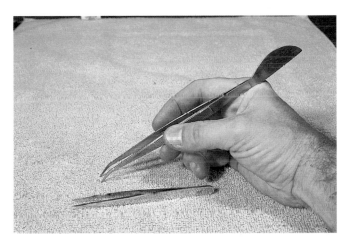

4–8

4–9

Folding Saw. Eventually you will run into a branch that will be too big to cut with the concave cutters. There are a number of fine-toothed saws made for bonsai (see **4–10**). They have at least sixteen teeth to the inch, and when folded, they are only eight or ten inches long.

Turntable. As mentioned in Chapter One (see **4–11** and refer to **1–10**).

Needle-Nosed Pliers. These are handy for winding wire around branches in cramped spaces.

Carving Set. Any tools suitable for wood carving or sculpture, even a Swiss Army knife, is useful (see **4–12**).

Tamping Trowel. It finishes the soil surface, fixes moss, moves gravel, etc.

Branch Splitter. Used for moving large branches, carving *jin*, cutting large roots. Similar to a concave cutter, except that the cutting blades meet at 180 degrees (see **4–13**).

Potting Sickle. For cutting pot-bound trees out of the container. You can sharpen the edge of a root hook.

Chisels. For hollowing out *sabamiki*, carving large *jin*, *shari*. Wood-sculpting tools with a mallet are nice.

Clamps. For bending large branches (see **4–14**).

Large Concave Cutter. This will become a great convenience as the size of your trees increases.

4–11

4–12

4–10

4–13

4–14

CARE OF TOOLS

My experience here in the Northwest has been that if any part of any tool can rust, it will, and it can rust overnight (see **4–15**). I have a small aerosol can of spray lubricant handy; it dissolves sap and resin residues from conifers, and after wiping with a dry cloth, it leaves behind a thin protective layer against rust. Some say mineral oil is best, but my spray lubricant is very convenient.

Never use a file to sharpen your bonsai tools. I speak from experience, bad experience. There is usually only one surface that needs sharpening on most bonsai tools (see **4–16**). By using a file, no matter how fine, you drive small particles of metal to the other side of the cutting surface, and these will interfere with the opposing blade. Your tools will be ruined! If you choose to sharpen your own tools, use an Arkansas Stone or similar oil stone; first medium grit, then fine grit to finish. I urge you to take your tools to a bonsai specialist who can either sharpen them or make a definite recommendation.

Store your tools in a clean, dry, cloth-lined drawer or leather pouch. Keep all sharp surfaces pointing in the same direction (see **4–17**).

When travelling, pack extra cloth between each tool to avoid nicks and scratches. For workshops, mark *your* tool handles with nail polish or engrave your name.

Get into the routine of removing soil to one side of your turntable and parking your tools on the other side (I recommend soil to the left, tools right). Small tools can easily end up in the trash as you clean up. Keep only the same five favorite tools on the workbench; leave the others in the drawer or pouch. During cleanup simply count your tools to account for them.

Sterilize your tools after working on infected trees—removing galls, blight, rot, fungus, mildew, virus, or small insects, such as mites, aphids, or whitefly. A thorough wipe with isopropyl alcohol or a strong bleach solution will do. Wipe the tools dry and recoat lightly with oil.

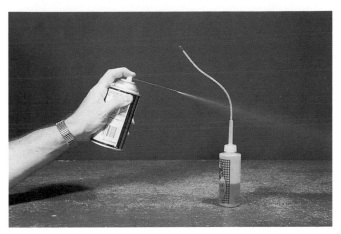

4–15

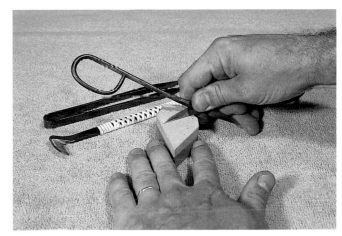

4–16

4–17

WOUND SEALERS

I recommend wound sealers for the following reasons:

1. Fast-growing deciduous material, such as birch, willow, elm, maple, hornbeam, and alder, have a nasty tendency to die back to the next bud behind the bud you selected during pruning. Wound sealer tends to conserve moisture around these important buds and allows controlled healing to occur. The resultant new growth is where you wanted it to be and in the right direction.

2. In both collected and nursery material, I am aware that some of the twigs and branches I am removing might be dead due to fungal or bacterial infection. I seal the wounds because I want to do all I can to keep these diseases from spreading.

3. Bonsai is an art form. I use wound sealers to cover up recent scars so that my trees look better. If a scar has no possibility of healing over, I use it as part of the design to create *jin* or to carve curves and hollows. A wound sealer with pigment, such as shoe polish or mud, makes a wound less visible. Japanese wound sealers also contain growth hormone to speed the healing process. Add powdered rooting hormone to your wound sealer for a similar result.

PRUNING TECHNIQUES

These suggestions do not take into account the design of the tree you are pruning. For example, when pruning back to a particular bud, the assumption is made that this pruning will help accomplish your design goals.

PRUNING A BRANCH COMPLETELY OFF

For small branches this is the easiest pruning you will ever do on a bonsai. Simply snip off the branch as close to the trunk as is physically possible (see **4–18**). Run your finger across the scar. Is there any bump or rise where the branch formerly was? If so, use a concave cutter to shape the area until it is perfectly smooth.

For medium-sized branches—about the diameter of a pencil—make your first cut about one quarter of an inch away from the trunk (see **4–19**). The branch's weight and bulk will then be out of the way for further touching up with the concave cutter (see **4–20**). There is never any need to cut off a branch with just one cut. The concave cutter, or its improved cousin, the knob cutter, does best when several cuts are made (see **4–21**). You should plan to "chew away" at the area until just the right contour is achieved. Run your finger over the cut area a few times and keep trimming until a smooth cut is achieved.

For large cuts—one-half-inch-diameter or greater—two options appear, *jin* or concave cut. If the only *jin* on your tree is one medium-sized branch, your tree will look as though one branch died last winter and you haven't gotten around to removing it yet. But, if you have many and varied branches peeled, twisted, and glistening with driftwood-grey hues, the design impact makes more sense.

4–18

4–19

4–20

4–21

4–22

4–23

MAKING JIN, SHARI, AND SABAMIKI

By now you probably understand that any deadwood remaining on a bonsai intentionally becomes a design element known as *jin* or *shari*. *Jin* is found at the top of the tree and is inspired by lightning-struck trees in the wilderness. *Shari* is deadwood located on a branch; it comes from frost-damaged or snow-broken branches on timberline trees. Each tree has a characteristic way of displaying deadwood; for example, dead branches on an old apple tree look quite different from dead branches on an ancient pine tree at timberline. Whenever you get the chance, photograph or sketch good examples from nature, and refer to them when carving your *jin* or *shari*.

MAKING SMALL JIN OR SHARI

One small *jin* will look out of place on your tree. Locate other areas that will repeat your theme. To peel bark easily, lightly crush the live twigs and small branches with a pair of pliers so that the cambium layer has been loosened. Pinch lightly around each twig from many angles so that the cambium is evenly loosened all around the twig. When the cambium is fully loosened from the heartwood inside, the bark comes off easily.

You may have to scrape some areas clean (see **4–22**). Define the edge of the *jin* with a clean cut with a knife and take care to protect the good cambium from accidental damage while cleaning the *jin* (see **4–23 and 4–24**). Important! While the wood is still soft, you may choose to wire it into place to complete the design. Once the deadwood is dry, it is too brittle to move.

4–24

4–25

After three months of drying out, lightly paint the *jin* with full-strength lime sulfur. This is easiest done with a small artist's brush (see **4–25**). The lime sulfur will protect the deadwood from disease and will impart a nice driftwood-grey tone to the wood like what is found in nature. Protect the soil surface with a cloth during painting.

MAKING MEDIUM-SIZED JIN OR SHARI

This is basically the same as above. Some consideration must be made so that the branch size balances the rest of the tree. If a medium-sized branch is found towards the top of the tree, it is better to scrape, peel, split, or otherwise reduce its diameter so that its heaviness does not stand out among the smaller branches.

MAKING LARGE JIN

A large *jin* is a substantial design element for a bonsai. A hastily designed major *jin* could ruin the appearance of an otherwise natural-looking bonsai. Consider the following guidelines.

1. The *jin* should communicate a story or scenario. For instance, consider carefully the different appearances resulting from damage due to snow overload versus a lightning strike.

2. A large *jin* could overwhelm the tree, particularly if this technique is being used instead of leaving a large pruning scar. Plan carefully to use only the best portions of the dead branch; no more and no less.

3. Take into consideration the natural flow of the grain of the wood. Nothing makes a *jin* look more ugly than to carve a curve into straight-grained wood. Many current bonsai artists use various power carving tools. For patient, fastidious bonsai enthusiasts, a simple set of hand-carving tools will give hours of pleasure at a relaxed, pensive pace.

MAKING SABAMIKI

Hollowing out a trunk is the third major form of bonsai deadwood, called *sabamiki*. This is often found on fruit trees such as apple, cherry, and wild plum; nut trees such as walnut and oak; and further, on such hardwoods as myrtle. But most often, this hollowed-out trunk is found on softer woods because of the inability of the tree to maintain *jin* or *shari*. Such species as pine, buttonwood, bald cypress, olive, willow, birch, sequoia, larch, redwood, etc., will often have an exaggerated root buttress due to some dieback of a strip of cambium close to the base of the tree. Even large succulent trees such as the East African baobab, thorn trees, sausage trees, or bougainvillea exhibit this trait with increasing age.

To make *sabamiki*, carve away enough trunk to make a significant impact on the design. At least one third of the trunk should be involved, both vertically and horizontally. Carve deep and irregularly. Treat with lime sulfur, as always.

A *Juniperus chinensis* "San Jose" is shown in **4–26** that I found in a bonsai nursery a few years ago. It has been in training for three years. The *shari* had been started by nature and chased down with carving tools. There are two points on this tree where the living cambium layer is only one-half inch wide, yet the tree thrives. It is twenty-one inches high with a two-and-a-half-inch trunk. The reddish brown container is a Japanese fourteen-inch oval.

4–26

HOW TO STYLE JIN, SHARI AND SABAMIKI

I think you can see in **4–27** that the tree is unusual. It is an Alpine fir, *Abies lasiocarpa*, collected from the mountains two years earlier at an altitude just above 5000 feet. It has never been pruned. The large cut end on the left was a longer dead end that was cut for ease of transporting the tree. The rings on that cut end are too numerous to count—even with a magnifying glass—but they certainly exceed two hundred. At these high altitudes, as well as in the desert, trees in some years will form two rings. In spring, new growth will form the first ring, usually in June. The intense ultraviolet of July and August forces the tree into a summer dormancy. In a warm September the tree takes advantage of early rains, if they come, to push new growth. This second growth ring is sometimes mistaken for an annual ring. A high-alpine tree with one hundred rings is unlikely to be one hundred years old; it is also just as unlikely to be fifty years old. At 5000 feet, the chances of a warm, wet September are about one in three; therefore, one hundred rings may actually represent about eighty-five years. Similarly, this fir tree is possibly more than one hundred seventy years old.

The back of the tree is shown in **4–28**. The trunk curves away from the viewer as do the three possible tops. In addition, the interesting lower *sabumiki* is absent. It is the *sabamiki*, or hollow trunk, which has forced the cambium to flare out sideways; this gives the tree its huge taper and root buttress.

The portion of the trunk shown in **4–29** gives a glimpse of what may be in store for this tree. Large areas of dead bark remain attached to the tree. This bark must be removed to help the tree combat insects and disease. If the dead portions are carved away carefully and slowly, eventually the live strips of bark can be located to help the artist style the tree.

Wiring the branches into place first only interferes with the artist's ability to carve the wood. Only remove those branches that are definitely not needed. The dead

4–27

4–28

4–29

branch shown in **4–30** is superfluous because it is small in diameter as well as long and leggy in appearance. By the time the artist is done with this tree, there will be sufficient deadwood of importance that such a distraction need not be retained.

Surrounding the remaining branches are dead twigs that originate from live branches (see **4–31**). These twigs should be retained, but shortened so that they are not distracting. They will be torn away to maintain a strictly natural appearance.

Excess dead twigs have been broken away in **4–32**. The next step is a large one: that of trying to locate live cambium while removing dead bark. This process will take a couple of days' work; but with patience and care, the fir tree will be in no danger.

A portion of the dead bark has been removed from the upper right-hand side of the tree in **4–33**. Bonsai master Kimura is well known for his ability to trace living cambium over the trunks of collected *Shimpaku* juniper. The secret is to go slow and easy with a very sharp carving tool. When live cambium is reached, the carving tool pushes readily through the soft layer, exposing a thin line of new red bark outside a bright yellow slippery cambium layer. Go no farther, but follow

4–30

4–32

4–31

4–33

the line formed by the adjacent cambium finds. On the right side of the bark–deadwood interface in **4–33**, the red and white lines are visible. Do not, under any circumstances, start stripping bark off that has not been tested in the above manner.

Down at the base of the trunk, the cambium layer is located by using a push-type bonsai carving tool (see **4–34**). When the soft red and white layer is found, the tool is set a bit higher. Gradually the trunk is ascended to reach the *shari* area high up on the right side of the tree.

The knob that is protruding from the center of the *sabamiki* is ugly and needs to leave (see **4–35**). A pair of pliers does the job.

It is much better without the knob (see **4–36**). Actually, there is live cambium at its base, indicating a strong rootage on the back side of this flared root buttress. Once the total cambium layer has been identified, the dead area can be treated with lime sulfur to even out the color.

In an effort to trace the cambium layer on the left side of the *sabamiki*, I had to dig down to locate the trunk's beginning point at the soil line. After a little exploration, I discovered about an inch and a half more trunk, all twisted, gnarly, and hollowed out (see **4–37**).

4–34

4–36

4–35

4–37

After repotting, which was then necessary, this trunk threatened to extend its diameter across the entire pot.

The cambium layer has been identified up and down the lower trunk (see **4–38**). I discovered that there are no dead areas on the upper third of the tree. The *sabamiki* on the trunk gradually tapers to *shari* farther up and stops abruptly at the uppermost portion of the tree.

The *jin* on this end of the tree, shown in **4–39**, will have to be independent of the *shari* and *sabamiki*. The *jin* will have to serve three design functions. First, it will have to harmonize with the existing dead areas in terms of texture, physical size, and internal consistency of style. The *shari* is fairly smooth and follows the trunk contours explicitly. The *jin* should show no more than one third of the total diameter to continue in the same visual impact. The *jin* must show the wearing down of wood rather than some violent style such as the breakage of branches to be in keeping with existing *sabamiki*. Second, this *jin* will have to provide realistic taper to the apex, thereby disguising that the end was cut off with a pruning saw. Third, it must provide an explanation for its existence. In this case, it has to be visually convincing that the exact same forces of nature which created the *shari* and *sabamiki* were at work on forming the *jin*. Given the extreme left-to-right sweep, the forces that shaped this tree were primarily wind and ultraviolet light. Wind accounts for the sweep of the foliage and summer

4–38

4–40

4–39

4–41

4–42

4–44

4–43

4–45

sun explains why there is no strong upward-pushing apex and extensive *shari* along the top of the trunk.

The wood shown in **4–40** is extremely hard due to its age. Fragmented sections of trunk can be retained to resemble branches. These will help explain why the tree tapers so quickly in this area and also provide more visual interest.

The completed *jin* is shown in **4–41**. I am afraid to come any closer to the two end branches, one will become the apex, and the other, a significant branch, since there are few branches on this tree. It is not worth losing these two branches for the sake of good *jin* taper.

These two end branches are shown in **4–42** wired so that they can be bent into their final shape. The outermost branch on the left is best for the apex; the other will be brought down severely to resemble the other branches.

The apex and top branch are shown in **4–43** in place. They both required two separate winds of ten-gauge copper wire to move. The long branchlets to the left should be removed to be consistent with the "wind" direction. The apex must also be slanted slightly towards the right.

The branch shown in **4–44** originates not only from the same location as the one next to it, but the foliage contributes nothing to the design. Rather than retain it as greenery, it is better to remove it and show off the *shari* a little more.

The branch is cut slightly with the concave cutter, then torn off upward to strip off the bark (see **4–45**). If

4–47

height of the bonsai is twenty inches. The wire may have to remain for two years due to the heaviness and age of the tree.

SHAPING A TREE

Familiarize yourself with the degree of apical dominance of your bonsai before attempting to prune. What does the tree tend to do when left alone? Is it a strong upright grower? Does it tend to grow about as wide as tall? Does it tend to hug the ground? Some pines are strong vertical growers and others hug close to the ground. Some bud back on bare wood and others always must have a green growing tip. Learn as much as you can about your tree before trying to prune it as a bonsai.

Most bonsai will have about two thirds foliage and one third bare trunk. Make sure that these proportions are roughly kept. If the lowest branch on the bonsai is high, simply allow the top to grow higher. The relative proportions of your tree will improve with age as its total height increases, and, therefore, the lowest branch will start looking better.

If the lowest branch is too low, reduce the height of the tree and, at the same time, reduce the overall foliage outline (see **4–48**). Simply find a convenient forward-facing branch near the top of your tree and wire it up to make a new apex. You may choose to remove the trunk immediately above this new apex or let it remain for a season (see **4–49**).

this branch were simply cut off, it would look artificial. While it is still green and moist, it can be curved slightly by overbending it with a pair of pliers.

The wiring is now complete as shown in **4–46**. Some branches may still be trimmed, but the basic style is established. It is an unusual *Fukinagashi* shape in that most windswept forms in the mountains will not allow the trunk to point towards the wind. This form is most likely to occur on the coast.

The tree was raised in the container just to show off the eleven-inch trunk (see **4–47**). Lime sulfur bleached out the *jin*, *shari*, and *sabamiki* overnight. The total

4–48

I find it extremely useful, although temporarily ugly, to utilize the upright trunk as a support for the new top (see **4–50**). The advantage is that there is no bulge towards the front, right below the new top, as there is when the new top is simply wired up. Green floral tape makes an ideal wrap because it is wide and flexible and will not leave a scar as other materials might (see **4–51**).

4–49

SHAPING A BRANCH

Get into the habit of approaching the branches with your hands lower than your pruning scissors. This way, the outermost extension of the branch will always be at the bottom edge. By always pruning in this manner, the new buds will have a tendency to form on the downward side—and as new growth comes out of the terminus, it will tend to be flatter rather than straight up.

4–50

SHORTENING A BRANCH

If foliage is present all along the branch length, then it is easily shortened merely by pruning at the tip of the branch. If foliage is not present close in to the trunk, then measures must be taken to achieve this foliage first. New buds are allowed to swell to their maximum size, then the buds at the tip of the branch can be removed. This will usually create new buds farther in towards the trunk. Repeat this process until growth on the branch has been established close to the trunk; then shorten the branch by pruning as needed.

4–51

LENGTHENING A BRANCH

To lengthen a branch, slowly allow the branch to develop outwards. This means pinching back at regular intervals. By allowing the branch to develop slowly in stages, you can avoid the barrel-shaped branches of a fast-growing tree. Do not prune back your branch if you are trying to develop length; merely pinch new buds in half as they develop so that they will divide.

FATTENING A BRANCH

Almost every bonsai has flaws to some degree or another. One flaw that is seen often is that there is no consistent decrease in the diameter of branches from bottom (the thickest) to top (the thinnest). On bonsai, we often overlook or compromise this relationship in order to prevent bare spots on our trees. This is understandable and sometimes unavoidable, but it is possible to fatten up a branch diameter. Following are several methods.

Method 1. Similar to fattening a trunk, find a backwards-facing branchlet that is largely hidden from view. Point this branchlet towards the sun, and let it grow unhindered for a season or more; then remove. The branch will be forced to grow thicker to supply the extra growth.

Method 2. Several times a week, grasp the small branch, and wiggle it back and forth. It is not necessary to see cracking in the bark or damage in any way. The more often, the better.

Method 3. Carefully slit the branch lengthwise with a razor blade. Make small slits along the branch, primarily on the top and bottom, especially close in to the trunk and decreasing as you extend out onto the branch. Do not remove bark! Merely score it deeply, leave it alone for a month, and do it again until the branch starts to look thicker. Try to mimic the natural cracking pattern the bark makes as it gets older. Rubbing rooting hormone into the cuts will accelerate the results.

THINNING A BRANCH

Growth always progresses from small to large. When dwarfing a plant, it is inaccurate to think of it actually shrinking. By thinning out a branch all you are doing is removing some of the green substance where photosynthesis takes place and thereby inhibiting further growth of the branch that supplies that foliage. It is easier to accelerate the growth of a small branch than to slow down a larger branch. Maximum results are achieved by doing both simultaneously.

LEAF PRUNING

In young deciduous trees, it is possible to remove all the leaves in mid-June and still have enough time left in the year to develop a new crop of smaller, perfectly formed leaves that will develop superior color in autumn. Why? Why would someone want to cut all the leaves off a perfectly healthy maple tree in the middle of summer? This process, known as leaf trimming or defoliation, accomplishes three things and *doesn't* accomplish three things. These are listed below. Obviously, this technique is not appropriate for all trees all the time. See also the description below of the technique under "How to Leaf-Trim."

Benefit 1. When all the leaves are out of the way, it is easy to prune the branches.

Benefit 2. The new crop of leaves that return in a few weeks will be smaller and more to scale. The bonsai will be more attractive and will look older.

Benefit 3. Autumn color seems to be enhanced in a tree that has been defoliated.

Drawback 1. General growth of the tree is set back. If you are trying to develop roots or trunk, this technique does not make sense.

Drawback 2. For trees that are very old, observation of this annual ritual gets a little scary. Taking the leaves off a 200-year-old maple is not something I would feel comfortable doing.

Drawback 3. A diseased, sickly, or recently transplanted tree might not recover from this treatment. Make sure your tree is in excellent health before defoliating it—and do not disturb the roots at the same time.

HOW TO LEAF-TRIM

Cut! Do not pull leaves off! Using a very sharp, pointed scissors (there are tools called leaf trimmers), cut exactly halfway between the leaf bud and the beginning of the leaf surface (see **4–52 and 4–53**). There is no need to cut off the leaf stem; it will fall off by itself within a week. The danger in cutting off the leaf stem is that you risk damage to the new leaf bud that is lying directly under the stem's base.

4-52

4-53

5

POTTING

I FIRST SAW A FOREST PLANTING ON A SLAB OF rock in a Japanese bonsai calendar. I cut out the twelve photos, had them matted, and stuck them all over my bedroom walls. I carefully studied each one, imagining its owner was consulting me on which branches should be attended to, possible improvements, and suggestions for future developments. Twelve years later I found myself in Omiya, Japan, staring in awe at not just one of these trees, but four of the twelve I had put on my walls. I had no idea these trees were so big! No wonder they were so detailed and the leaves were all in proportion; they were more than three feet tall! The forest planting on a slab of rock was five feet long and probably would have taken four strong men to lift! I was both in awe and a bit disillusioned.

WHAT IS A POT?

A pot is the *bon* for the *sai*. It could be a slab, a hollow log, a porcelain container, an antique Chinese vessel, or a homemade cedar planter. The important point is that the "pot" was an integral part of the illusion I experienced. I stood staring at these all too familiar trees and realized that in a different container, the illusion would have been lost. The *bon* blended perfectly with the *sai*, and an art form was realized.

As with all rules, there are the exceptions; but the following suggestions may help you select the best container.

You now understand the relationship between pot size and growth and development of the tree. Two bonsai sayings that really say the same thing are appropriate as a caution or disclaimer: "If you have ten bonsai, nine of them should be in training in the ground." "A bonsai tree should be 90 percent complete before it is promoted to a bonsai pot." In other words, the assumption is made that you understand that the bonsai pot is a powerful dwarfing tool; trees that need major development are not appropriate in any container.

SELECTING A POT

Observe your tree carefully. If the general outline is rough and angular, then a square or rectangular pot is more appropriate than a smooth oval or round pot.

Let your plant determine the size, shape, color, and texture of the pot. Select your tree first and determine what the ideal pot should look like, then shop carefully for it. Do not be tempted to prune or design your planting around the container. Even in the repotting process, try to imagine what the ideal pot should look like. Does the new pot need to be larger, smaller, thinner, taller? Is it the right color?

Containers with bright glazes will complement brightly colored trees. A pine never looks good in a bright glaze, and a flowering quince is muddied by a dull brown pot. But, don't try to match the colors.

When texture is present, some copying is subtle and nice. A cork bark elm looks better in a pot that is not perfectly smooth, whereas the smooth Zelkova bark is lost in a rough-hewn homemade container.

Determine the finished height of your tree. The length of the container should be about two thirds the height of the tree. If your tree is wider than tall, then use the width. The depth of the pot should be about one and one half times the diameter of the trunk. Let the tree thicken in time and approach the ideal dimension slowly.

There are exceptions, however. Ignore the above rules when working with semi-cascade and cascade trees. In a round, square, hexagon-, or octagon-shaped pot, for these styles the trunk is located in the center, not to one side. In an oval or rectangular pot, the trunk is placed about one third of the way in from either side.

THE POTTING PROCESS

Healthy bonsai are in a constant state of being partially "root-bound." If a very small rooted cutting in a large pot is allowed to grow for years without repotting, it gradually goes from perhaps one percent root-bound to 100 percent root-bound; whereupon it dies. Using this for reference, bonsai should be kept at least 50 percent root-bound, but not allowed to reach 85 percent root-bound. Below 50 percent, the foliage is too large. Above 85 percent, the roots become increasingly entangled so that it is difficult to tease or comb them apart during repotting, and the foliage is getting too stunted.

When you are potting or repotting, whether from collected stock or nursery container, the ideal is to cut off only those roots that impede correct placement of the tree in the pot, plus a bit of wiggling room. Cut off any large unproductive roots; only small white roots provide water and nutrition to the plant. Retain large roots only for display on the surface of the soil. If all the small root hairs are at the ends of large roots, what do you do? Cut off some large roots (not all!) and wait until the cut ends sprout new white root hairs. If the tree does not fit into an ideal pot right away, don't force it! You may have to overpot for a year or two.

REPOTTING

How often do you have to repot? Every three to five years for conifers, two to three years for deciduous trees, one to two years for fruit trees, and most tropical indoor bonsai every two to three years. These times should vary for unusually fast- or slow-growing varieties. Watch for disease or signs of poor development at all times.

Make sure you have all supplies and materials necessary at hand well before removing the plant from the container. Have several sizes of pots in case root pruning is heavier or lighter than expected. Prepare your soil in advance. Most beginners kill their first bonsai with love and attention to minute detail, slowly selecting each root to prune and which one not to prune.

Work indoors or in full shade, on a cool day. Schedule your potting to avoid freezing weather or hot spells. Keep your roots moist at all times! A spray bottle is a necessity; use it frequently. White root hairs only need a minute of dryness to die. If it takes you two hours to repot a bonsai, you are doing something wrong. Allow yourself only 20 minutes maximum from start to finish.

Checklist Before Potting or Repotting

- ideal pot
- substitute pot (a little bigger)
- prescreened bonsai soil suitable for the species (and plenty of it!)
- screen for drain holes
- wire to secure the drain hole screens
- string to secure plant in pot
- chopsticks for tamping soil
- spray bottle (with water in it!) or substitute my potting formula: one teaspoon each of vitamin B$_1$, rooting hormone, and D.M.S.O. per gallon of water
- turntable
- root hook

Now you are ready to pot/repot. Remove the root ball from the container and slightly mist the outside of the exposed roots.

Wash the old container now if you are repotting. Remove calcified scale with vinegar. Lightly bleach the container to remove scum and possible disease residues, and rinse thoroughly.

Tease the root ball gently apart. Remove stale soil pockets that smell stagnant. Check under the trunk for insects or signs of root rot. Clean this area especially well.

Try the tree in its new container. Assess where and how much rootage will have to be removed. Ask yourself if that much removal will maintain the health and foliage of the tree. Keep slightly more roots than foliage at all times. Slightly less rootage than foliage may cause the tree to shed an important branch. Much more rootage than foliage encourages root rot as unutilized roots decay.

Trim roots until the tree is properly placed in the pot. Check from the side to make sure the apex is over the midline of the pot; check and double-check from all angles. Exposed rootage should be visible above the rim.

Add small amounts of soil at a time, and thoroughly tamp the particles into place around the roots. Spend about ten minutes tamping soil particles into crevices and air pockets. Keep tamping until no more bonsai soil can be incorporated into the new planting.

Carefully brush the soil surface to create the landscape you desire. The soil level at the inside edge of the pot should be about one quarter inch below the rim. The height of the largest exposed roots should be about one third above the total height of the pot.

Secure with string or twine as necessary. Remember to allow for wind, birds, squirrels, etc.

BONSAI SOIL

Most bonsai enthusiasts are reluctant to accept that there could be such a thing as "bonsai soil." Somehow the concept that orchids grow best in an orchid-growing medium is easier. That specialized plants such as cactus, Venus fly traps, and Bird of Paradise need specially formulated soils is acceptable. But "bonsai soil"?

Near the turn of the twentieth century, when bonsai was first being introduced into Europe and America, bonsai failed to thrive, starting a myth that there was some "Oriental secret" to growing these plants. That myth has mostly been dispelled and replaced with basic botanical knowledge. One of the main so-called secrets was the concept of making bonsai soil.

Advantages of Good Bonsai Soil

- increased oxygen to the roots
- improved drainage
- easier to transplant without damage to root hairs
- roots comb out better for pruning
- greater surface area on which roots can grow
- increase in the number of root branches and frequency of their divisions
- less dangerous heat rise in the pot in hot weather
- correct pH of soil for species
- ideal conditions for ion exchange
- suitable medium for development of healthful bacteria
- excellent color for best display
- easier to apply and control nutrients
- less damage due to root rot
- reduced twig dieback on deciduous trees
- long-term success: your trees will be healthier each year

There are five main considerations when making bonsai soil: particle size, texture, soil composition, microorganisms, and aesthetics.

PARTICLE SIZE

Consider two cubes. I will assign sizes to these cubes to demonstrate a surprising and unexpected principle which is important to soils, especially potting soils.

Cube A is one inch on each edge. Two things can be said about Cube A: its volume (V) is one cubic inch, and its surface area (S) is six square inches. This can be expressed as:

$$V = 1 \text{ in}^3 \qquad S = 6 \text{ in}^2$$

Cube B is two inches on each edge. Its volume and surface area are expressed thus:

$$V = 8 \text{ in}^3 \qquad S = 24 \text{ in}^2$$

Roots grow on surfaces of soil particles, not just "in" the dirt. Seen through a microscope the meristematic area, or growing tip, seeks out pockets of readily available water that are adjacent to air. Residual water clings to surfaces of soil particles and air channels are found passing nearby. Where there is water but not air, and vice versa, there is no meristematic growth.

Which of the cubes makes the best soil particle, A or B? Cube A has a surface area of 6 square inches, whereas Cube B would provide 24 square inches. Cube B seems better; but on closer evaluation, Cube B would occupy eight times the volume in the pot as Cube A—not a good tradeoff for having only four times the surface area. This can be expressed as:

$$\text{Cube A} \quad \frac{\text{Surface}}{\text{Volume}} = \frac{6}{1}$$

$$\text{Which is better than: Cube B} \quad \frac{\text{Surface}}{\text{Volume}} = \frac{24}{8} = \frac{3}{1}$$

A cube half the size of Cube A would have a surface-to-volume ratio of 12, clearly superior to Cube A. This establishes the principle that as soil particles become smaller, they increase rather dramatically in their efficiency to provide soil surface for roots without using up very much room in the pot.

So how small can we make these particles? There is a limit somewhere.

Liquids have an unusual property associated with them called surface tension. What does this have to do with bonsai soil? If soil particles are so close together that the surface tension of water creates a capillary effect, the water will rise against gravity or cling to the particles. A bonsai pot filled with such a soil would not allow roots to grow, because most of the interstitial spaces would still be occupied by water and not air. Evaporation might briefly "dry out" the soil; the plant would have some oxygen, but would soon be fighting for water. Roots would perform poorly, new buds would be small, discolored, and weak. It would be difficult to get the soil wet once it was dry and difficult to get it dry once it was wet. Some roots would rot every winter, and finally, after about two and one half years, the bonsai dies. Sound familiar?

If soil particles are no smaller than 3/32 of an inch, the foregoing scenario can be avoided. Fortunately, this is an easy size to achieve; just discard any part of the soil that passes through a common window screen.

Getting rid of the large, inefficient particles (Cube B) is easy too; discard any particles that will not pass through 1/8-inch hardware cloth—sometimes called soffit screen. A square frame about 16 inches on a side and three inches high is all you need. Staple the appropriate screen or hardware cloth to the frame. Bonsai nurseries have inexpensive sifting screens available that will last a lifetime.

A related soil issue concerns the common practice of sprinkling loose gravel, clay pot chips, or some stones into the bottom of the pot in order to "improve drainage." Even Japanese literature shows the bonsai pot being striated or layered with a coarse soil mix in the bottom of the pot. Recent research in soil science indicates that this may actually be doing more harm than good. Water tends to move from a large particle towards a smaller particle. This results in an upward migration of moisture, creating a shortage of water for the deeper roots and causing a buildup of salts. Many bonsai masters are starting to agree: the pot that drains best is the one that contains a homogeneous mix from top to bottom, with no change in particle size and no interfaces between soil types.

TEXTURE

Consider two particles: one smooth, one rough (see **5–1**). They are the same size; yet, you can easily see that the rough particle has a much greater surface area per volume. The rough particle is therefore a more efficient soil particle for our bonsai pot.

Imagine two types of particles in separate bins; one is a washed river sand; the other is pumice. Through a microscope the roots of a bonsai maple slide and skid along between the polished surfaces of the river sand. In the other bin, seen microscopically, the maple's roots divide and redivide into thousands of tiny root hairs as they are "irritated" by the miniature irregular, rugged particles. A remarkable macroscopic result is that the branches are more twiggy, detailed, twisted, and exhibit

5–1

a higher degree of ramification; root character and development are expressed in the branch structure as well. Therefore, when selecting soil components, favor the rugged to the smooth, the irregular over the polished.

On a hot summer day, residual moisture in irregular, rugged soil particles becomes quite important in maintaining a modest temperature in the bonsai pot. Roots above 90 degrees F (32.2 degrees C) start to go dormant. They stop putting out new growth to protect from dehydration. Any further temperature increase causes damage. These moisture reservoirs in the soil particles act like tiny evaporative coolers and can assist the bonsai in making it through the summer without stress—without twig dieback or the curly brown leaf edges I despise. If you've ever grown a Japanese maple bonsai, you know what I'm referring to.

SOIL COMPOSITION

Most of us understand that an ideal soil for one plant, such as an azalea, would be unsuitable for a different plant, such as a juniper. Let's look at some of the reasons why.

A line graph that includes all the pH conditions under which plants can survive might look something like this:

pH 0 ——————————————————————— 100
    Acid   Alkaline

The numbers 0 and 100 are arbitrary ends of the scale rather than actual pH values. This is a bit theoretical and imprecise, but it serves to illustrate related factors. *Satsuki* azalea at 23, butterfly maple at 41, crab apple at 56, and *Shimpaku* juniper at 74 all grow in a different soil.

Optimum soil pH for such species is most often the pH found in the native soil. The azalea in nature grows as a small spreading bush found in shady areas under the spreading canopy of taller "climax" trees. The azalea roots are found in layers of decaying organic matter made up of fallen leaves, from itself and the trees. (The word organic means alive at one time—composed of carbon-containing compounds—not to be confused with the absence of pesticides.) The *Shimpaku* juniper, by contrast, are themselves climax trees. They grow mostly in pockets of decomposed rock formed by constant freezing and thawing of the ledges over time. What little organic matter the roots are growing in has been dropped by the juniper itself over a long period of time in sparse quantities. The high mineral content of the rock contributes to the high pH of the soil.

For further comparison here are some other line graphs.

Leaf Size ——————————•————————•———————
    0   azalea   juniper   100
    Large   Small

The azalea is located in the twenties for comparative leaf size whereas the juniper, because of its small needles, is found in the seventies.

U.V. Tolerance ——————————•————————•———————
    0   azalea   juniper   100
    Intolerant   Tolerant

There is a similar correspondence for ultraviolet light tolerance.

Soil Comp. ——————————•————————•———————
    100%   azalea   juniper   100%
    Organic   Inorganic

This line measures soil composition. Note the relative proportions of organic and inorganic materials for the azalea and juniper.

The serious bonsai enthusiast has two bins full of soil particles waiting at all times—screened of course. One of the bins contains 100 percent organic particles: bark, sawdust, leaf mould, shavings, steer manure, or compost from the garden. The other bin contains 100 percent inorganic particles: decomposed granite, sharp sand, pumice, vermiculite, perlite, lava cinders, etc. These particles have never been alive and are high in mineral content and high in pH.

As an example, suppose you are repotting a Japanese black pine. What is the soil composition?

pH
```
0            ( ? )              100
Acid                      Alkaline
```
You don't know, doesn't seem acid though.

U.V.
```
0                 80%        100
Intolerant              Tolerant
```
You know it tolerates a lot of sun.

Leaf
Size
```
0                 70?         100
Large                      Small
```
Big needles, bigger than juniper anyway.

Using the line graphs, an approximate composition for the Japanese black pine would be 75 percent inorganic. This actually is about right. Try these lines out on your own; they are useful for all species.

Some of the major species are listed in five groups as examples to help guide you to correct soil mixing. This plant list is by no means complete. Getting the composition exactly right is not so critical, because particle size is actually more important than pH.

Group 1.   ¾ Organic   ¼ Inorganic
Azalea, rhododendron, bald cypress, redwood, tropical foliage plants

Group 2.   ⅔ Organic   ⅓ Inorganic
Alder, birch, beech, hornbeam, elm, Zelkova, dogwood, maple

Group 3.   ½ Organic   ½ Inorganic
Pyracantha, wisteria, quince, fig, Corokia, holly, boxwood, apple, peach, pear, cherry, plum, Cotoneaster

Group 4.   ⅓ Organic   ⅔ Inorganic
Larch, ginkgo, fir, spruce, hemlock, cypress, Cryptomeria

Group 5.   ¼ Organic   ¾ Inorganic
Oak, pine, juniper, alpine and desert plants, jade, eucalyptus

MICROORGANISMS

Fertile soil is never sterile. The word sterile, though, is sometimes used commercially to indicate weed-free; a bag of potting soil will often tout the word sterile as reassurance that this bag contains good stuff, not bad stuff. If the soil were really sterile, it would house no bacteria, no spores, no seed, no mould, no fungi, no virus, no insects, no eggs, no larvae, etc. When potting soil says it is sterile, it means to put our minds at ease that it's not likely to contain insects and disease.

Many plants take advantage of microorganisms to accomplish life processes. Fertile soil is full of microorganisms. Many forms of bacteria contribute to the breakdown of soil. The effects are quite beneficial and contribute to what soil scientists call "ion exchange." Excellent ion exchange is associated with a superior soil. Poor ion exchange indicates a lack of important chemical interaction, resulting in reduced nutrient exchange, limited moisture uptake and, in general, a slowing down of the biochemistry that supports the life of the plant.

Soil Components to Avoid

A.   Any soil that does not have weeds growing in it.

B.   Roadside soil. It may contain asphalt residues, pesticides, and dust that is difficult to wash out. There will be no beneficial bacteria.

C.   Beach sand or soils. They contain salt and other minerals, and washing them out is inefficient and incomplete.

D.   River sand. The edges have been polished smooth over time; there are no beneficial cracks and crevices for roots, moisture, nutrients, or helpful bacteria.

E.   Manures as soil. They may contain straw and undigested organic material, but the remaining time that these will stay firm and particulate is limited. They will break down completely and soil compaction will result. A manure slurry fertilizer, however, is beneficial, and manure as a soil amendment is fine.

F.   High-mineral soils. Beware because these have often been formed as the result of sedimentation of alkali or brackish lakebeds in high desert areas.

G.   Discarded soil. It is tempting to reuse potting soil, but I cannot recommend it. Why didn't the former plant do well? What was the former plant treated with in its lifetime? Perhaps nothing, but possibly insecticides, fungicides, nonutilized fertilizers, etc. It is best to start anew.

H.   Used kitty litter. Even though you screen out the solid waste, the urine does not wash out easily or completely.

I.   Deodorized kitty litter. The little blue or green particles in this type of kitty litter contain dyes and fragrances that affect soil performance in a negative way.

J. Aquarium gravel. These gravels are highly polished—which is bad—or artificially colored, which is worse, or possibly coated with a substance to make them attractive under black lights.

K. Fine peat moss. These materials are nitrogen-starved. They will rob nitrogen from the plant faster than you can fertilize. When the nitrogen is finally at a level high enough for the material, it's then too high for the plant. A scum forms on the surface of the soil, blocking air and interfering with watering and drainage. Use only dark, well-rotted, and stabilized wood products. I prefer hemlock bark for its lack of slivers.

Perhaps the most interesting microorganism in bonsai soil, or any soil, is mycorrhizae, a fungus. An extremely beneficial organism, it attaches itself to roots in the form of nodules that are quite visible to the naked eye. Their relationship to the plant is symbiotic. The mycorrhizae derives water and nutrients from the root, thereby eliminating the necessity for leaves. The plant benefits from the nodule because the fungus can process atmospheric nitrogen as a nutrient. Your bonsai can benefit from its existence if you inoculate your bonsai soil with a known population of mycorrhizae.

When transplanting bonsai, I usually retain a bit of the old soil and transfer it along with the tree. When collecting trees from the woods, make sure you bring some well rotted organic material along with the tree. Simply find an established, mature tree of the same species; brush off the top layer of recently fallen needles and look for a slightly moist, partly rotted layer of needles below. This layer appears slightly frosted with beneficial moulds and fungi and has a characteristic rich, woodsy smell similar to Camembert rind. Dig up a couple of handfuls, making sure to include the top layer of soil as well. Keep this soil moist in a plastic container until ready to plant your tree, then make a slurry or suspension of your mouldy needles by stirring them briskly in a bucket of water. Pour the container of water over the root area of your newly transplanted specimen. This technique benefits trees planted in the ground equally as well as trees planted in a container and can be applied to all species, not just pine.

AESTHETICS

I like to think of bonsai as half horticulture and half art. That way of thinking serves me well when I want to stress the importance of a soil's color. From a purely horticultural standpoint, the tree could care less about the color of the soil from which it is growing. I must admit, however, my personal dissatisfaction with white-colored particles in some bonsai soils. There is something unsettling, rather cluttered, and messy about seeing perlite in bonsai soil. I find some pumices to be a bit better, but still quite obvious after a summer rain. Even vermiculite has rather crystalline flecks in its makeup, and similarly, red lava cinders are a distracting hue to my artistic sense. Over time I have come to appreciate black lava cinders and decomposed dark rock as two superior inorganic soil components. They hold their color well, yet exhibit a wet–dry color change obvious enough to assist in setting watering schedules.

My favorite organic particle, as I mentioned earlier, is hemlock bark. After having been aged for a year in the presence of steer and chicken manure, it turns a dark rich brown, almost black color. It holds its particle size for about five years, making it one of the best organic materials around for older potted specimens that enjoy infrequent repotting.

With all soils, the final test of a good soil is its performance with plant material. I highly recommend that you try to grow radishes in your prospective bonsai soil mix. Set up small experiments adding Vitamin B_1 to one and not another, or plant seeds in your organic or inorganic mix alone and in various proportions. These experiments will help take the guesswork out of your bonsai soil. Observe the radish plants carefully. A plant that starts out with a flourish only to yellow, weaken, and become nonproductive will guide you to what you need to add to your soil to keep your bonsai happy with time. A lush radish tip, but no vegetable root, tells you that you lack phosphorous and potassium. You need to nurture bonsai growing in this medium with 0–10–10 each winter. Look for chlorotic leaves. They can tell you that iron, sulfur, nitrogen, or trace minerals are lacking. Keep trying to grow that perfect radish. In the end, your persistence and unbiased observation will lead you to the bonsai soil that works best for you, taking into account your individual watering habits, your personal schedule and, of course, your local climate.

6

BONSAI TRAINING

PRIOR TO THIS CENTURY, HUMAN INTERVENtion influencing bonsai design was limited to the much revered Lingnan pinch-and-grow method developed by the ancient Chinese philosophers responsible for the Literati school of landscape painting and design. The Japanese around the turn of the twentieth century, in an attempt to achieve natural shapes in an expedient amount of time, developed wiring as another training technique suitable for bonsai. These two schools of thought persist today.

There appears to be a great philosophical difference between these two training techniques, but most bonsai hobbyists apply a combination of the two methods, often without giving the decision much thought. I recommended that you learn both methods and utilize each as appropriate for your tree. Some brittle, sensitive, and cantankerous species, such as ginkgo, quince, pyracantha, jade, and bald cypress are simply easier to grow with the Chinese philosophy. Other species, such as azalea, respond better when wired. Forming a classic *Matsu Zukuri*–style *Satsuki* azalea with the pinch-and-grow technique only would take two generations; a time schedule of no interest to most contemporary bonsai enthusiasts.

HOW TO WIRE YOUR BONSAI

Copper has many useful attributes as applied to bonsai horticulture. Perhaps you have noticed the signs in front of koi ponds at a Japanese garden; they ask you not to throw coins in the water. Of all coins, the copper penny is the most destructive to water plants and fish. Several handfuls of pennies is enough to stress the animal and plant life, the primary result being stunted growth.

One of copper's attributes, as applied to bonsai, is that a small amount of copper shortens nodes, restricts the full development of needles and leaves, slows the development of larger shoots—contributing to the process of creating a cultural dwarf. Low fertilizer, controlled water, high sunlight, small container, and coarse soil are some other factors that are already familiar—and each is probably more influential than copper alone.

Bonsai receive copper most directly from copper wire buried in the soil—from copper wire staples used to secure drainage screens, or from wraps of copper wire around the roots used to support the tree in the pot. Bonsai also receive copper from wires that are wrapped around the branches and trunk. Every time the bonsai is watered from overhead, a minute amount of copper leaches off the corroding wire and enters the bonsai soil, imparting its dwarfing effect. Copper staples are convenient and the concentration of copper around the drain holes helps to keep insects and disease out. The copper also limits root growth around the drain hole, increasing drainage. On the other hand, any bare wire used to support the tree after potting or repotting really has no merit. Additional metals are being added to the soil at a most critical time in the life of the tree, making it harder for a recently transplanted root to absorb water. I prefer the use of "neutral" fibres for this purpose, such as nylon fishing line or string.

Another attribute of copper is its property to harden when worked and to soften on heating. Most metals must be worked when they are hot; copper is worked when cold. Heated to a cherry-red color to soften, the copper is then quickly plunged into cool water. It comes out clean and bright. After a little bending and shaping, the copper gradually toughens up and the annealing process must be repeated to restore the softness. Commercially available copper wire is normally bright and annealed already. After it is bent around a branch, the wire gradually toughens up—holding the branch in place. It is easy to make the mistake of trying to twist the wire back off again after a few months, only to notice too late that the copper is much too stiff to be removed without injuring the tree. Always cut off copper wire.

An attribute of copper that is sometimes overlooked is its pleasing appearance. As the copper is exposed to rain and sun, it develops a grey-green patina, called verdigris. Wired trees are allowed in formal exhibitions, but the wire must be copper! A well-wired tree with no crossing wires, no badly spaced loops, and a myriad of fine secondary wiring is highly appreciated and respected. Understand as you learn how to wire that the skill takes practice, practice, and more practice.

Aluminum is slightly less expensive than copper, but it ages to a sort of brown, brassy color, and you have to use twice the size of wire to accomplish the same objective. Some argue that it is "easier to bend," but why bother?

To choose the correct size copper wire to use, a good general rule of thumb is to hold the prospective wire next to the branch to be bent. If the copper wire is about one third the diameter of the branch, it is about right. (Aluminum wire must be about one half the diameter of the branch.) As a second test, while you are holding the wire next to the branch, give the wire a small bend in your hands, then bend the branch similarly. If the wire feels ever so slightly tougher than the branch, it is just the right size. Branches of various species have different strengths and some adjustment is necessary. If the wire you have selected is "too big" but you are able to get it on the branch, absolutely no harm has been done. If, after you wire the branch, you find that the wire is too small to hold the branch, it is easily fixed. Simply add another wire next to the one you just applied. There is no need to remove the original wire.

In discussing wiring I assume that you not only want to wire your tree, but that you know where you want the branches to go. If one of the wiring diagrams shows you how to wire a branch down, you may go ahead and apply the wire as in the diagram. Then after the wire is on, bend the branch up, or to the side, or forward, etc. For help in styling your tree see Chapter 3 on styles.

Bending a Trunk. Once you have selected the proper size wire, measure the length of the trunk, and cut your wire about twice that length. Then begin by inserting a small length of wire into the root area of the tree, right behind the trunk. Insert only enough wire to add stability to the beginning end of the wire—about two inches is enough.

Proceed to turn the wire around the trunk either clockwise or counterclockwise, it doesn't matter which. Keep each loop at about a 45-degree angle as you proceed up the trunk, and make sure you allow for future growth of the tree—in other words, do not wrap too tightly. Each loop should have a bit of daylight between the wire and the trunk. Continue wrapping the trunk, maintaining the 45-degree angle and avoiding branches and leaves by gently teasing them out of the way. When you have reached the top of the tree, bend the wire back on itself to secure the end; then trim off any excess.

Wiring Branches. Begin with two good winds on the trunk (in the same direction as the trunk wire) and follow along the various curves and undulations of the main branch or branchlet to its tip. Secure the end of the wire as before, and trim off the excess. If additional wiring is needed, repeat this process with the appropriate wire size. Attach an additional wire by winding alongside the existing wire at least two full turns. Do not cross wires. Not only is it unsightly, but the wire tends to mark the tree at those points. You should be able to completely wire a tree without crossing any wires.

Wire up from the base of the trunk at a 45-degree angle, clockwise or counterclockwise.

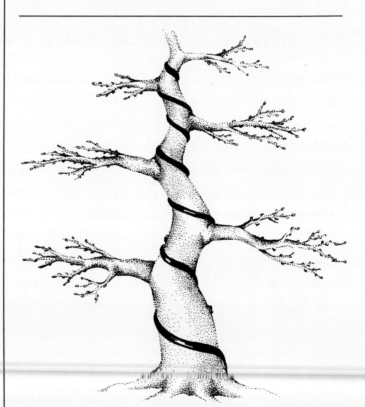

This wire is too tight. There is no room for the tree to expand as it grows.

This wire has been applied too loosely. The wire will not hold as well as it should.

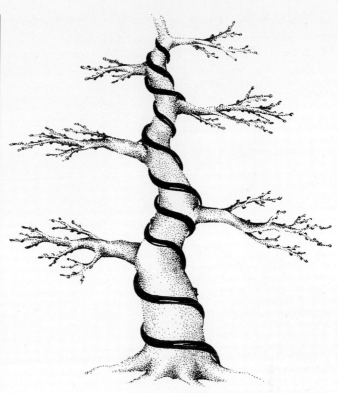

This tree has been wired with too many turns of wire. Keep a steady 45-degree angle.

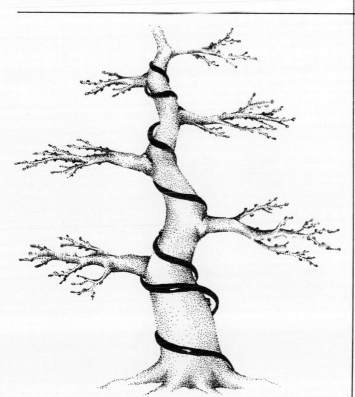

In this case, the wire has been applied sloppily and irregularly; some of it is too tight and some too loose.

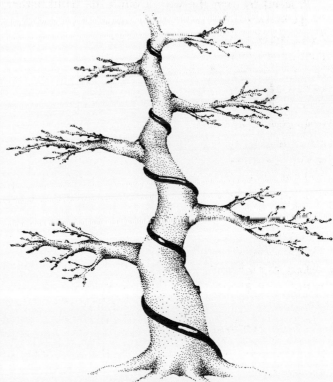

This tree has been wired with too few turns. The wire is most effective when the turns are a bit closer together.

The wire that is just under the base of the branch will make it difficult to bend the branch down.

This is way too long a reach. The wiring will not be stable and the branch will not bend.

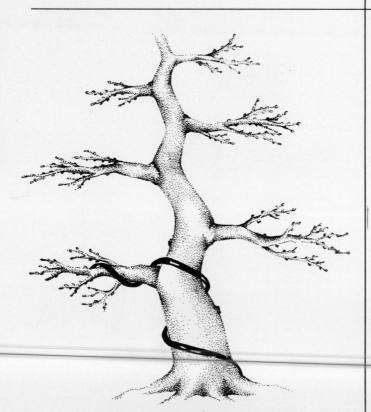

Not a bad wiring job, but try to get at least two turns on the trunk before going out onto the limb.

The wire on the trunk is too high. As you pull the branch down, the wire will shift position.

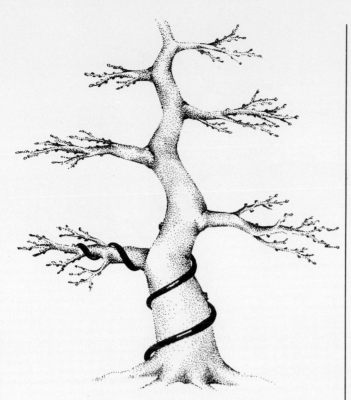

Good wiring job. Two bends on the trunk and a useful reach out onto the branch.

This method is very unstable. When you bend one branch down, the other will be pulled up.

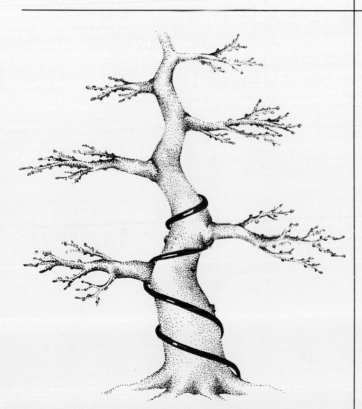

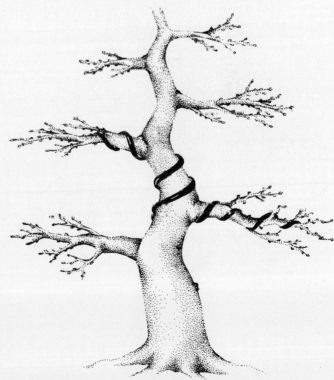

Not a good technique. You have changed directions. This wire will cut into the branch base.

This wire is a little tight. The bottom loop on the trunk is too low before going to the branch.

It would have been better to go clockwise up the trunk from the lowest branch.

Nicely done. The two branches are the same size and there are two winds around the trunk.

Sloppy wiring at the branch tips. Wire carefully around twigs and branchlets to avoid damage.

Do not leave excess wire extending from the ends of branches. Trim off any extra length.

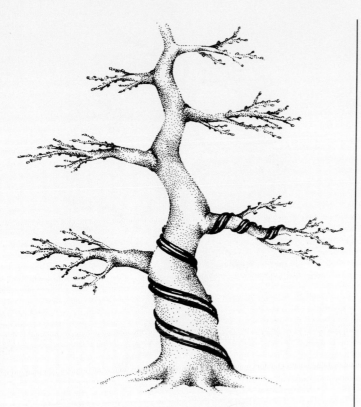

Good technique. If extra strength is needed, just follow along parallel to the first wire.

Do not secure wire to the trunk like this. Three winds below the branch holds better and looks better.

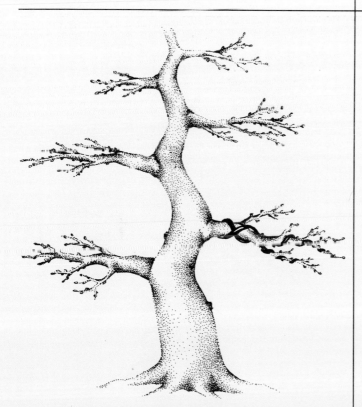

This will hold the branchlets, but where the wires cross each other, the bark will be damaged below.

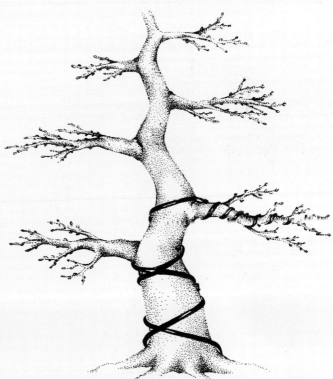

Never cross wires like this. You will scar the trunk and the wiring job looks unsightly.

You will need two turns around the trunk to stabilize these branches. Do not change directions on the branch.

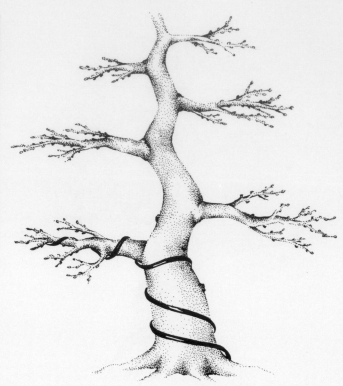

This wire is too tight under the base of the branch. You will not be able to turn or rotate the branch either.

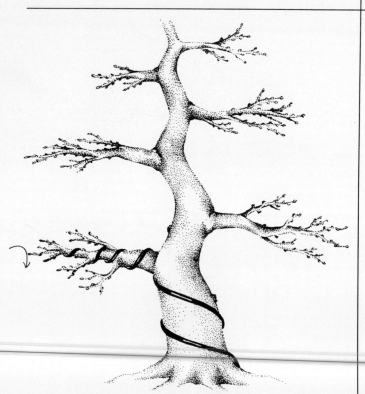

This is a good technique for rotating the branch lengthwise in a clockwise direction.

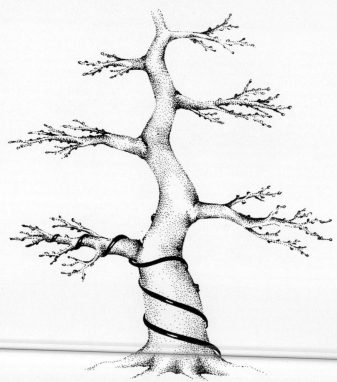

If necessary, make a small crack at the top of the base of the branch to help bring the branch down.

This is a good wiring job. All three branchlets are secure and the wires are all parallel.

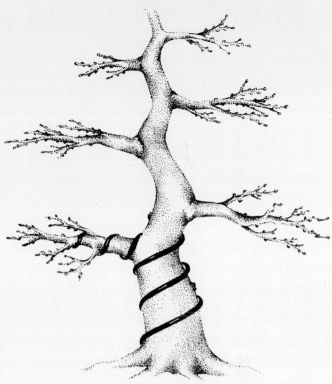

Too much wire located under the base of the branch. One fewer turn on the trunk is better.

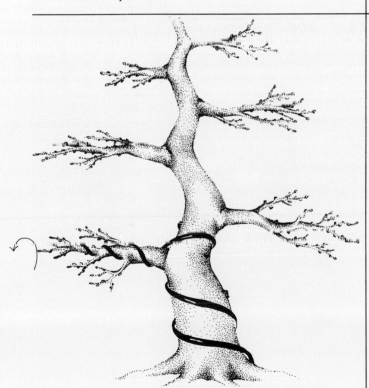

Almost good technique. When you try to rotate the branch lengthwise and counterclockwise, the top trunk loop will loosen.

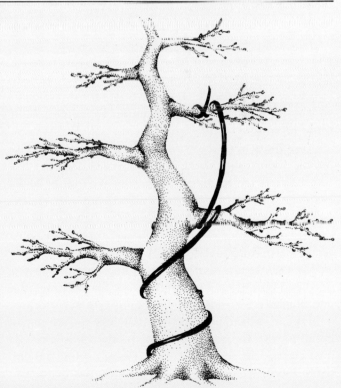

I hope you can see the difference between good wiring and sloppy wiring by now. Keep practising!

OTHER TRAINING HINTS

Training Large Branches. For large branches that are difficult to bend, it is sometimes helpful to split them lengthwise with a tool made for this purpose. A branch splitter looks similar to a concave cutter except that the two cutting jaws meet each other at 180 degrees. Split the branch horizontally, making sure to include the most difficult or thickest area, and extend the cut along the branch about halfway; do not split the entire length of the branch. Keep the tip uncut. This type of cut effectively "delaminates" the heartwood and helps to move a branch up or down. If you desire to move the branch to the right or left, simply split the heavy area vertically instead of horizontally.

Wilting Technique. Some species can be successfully "wilted" before the branches are bent. Branches that would normally break during bending can then be moved. Allow the plant to dry out slowly until no more moisture can be detected in the pot. Mist the tree lightly and keep it indoors overnight without further water. The next day, wire and train the branches carefully, moving the heaviest branches first. That evening mist the tree several times without watering the pot. The following morning water as usual.

Slow Bending Over Time. For especially tough branches, it may be necessary to move them slowly over a long period of time. I have used with great success a variety of turnbuckles, clamps, and weights. It is fairly easy to set up hardware on a tree. Study the direction in which you want the branch to move. Fabricate a solid point of resistance; this could be the pot, root system, another branch, or the trunk itself. Don't overlook fastening opportunities such as the bonsai bench, an adjacent fence or even another large tree! No matter what, however, protect the live tree tissue with soft cloths, rubber tubing, or similar soft material. When you are pulling or pushing a large branch over time, it is easy to scar the tree without this additional cushion.

The use of the bonsai clamp bending a trunk is shown in **6–1**. This device has been in place for eight months and is ready for removal. This juniper had a boring, straight middle trunk section that was too large for bending with copper wire; so this method was selected. The clamp was tightened slightly every other day for three months, and the straight section has been successfully bent.

The San Jose juniper, *Juniperus chinensis* "San Jose," shown in **6–2**, displays a more pleasing curve than it had

just a few months ago. It is eighteen inches high with a three-inch trunk. The container is a two-tone unglazed signed Japanese piece. The juniper is fifteen years old from nursery stock. The *shari* was created artificially.

6–1

6–2

THE LINGNAN PINCH-AND-GROW TECHNIQUE

With this method, the initial styling of a tree appears quite drastic and even brutal. The potential bonsai material is reduced to the extent that often the only design element remaining on the tree is the trunk line. If any branches remain, they are typically small, narrow, or short branches that are already in perfect position. Then begins the patient task of adding to this basic "skeleton." New shoots erupt from everywhere, especially around old latent bud scars and the bases of the removed branches. The grower carefully selects buds that are going to grow naturally in the desired direction. If no such bud forms immediately, don't worry; one will eventually appear.

Be patient; newly formed branches will develop slowly. Allow favorable buds to extend themselves slightly before removal. This promotes more back budding and helps the tree become compact and twiggy instead of long and leggy. Buds always form at the base of old leaf nodes and you can always predict their growth direction based on the position of the leaf. If you want new growth to come from the underside of a branch tip, find a leaf node that is located on the underside of the branch and trim carefully just beyond that point. It is sometimes necessary to use a wound sealer to keep the desired bud from drying up. Do not prune too close to the potential bud; it is better to allow half an inch of twig beyond the bud and use wound sealer on the cut. Make an additional cut later to remove the stub after the new sprout has extended itself. By directing all new growth carefully, you can achieve a virtually scarless tree and avoid the use of copper wire entirely. This method is especially suitable for brittle species that are difficult to wire.

TRAINING PINE BONSAI

Pine buds, known as candles, are normally trimmed just as the needles are starting to separate from the tender stem to which they are fastened. Pruning earlier tends to damage some needle tips and reduce favorable results. Pruning too late, when the needles have extended themselves, is not desirable because the stem hardens quickly into a woody branch which necessitates trimming with scissors.

However, there is considerable debate on how to prune pine candles that has been going on for centuries and continues to this day. I had an opportunity some years ago to work with a wide selection of pine species in evaluating growth after applying one of four commonly cited pruning methods. I call these methods A, B, C, and D, and offer some of my personal observations.

Method A. This is the ever-popular technique of varying the amount of candle removal in indirect proportion to its size. In other words, if a candle develops slowly—and is the smallest on the tree—only about one quarter of it is twisted off the tip when it achieves its fullest extension. On the other extreme, those candles which are developing rapidly—and are quite long compared to the others—are pruned quite drastically by twisting off as much as nine tenths of their total length.

Results with A. The pines reacted to Method A by pushing available growth into what remained of existing candles. The needles were somewhat shorter than they would have been if left untrimmed, but tended to be larger still than the last year's growth. Budding back on the branch was minimal to none. A few new sprouts were seen where one- and two-year-old needles were still attached and where plenty of sunlight could penetrate.

Method B. This consists of timing total candle removal to correspond with the development of the majority of the candles on the tree. When most of the candles are just at the peak stage for removal, not too compact and not too opened up, all candles on the whole tree are totally removed, regardless of size or stage of development. For the climate of my home in Oregon, this seems to be early May.

Results with B. By late June a tremendous number of new buds developed. Most new buds were concentrated around the old candle sites. Where one candle had been removed, three, four, or five new buds were now growing. Where sunlight touched the bark, especially near old pruning scars, additional buds formed. By late summer the tree was covered with beautifully formed short-needled growth. New growth was so profuse that on some easily budding species, e.g., black, white, and bristlecone, it was necessary to thin out new buds so that the remaining ones could grow without competition.

Method C. For this experiment, I allowed the developing candle to come to its moment of perfection before removing it in its entirety. As each candle achieved its ideal moment for removal, it was twisted off gently, regardless of its length. If a small candle started opening up, it was removed. If a large candle had reached out three, four, or even five inches without starting to open up, it was still not removed until the proper moment. Candle removal for these trees stretched out over a period of about three weeks for most species.

Results with C.
Poor areas of growth remained poor. Where a small candle had been removed, only one or two small buds would return; and they would grow slowly, and develop into small candles with short needles. Where long, strong candles were removed, as many as a dozen small buds would return, all clustered around the base of the old candle. Left untrimmed, these buds would develop into many short, strong, and stiff shoots that had to be thinned to minimize the "poodle" appearance.

Method D.
This technique requires that the grower anticipate the growth of the tree. Overall candle development is examined, and then the date when the majority of the candles will be at the perfect state for total removal is projected. For example, you estimate that your tree, based on its present rate of growth, taking the weather into consideration, will be prime for candle removal on May 15—similar to Method B. This time, however, you totally remove the smallest candles two weeks earlier, on May 1. The candles that you remove are all in various stages of development; some are tight, some have started to open up perhaps, but they are all the shortest candles. Remove one third of all candles at this time. One week later, on May 8 in this example, you remove another third of the candles. This now constitutes removing half of the remaining candles on the tree. The candles that you remove are, again, the smallest on the tree. This leaves the largest candles on the tree scheduled for removal the next week, on May 15, your estimated date for total removal.

Results with D.
The results were not what I expected, and I think they will surprise you as much as they did me. Bud development was moderate—not as good as Method B—but the rewards were that this method tended to even out growth areas around the tree. At the base of a former small candle came one or two moderately sized candles. At the base of a formerly medium-sized candle came two or three medium-sized sprouts. Best of all, strong growth tended to be limited to only four or five modestly sized shoots instead of the "poodle" effect that resulted with Method C. Apparently allowing additional time for the small candles to start setting new buds is what evens out the redistribution of meristematic hormone throughout the plant.

Pine Candle-Pruning Conclusions.
Method A is probably the best known technique used on pines. It is the easiest to comprehend and the least traumatic to both the plant and its owner. For the average bonsai enthusiast, however, who has a spindly, leggy pine that could use some compaction, Method B is far and away the favored way to go. A word of caution here: if your tree is not healthy and is not producing large, long candles, work on your container growing skills before attempting Method B on a barely alive pine. For hard-to-bud species such as Scotch, Austrian, and other low-altitude pines, Method B has some decided advantages over the more widely accepted Method A.

Method C has little redeeming value except possibly to help growers of pompom trees. Method D has perhaps the most significant contribution to bonsai by being a method that helps even out the growth of styles that are difficult for some species. With Method D, I can promote stronger buds along the long lower branch, for example, without resorting to tipping the pot on its side as some growers recommend.

Method "R."
There is one other method—sort of—that I call Method "R," named after "Rich Idwithfear." This is actually quite popular; you do nothing to your pine in the spring. When fall comes, you bring your pine to a club workshop and seek out advice on how to make it less leggy and more compact. I tell you this in jest, but unfortunately it is a widely used technique. Seriously, I encourage you to try one of the other methods this coming year.

WORKING WITH A VISUAL PLAN IN MIND

The above training methods are only helpful if you have a vision of what you would like to accomplish. I recommend that you make a drawing of your tree as you intend it to be in ten years. If you cannot visualize this, training your tree may become very difficult, because you may just wind up applying random rules. Whether your drawing is a work of art or not doesn't matter; it forces you to commit to an established style. It assists you in determining which shoots to retain and which ones to prune away. The drawing also helps you evaluate whether your pruning and pinching efforts are achieving the desired results.

Document your bonsai's training progress with photos. If your bonsai looks right in a photograph, it is a kind of objective confirmation; you should be proud.

An annual photographic record is a rewarding chronicle and doubles as evidence for insurance purposes should the unthinkable happen and your bonsai be destroyed or get legs and disappear.

Be self-critical, and do not succumb to the natural urge to procrastinate. John Naka has said, "If your tree has a problem, cut it out and it won't have a problem anymore." Do your major pruning right away, then there is plenty of time for the tree's healing and your enjoyment of your creation.

6–4

HOW TO MAINTAIN AN EXISTING PINE BONSAI

The Scotch pine, *Pinus sylvestris*, shown in **6–3** has been previously shaped with wire in the *Moyogi* style. The wire was removed one year ago, and the strict horizontal branch formation has stimulated many new pine buds, or candles. These candles are now in the perfect stage for candle pruning, the process where the new growth is gently twisted apart between the thumb and forefinger.

6–5

6–3

6–6

Candles on an established tree are reduced in the manner shown in **6–4 through 6–7**. Short, stubby, and underdeveloped growth is left alone. Medium-strength growth is reduced by half, and the largest, thickest, and longest candles are reduced by seven eighths of their length. To trim off a candle, grasp the new growth gently between thumb and forefinger of both hands, and, ever so slightly, bend, twist, and pull apart the candle at the appropriate place. If the candle is too

6–7

old needles should all be pulled off. Gently pull off all needles from second-year growth that are pointing downwards. Old pine specimens have all of their new growth aimed upward. Part of creating the illusion of age consists of copying natural older trees.

Pine trees seem to bud back best where two key elements exist: sunlight and recent scarring of tissue. By pulling off the lower needles, we not only let in more sunlight, but we create small scars where future buds are likely to form. Another benefit of these scars being positioned on the bottom or sides of the horizontal main branch is that this is the best location for new buds. A new bud on top of a branch is useless, because it contributes neither to the length nor to the width of the branch.

young, it will still be brown. If the candle is too old, the needles are well separated from the core; when you try to pull it apart, some of the core remains behind, making it necessary to trim with scissors instead of with your fingers. Try to time your pruning so that the majority of the candles are just right for it.

The top of a tree before and after candle pruning is shown in **6–8 and 6–9**.

The candles have been trimmed back on the pine shown in **6–10**. Note that the strongest buds have been reduced the most, and the weakest buds remain untouched. This will even out the growth of the tree. In three weeks, the new needles will all be opened up, and the branches will fill out and thicken. Additional thinning may be needed. I find it helpful to pretend that my eyes are the sun. If I cannot see some portion of the pine tree quite clearly, it is time for more thinning. If you do not thin your tree, it will become bare inside just like the inside of a hedge. Some species of pine that bud back quite easily are bristlecone, white, black, limber, pinion, Jeffrey, Mugho, and other hardy high-altitude pines. Those that do not bud back readily are the Scotch, ponderosa, lodgepole, Canary Island, jack, and other lowland pines. With this latter group, it is extremely important to maintain buds close in to the trunk, because once they are lost due to the grower's neglect, they are unlikely to come back. Late April or early May are critical times for pine bonsai. Do not miss this important time of the year or your bonsai will become only bigger, not better.

Pine trees grow best in full sun, and pine branches are at their healthiest condition when they can receive maximum light and air circulation (see **6–11**). By pulling off superfluous needles, you can enhance light and air circulation in and around the branches. Three-year-

6–8

6–9

6–10

6–11

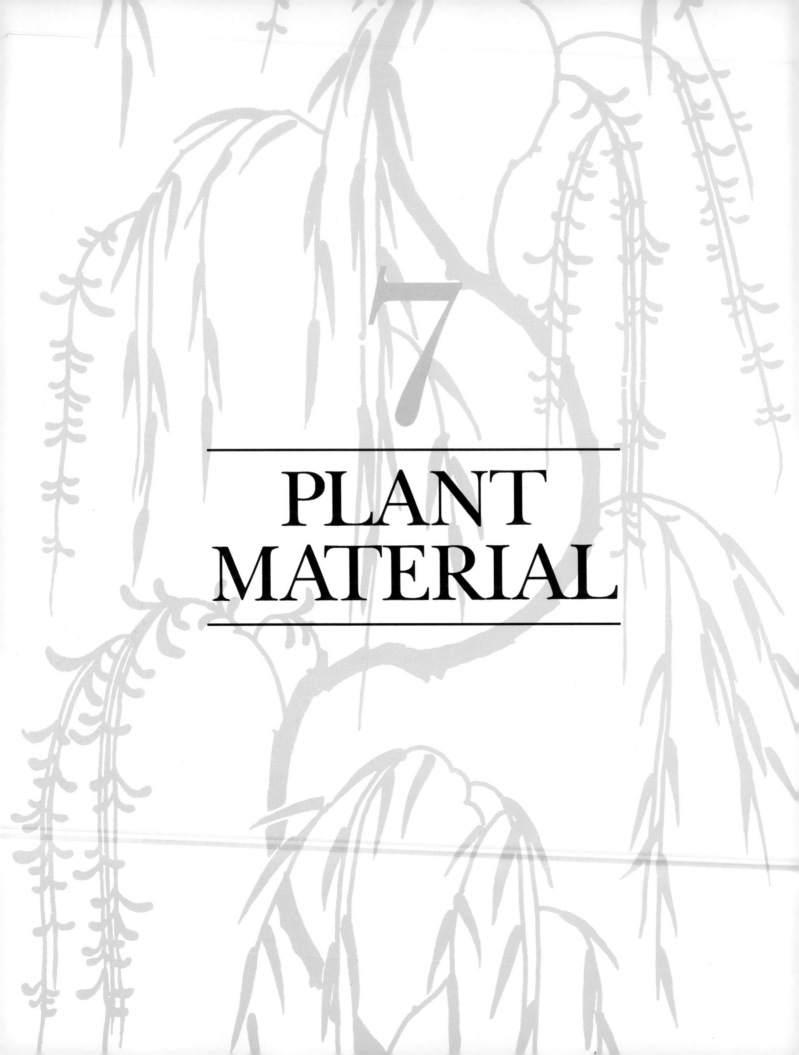

7

PLANT
MATERIAL

THROUGHOUT THE LONG HISTORY OF BON-sai, the particular plant materials available have had a profound impact on the development of both its art and its science. With each success and failure, the bonsai tradition has learned the tolerances of certain plant species. The pinch-and-grow technique was developed largely because of the specific growing characteristics of the Chinese fukien tea plant. Knowledge of the budding tendencies of pine has its origin in the Japanese black pine. Inspiration for rock plantings derives from Japan's Inland Sea.

BONSAI FROM NATIVE PLANTS

What we have learned from these earlier experiences we can now apply to the world's flora. Each region has its variety of native plant life. We can, each of us, in our own local area, take advantage of what nature has to offer.

Where Japan boasts of its Ezo spruce, the Northwest of the United States has Engelmann spruce; it is just as compact, the needles are similar in size, it buds back equally as well, and the plants are easily obtainable. The Japanese white pine is widely known for its soft and stunning silver-striped needles and creamy bark. Oregon, where I live, has at least two equivalents in the

Western white pine and the high-altitude white bark pine; both are five-needled pines. The Japanese maple is similar to the vine maple. Each region has its own superior bonsai material. Hawaii has its figs; California its desert juniper. The Swiss have their Mugho pine, and Florida has its buttonwood.

Take advantage of these local natives. They are hardy, they are available, and they help make a regional contribution to the world of bonsai material.

LOCAL NURSERY STOCK

Almost every town has a garden center nearby. Even some grocery and hardware stores will carry seasonal plant material. These are fairly inexpensive sources that you should consider. Remember, bonsai material is best when it is a bit unusual. In a row of juniper, there is always one that grew just a little bit odd. It may be hanging over the edge of the pot and be ideal for a cascading bonsai. It may have died back a few winters ago and have a large trunk and beautifully scarred branches. You can find potential bonsai wherever plants are sold. They can be easily transplanted at any time of the year.

BONSAI MATERIAL FROM THE LANDSCAPE

Driving down the road one day, I passed a neighbor who was taking out some juniper that had overgrown its allotted space next to the driveway. I asked him if I could have some of the pieces that still had roots attached. I got many nice bonsai out of those fragments. You may have some overgrown material around your home or know of someone who is removing some. It is surprising what you might find. You certainly can't beat the cost and it is a fine way to "collect" suitable specimens nearby.

Acer palmatum, *Japanese maple*

Juniperus squamata *"Blue Star," Blue Star Juniper.*

THE ZONE SYSTEM

Whatever bonsai material you choose, it is imperative that you get information about the species as to its cold hardiness. The Zone System is commonly used to describe local weather characteristics. For example, I live in Zone 6, which is described as perfect for the development of nandina, roses, rhododendrons, azaleas, and *Pieris*. This valley in Oregon grows much of the United States' fruit and shade trees as well; so it is no wonder that Japanese maple, Zelkova, and *Prunus mume* do well in my backyard. Be aware of your local conditions and compile a list of plants that do quite well in your area. These plants will offer you the greatest chance of success as bonsai. When you choose to attempt other species, it is with the knowledge that horticultural adjustments will have to be made. For example, I know that we

are not quite high and dry enough for most pine; so I compensate by keeping my pine bonsai a bit on the dry side, and I try not to moisten the foliage when watering. For plants that are from a more tender zone, it means that when winter comes I'll have to keep a careful eye on the thermometer outside. When cold conditions arrive, these tender plants temporarily come into an unheated area of the house. Know your local weather zone, and match it with your bonsai material for the greatest chance of success.

Acer palmatum, *Japanese maple "Waterfall."*

SUGGESTED BONSAI MATERIAL

Acer palmatum, *Japanese maple* "Shojo Shidare."

The following list is quite extensive, although not complete. The material is listed by species to assist you in selecting local material. For example, if you cannot locate Japanese white birch (*Betula platyphylla Japonica*) in your area, you might consider substituting pyramidal white birch (*Betula alba fastigiata*). As with all material, get to know its seasonal limitations. If you live in Guam, for instance, you should avoid trees like Himalayan beech and alpine fir.

Acer ginnala	Amur maple
Acer griseum	Paper bark maple
Acer Japonicum	Fullmoon maple
Acer Japonicum "aconitifolium"	Laceleaf fullmoon maple
Acer Japonicum "aureum"	Golden fullmoon maple
Acer oblongum	Evergreen maple
Acer palmatum	Japanese maple
Acer palmatum "Arakawa"	
Acer palmatum "butterfly"	Japanese butterfly maple

Juniperus procumbens nana, *Japanese green mound juniper.*

Abies amabilis	Silver fir
Abies balsamea nana	Dwarf balsam fir
Abies Koreana	Korean fir
Abies lasiocarpa	Alpine fir
Abies lasiocarpa "Arizonica"	Cork fir
Acer buergerianum	Trident maple
Acer campestre	Hedge maple
Acer campestre "compacta"	Compact hedge maple
Acer capillipes	Japanese red maple
Acer circinatum	Vine maple

Acer palmatum, *Japanese maple* "Viridis."

Acer palmatum, *Japanese maple* "Beni-Hime."

Acer palmatum "Kiyo Hime"	
Acer palmatum "Koshimino"	Dwarf Japanese maple
Acer palmatum "linearilobum"	Thread leafed maple
Acer palmatum "Sango Kaku"	Coral barked maple
Acer palmatum "Shishigashira"	
Acer paxii	Lobed evergreen maple
Acer rubrum	Red maple
Acer saccarinum grandidentatum	Rock Mountain maple
Acer tataricum	Tatarian maple
Acer truncatum	Chinese maple

Acer palmatum, *Japanese maple* "Otto's dissectum."

Acer palmatum, *Japanese maple* "Shishigashira."

Acer palmatum, *Japanese maple* "Beni Maico."

Albizia julibrissin	Mimosa or silk tree
Alnus tenuifolia	Mountain alder
Arctostaphylos manzanita	Manzanita
Arundinaria disticha	Dwarf fernleaf bamboo
Arundinaria marmorea	Dwarf black bamboo
Betula "nana"	Dwarf Arctic birch
Betula pendula "laciniata"	Cutleaf weeping birch
Betula pendula "fastigiata"	Pyramidal white birch
Betula pendula "purpurea"	Purple birch
Betula pendula "Trosts dwarf"	Trosts dwarf birch
Betula platyphylla Japonica	Japanese white birch
Buxus microphylla compacta	Dwarf boxwood
Buxus microphylla Koreana	Korean boxwood
Buxus microphylla "Morris midget"	
Calocedrus decurrens	Incense cedar

Camelia sasanqua	Sasanqua camelia
Camelia Sinensis	Tea
Camelia vernalis	Vernalis camelia
Carpinus betula	European hornbeam
Carpinus Caroliniana	American hornbeam
Carpinus Turczaninovii	Turkish hornbeam
Cedrus brevifolia	Cyprian cedar
Cedrus Libani	Cedar of Lebanon
Cedrus Libani "nana"	Dwarf cedar of Lebanon
Celtis Sinensis	Chinese hackberry
Cercis Chinensis	Chinese redbud
Cercocarpus ledifolius	Curl-leaf mountain mahogany
Chaenomeles Japonica	Japanese flowering quince
Chamaecyparis Lawsoniana "Ellwoodii improved"	Ellwood cypress
Chamaecyparis Lawsoniana "minima glauca"	Dwarf blue cypress
Chamaecyparis Nootkatensis "compacta"	Dwarf Alaska yellow cedar
Chamaecyparis obtusa "filicoides"	Fernspray cypress

Albizia julibrissin, *Mimosa or silk tree.*

Cedrus deodora pendulum, *Weeping Deodora cedar.*

Chamaecyparis obtusa "Kosteri"	Koster cypress
Chamaecyparis obtusa "nana"	Dwarf *Hinoki* cypress
Chamaecyparis pisifera	*Sawara* cypress
Chamaecyparis pisifera "filifera"	Threadbranch cypress
Chamaecyparis thyoides andelyensis "conica"	"Andelyensis conica" cypress
Chrysanthemum morifolium	Chrysanthemum
Citrus	*Nagami* kumquat
Clematis montana	Anemone clematis
Coffea Arabica	Coffee
Cornus kousa	Korean dogwood
Cornus mas	Cornelian cherry
Corokia cotoneaster	Corokia
Corylus avellana "contorta"	Harry Lauders walking stick
Corylus colurna	Turkish hazelnut
Corylus maxima "purpurea"	Purple filbert
Cotoneaster congestus	Congested cotoneaster
Cotoneaster microphyllus thymifolius	Thyme leaf cotoneaster

Crassula argentea "Crosby's dwarf"	Dwarf jade
Crassula tetragona	Succulent pine
Crataegus ambigua	Russian hawthorn
Cryptomeria Japonica "Bandai-sugi"	Conical cryptomeria
Cryptomeria Japonica "Jundai-sugi"	Globular cryptomeria
Cryptomeria Japonica "pygmaea"	Dwarf cryptomeria
Cryptomeria Japonica "tansu"	Tansu cryptomeria
Cupressus Forbesii	Telcate cypress
Cupressus macrolarpa	Monterey cypress
Eurya emorginata micro-phylla	Japanese fern tree

Chamaecyparis obtusa "Mcroke," Hinoki *cypress.*

Fagus sylvatica "asplenifolia"	Cut leaf beech
Fagus sylvatica "atropurpurea"	Copper beech
Fagus sylvatica "lanciniata"	Laceleaf beech
Fagus sylvatica "rohanii"	Oak leaf beech
Fagus sylvatica "Spaethiana"	Purple beech
Fagus sylvatica "tricolor"	Tricolor beech
Fagus sylvatica "Zlatia"	Golden beech
Fuchsia "Isis"	Fuchsia
Ginkgo biloba	Maidenhair tree
Grevillea rosmarinifolia	Rosemary tree
Hakonechloa macra "Aureola"	Japanese forest grass
Hamamelis mollis	Chinese witch hazel
Ilex crenata "Mariesii"	Dwarf Japanese holly
Ilex dimorphophylla	Okinawan holly
Imperata cylindrica "rubra"	Japanese blood grass
Juniperus Chinensis "parsonii"	Prostrate juniper

Juniperus X Media "Shimpaku," Shimpaku *Juniper.*

Juniperus horizontalis "Wiltoni," *Wiltoni juniper.*

Juniperus Chinensis procumbens "nana"	Japanese green mound juniper
Juniperus Chinensis "sargentii"	*Shimpaku*
Juniperus Chinensis "Blaauw"	Blue *Shimpaku*
Juniperus Chinensis "torulosa"	Hollywood juniper
Juniperus Chinensis "skyrocket"	Skyrocket juniper
Juniperus communis compressa	Dwarf columnar juniper
Juniperus squamata "Blue Star"	Blue Star Juniper
Larix decidua	European larch
Larix kaempferi	Japanese larch
Magnolia parviflora	Oyama magnolia

Larix decidua pendula, *Weeping larch.*

Picea glauca "conica"	Dwarf Alberta spruce
Pieris Japonica "compacta"	Dwarf andromeda
Pinus albicaulis	Whitebark pine
Pinus aristata	Bristlecone pine
Pinus balfouriana	Foxtail pine
Pinus bungeana	Lacebark pine
Pinus cembroides monophylla	Blue Pinion pine
Pinus contorta "Murrayana"	Mountain lodgepole pine
Pinus densiflora	Japanese red pine
Pinus densiflora "umbraculifera"	*Tanyosho* pine

Picea orientalis "Gracilis nana," *Dwarf Oriental spruce.*

Malus "Dorothea"	Yellow crab apple pink flowers
Malus "radiant"	Red crab apple red flowers
Malus zumi calocarpa	Red crab apple white flowers
Malus floribunda	Japanese flowering crab apple
Myrtus communis "microphylla"	Dwarf myrtle
Narcissus "minimus"	Dwarf daffodil
Narcissus "triandrus"	Angel tear daffodil
Nothofagus Antarctica	Antarctic beech
Olea Europaea "little Ollie"	Dwarf olive
Parrotia Persica	Persian beech
Phoenix roebelenii	Pygmy date palm
Picea abies "mucronata"	Dwarf spruce
Picea abies "pygmaea"	Pygmy spruce
Picea Engelmannii	Engelmann spruce

Pinus edulis	Pinion pine
Pinus flexilis	Limber pine
Pinus halepensis	Aleppo pine
Pinus monophylla	One needle pine
Pinus monticola	Western white pine
Pinus mugho mughus	Dwarf Mugho pine
Pinus pinea	Italian stone pine
Pinus strobus	Eastern white pine
Pinus strobus "nana"	Dwarf white pine
Pinus sylvestris "nana"	Dwarf Scotch pine
Pinus thunbergiana	Japanese black pine
Pistacia Chinensis	Chinese pistachio

Picea orientalis "Repens," *Oriental spruce.*

Picea sitchensis, *Sitka spruce.*

Pinus contorta globosa, *Lodgepole pine.*

Platanus Occidentalis	Buttonwood
Podocarpus nivalis	Alpine yew
Populus tremuloides	Quaking aspen
Potentilla fruticosa	Shrubby cinquefoil
Prunus Hally Jollivette	Pink flowering cherry
Prunus serrula	Birch bark cherry
Prunus serrulata	Japanese flowering cherry
Prunus cistena	Dwarf flowering plum
Prunus mume	Japanese flowering apricot
Prunus tomentosa	Nanking cherry red fruit
Prunus Virginiana	Choke cherry
Pseudolarix kaempferi	Golden larch
Punica granatum "nana"	Dwarf pomegranate
Pyracantha "red elf"	Compact firethorn
Pyrus Kawakamii	Evergreen pear
Pyrus salicifolia "pendula"	Willowleaf pear
Quercus dumosa	California scrub oak
Quercus ilex	Holly oak
Quercus myrsinifolia	Japanese evergreen oak
Quercus phellos	Willowleaf oak
Quercus suber	Cork oak

Pinus strobus *"Griegs," White pine.*

Pinus mugho mughus, *Dwarf Mugho pine.*

Picea pungens glauca nana, *Dwarf Colorado blue spruce.*

Pinus strobus "nana," *Dwarf Eastern white pine.*

Pinus strobus pendula, *Weeping white pine.*

Quercus vacciniifolia	Huckleberry oak
Rhododendron "blue diamond"	Lavender
Rhododendron "bow bells"	Pink
Rhododendron "Ginny Gee"	Pink to white
Rhododendron "hotel"	Yellow
Rhododendron Kiusianum	
Rhododendron "mucronulatum"	Deciduous purple
Rhododendron "Nancy Evans"	Orange
Rhododendron "Trilby"	Red
Rhododendron Satsuki azaleas	Many colors
Rhododendron Kurume azaleas	Many colors
Rhodohypoxis baurii	Dwarf bulbs
Salix purpurea "nana"	Dwarf Alaskan blue willow
Salix sachalinensis "setsuka"	*Setsuka* willow

Schefflera arboricola	Hawaiian elf schefflera
Serissa foetida	Chinese snow rose
Sorbus reducta	Dwarf ash
Sorbus Tianshanica	Turkestan mountain ash
Styrax Japonicus	Japanese snowbell tree
Syringa Koreana	Korean lilac
Taxodium distichum	Bald cypress
Taxodium mucronatum	Montezuma cypress
Taxus cuspidata "nana"	Dwarf Japanese yew
Taxus media "brownii"	Brown's yew

Ulmus parvifolia "Seiju," Seiju *elm.*

Tsuga Canadensis "redula," *Weeping hemlock.*

Thuja Occidentalis "little giant"	Little giant arborvitae
Thuja Occidentalis "nana"	Dwarf arborvitae
Tilia cordata	Little leaf linden
Tsuga Canadensis "redula"	Weeping hemlock
Ulmus parvifolia	Chinese elm
Ulmus parvifolia "Hokkaido"	*Hokkaido* elm
Ulmus parvifolia "Seiju"	*Seiju* elm
Wisteria floribunda	Japanese wisteria
Wisteria Sinensis	Chinese wisteria
Zelkova serrata	Sawleaf Zelkova
Ziziphus jujuba	Chinese date tree

Tsuga Canadensis *"Everet Golden," Canadian hemlock.*

8

CREATING A BONSAI

8-1

8-2

8-3

MOST STUDENTS JUST STARTING OUT BEGIN with the mistaken notion that these trees are all about one foot tall and about as wide. Actually, there is a full range of bonsai sizes available from the "pea-sized" *Keshitsubu* bonsai, which can be held on the tip of one finger, all the way up to the "imperial" or sixteen-handed bonsai.

The large bonsai shown in **8–1** require sixteen hands to lift, or eight people. They are common at the Imperial Palace and, hence, the name. Some of these larger trees are ten or twelve feet tall and have magnificent trunks on them up to three feet in diameter. Their gorgeous ornate pots are priceless.

A *Mame*, or miniature bonsai, rhododendron is shown in **8–2**. This is a two-year-old plant of the variety "*Kiusianum* Pink." It has three blossoms already and a nice little bend in the trunk. The pot is less than an inch high. These small bonsai are, of course, highly portable, but their charm is tempered by their frequent need for water—sometimes ten times a day!

A *Mame*, or palm-sized, bonsai only six inches tall yet thirty-five years old is shown in **8–3**. It is a Manzanita, *Manzanita Columbiana*, collected from the wild. The container is a beautiful handmade signed piece from Japan.

PERSONAL GOALS

You should select the size that you find most appropriate. If you are not often at home, the small *Mame* or *Shohin* bonsai will suffer. In the summer, they require water several times each day; in winter, smaller containers are more vulnerable to a sudden frost than larger ones.

A large bonsai is easier to maintain in both summer and winter, but if you cannot lift the bonsai easily by yourself, the hobby can be frustrating. You have to be able to rotate your trees easily so that sunlight can reach all sides of the branches for even development. Also, there is usually never one spot in your backyard that is perfect for all four seasons. Work with plants that are only as large as you can comfortably move.

Some amount of investment will help add to your enjoyment of this art. A good imported container, some adequate tools, choice plant material, and some bonsai books will get you off to a satisfying start. A realistic figure to start with would be about a hundred dollars (US). This will get you a modest plant, pot, soil, a beginning tool, and an inexpensive book. Your second bonsai will require much less of an investment, since you are already on your way.

One aspect of training bonsai that is often overlooked by the beginner is the commitment of time. Those that are most successful at growing trees enjoy the quiet time spent making them look better. If you feel that pruning, watering, and potting is a waste of time or a bother, I cannot recommend bonsai as a hobby for you.

Other personal decisions also affect the degree of enjoyment we get from our trees. If we force an upright plant into a cascading style, we also increase the amount of attention the bonsai will require. For some people, this challenge is part of the fun. For others, it destroys the fun. Select indoor plant material if you would rather not work outdoors. Your bonsai will suffer if you aren't willing to go out in the rain or cold to tend them properly. Match your personal needs to your bonsai. If you set aside a time and a place to work, your enjoyment will likely double. Work with adequate tools and containers. Read as much as you can on the subject. Attend local bonsai meetings if possible. Your success will magnify your enjoyment.

GROWING BONSAI FROM SEED

For some bonsai growers this is the most satisfying method to grow bonsai. Growing from seed has its advantages and disadvantages. What is seen by some as inconvenience brings tremendous satisfaction for others as they watch their bonsai grow and develop from a tiny speck.

Some seed catalogs will have appropriate bonsai material listed. Refer to Chapter Seven for some suggested plants to try. A bonsai nursery, if one is nearby, might sell seed or refer you to a source. Try bonsai journals, catalogs, or newsletters for sources of mail-order seed. Another good source is from older trees themselves. Your local library or college can probably assist you in locating plantings that set seed every fall. Don't forget your local countryside, mountains, or beaches.

Store your seed in a dark, cool place, and keep it dry and clean until use. Get as much information as you can about the proper method of germinating the seed.

GENERAL RULES FOR GERMINATION

Fresh seed collected in the fall should be sown in the ground immediately or dried for use the following year. Do not store fresh seed in a moist condition; it will decay. Most tree seed requires a cold period before it will sprout. You can achieve this naturally outdoors or in your refrigerator. Typically sixty days of temperatures near 35 degrees F is sufficient. If you are using dried seed, soak the seed for two days in a bucket of water that has been heated to bathwater temperature. There is no need to add further heat; just use a large container so that the heat will gradually disperse.

Sow your seed in well-aerated, loose soil. Cover with a half inch of soil, and keep moist but not soggy. Sometimes it takes a second winter to properly stratify some species; so don't be too quick to throw the seed away. If you have garden fauna that eat seeds, sow your seeds in a wooden box protected with screen.

Growing your seed in a container gives you the added flexibility of moving it around in case of inclement weather or pests.

Small containers dry out quickly and require careful attention to watering. They also respond quickly to frost and midday heat. I recommend a cedar box measuring about 24 inches by 18 inches and about 4 inches deep (see **8–4**). Fill the container with fresh, weed-free, screened bonsai soil, prepared just as you would for finished bonsai.

Lightly spread the seed into neat rows on the soil surface; label carefully with the date, stratification information, variety, and seed source in addition to the customary common name (see **8–5**). This information will help you later, successful or not.

Use an indelible pen to mark plastic markers (see **8–6**). Delineate your rows to provide adequate separation between species.

Cover the entire container and rearrange the seed if necessary (see **8–7**). You may plant conifers and deciduous together; it does not matter. You can transplant the seedlings as they are ready regardless of their proximity to other underdeveloped seed.

Cover with a light layer of bonsai soil, no more than the thickness of two seed diameters (see **8–8**).

Tamp the soil down with a trowel (see **8–9**). Use moderate force without concern over too much compaction. The screened soil will still drain extremely well.

Water well with a light bonsai watering hose or similar watering device. Take care to water lightly enough to avoid dislodging or washing out the seed, yet water deeply enough to remove tannins from the soil (see **8–10**). Any bark products must be washed well to avoid toxic effects to developing seedling roots.

After a few weeks, the first new sprouts start to appear (see **8–11**). Weed carefully to avoid removing the plants you are trying to grow. Remember to wait for the true leaves to appear after the cotyledon before making a judgment on the identification of a plant.

The plants can receive their first fertilizer as soon as they are visible. Apply a light amount of liquid fertilizer (see **8–12**). Do not sprinkle with granular fertilizers. A well-balanced 5–10–5 seems to work best. Transplant to a large container when the roots are about three inches long. Transfer quickly to avoid drying out the tender new seedling.

Trim off the extreme end of the root to encourage side roots (see **8–13**). Some species, such as oak, have a dominant tap root. Others, such as pine and maple, have natural side roots.

In your new container, form a small cone-shaped hole in the soil (see **8–14**). The point of your small scissors or a chopstick does this quite well. Then carefully place the freshly pruned seedling into the soil cavity.

With the plant at the proper level, compress the soil around the roots carefully (see **8–15**). It is not necessary to use much force.

As you water the new seedling in, you will notice the soil settling in around the plant and you may have to add a bit more soil on top (see **8–16**).

After a few weeks of growth, fertilize again with a good drench of fish fertilizer from a watering can (see **8–17**). Don't use granules; they encourage slime, mildew, and liverwort.

As the plants develop, take care to give them the appropriate amount of sunlight, water, and nutrition (see **8–18**).

Make sure they are labelled properly (see **8–19**). Some closely related plants are impossible to distinguish when they are so young. Start to train for bonsai immediately by pinching back strong shoots and establishing a dominant trunk line by pruning away competing tops. Do not wait until they are so big that scars will result. Certainly begin training by the first year. If using copper wire, extend your trunk for a while to get some diameter and strength on it before risking damage. Watch especially for fungus and mildew. Water only when necessary and always make sure your soil drains very well.

A simple trident maple grove, *Acer palmatum buergerianum*, is shown in **8–20** made from seven four-year-old seedlings. Plantings of this type are quick and easy; I recommend them for beginners. Maples of all types transplant easily, requiring little care. Their pruning requirements are not complex, and the leaves start to miniaturize after only one season in a container.

The planting shown in **8–21** is a grove of English hedge maple, *Acer campestre*, grown from seed. I have always enjoyed the imprecise growth habits exhibited by plants developed from seed. The autumn color of this maple forest is just as unusual as the trunk formation. Each tree develops its own display at a different time. The planting is seventeen inches tall in a nineteen-inch brick-red Japanese container.

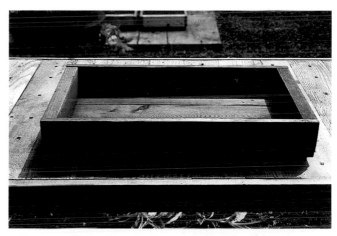

8–4

8–5

8–6

8–7

8–8

8–9

8–10

8–11

8–12

8–13

8-14

8-15

8-16

8-17

8-18

8-19

8-20

8-21

BONSAI BY DIVISION

Many plants such as lilac, quince, bamboo, and azalea can be easily propagated by division. This means simply that you can divide up your plant into pieces like overgrown tubers or corms. If you chop straight down through a lilac bush, you end up with two lilac bushes. If you rip up a bit of bamboo root, it will likely sprout a new plant. If you want to try propagation by division, use a piece with both root and stem for best results. Allow the new plant to develop on its own for a year before trying to train it as bonsai material. This extra time will help the old scars heal and assure its survival before you invest a great deal of time. Propagation by division produces a plant that is genetically identical to the parent plant. This is especially useful on flowering species like quince. The new plant will bloom at the same time as the parent plant; it will be the same color, shape, and the leaves and flowers will be the same size.

BONSAI FROM CUTTINGS

A fairly quick way to procure bonsai material is simply to cut a twig off an existing plant and place it into some rooting medium and start a new plant. Obviously, some plants root better than others. Some easy plants to try are maple, elm, beech, birch, hornbeam, azalea, rhododendron, and Zelkova. Prune off about three inches of new growth some time in May or June. Immediately coat the cut end with liquid or powdered rooting hormone, and plant in sand or perlite. Water or mist as often as you can; in about three weeks, a few of your cuttings will have sprouted new roots. For plants that are harder to root, like conifers, it is helpful to heat the sand or perlite slightly by placing a light bulb below the propagating pot. Even so, most of your cuttings will fail; so always cut more than you need to ensure success.

Once the roots are about an inch long, begin feeding with a low-nitrogen fertilizer in small doses until the roots grow to about three inches. Then, move the cutting into a larger container with potting soil, and feed regularly with a well-balanced fertilizer. Treat this new plant as you would a year-old seedling. Begin bonsai training as soon as it is feasible. Remove unwanted shoots as they appear, and wire the trunk while it is still young and flexible.

ROCK-GROWN MAPLE FROM A CUTTING

To create this planting, you will need an appropriate maple source for the cutting, an interestingly shaped rock slightly larger than a softball, and time.

I used a trident maple, *Acer buergerianum*, although any Japanese maple works well—as do *Acer rubrum*, *Acer ginnala*, *Acer campestre*, and *Acer griseum* (see **8–22**). To make a cutting, choose an actively growing branch sometime in April or early May, and cut off a section that is no bigger than a pencil.

Strip the leaves off the bottom three inches of the cutting with your hands (see **8–23**). It is better to tear them off rather than use sharp tools. Prepare a solution of liquid rooting hormone or powdered hormone if liquid is unavailable.

With a very sharp pair of scissors or a grafting knife, cut through one of the lower nodes at a diagonal while the cutting is immersed in the rooting hormone (see **8–24**). This takes advantage of existing plant hormones inside the stem that have concentrated in the region of the former leaf stems. Where the recently torn-off leaves were is where you have the greatest chance of growth—either new leaves or new roots. In this case, the cutting will produce roots since it will be buried in soil.

While still dripping wet with liquid hormone, immediately plunge the cutting into a container holding appropriate rooting media (see **8–25**). Perlite or pumice works best for hard-to-root species such as pine and dwarf conifers. Sharp mason's sand seems best for fruiting and flowering trees; for easily propagated plants such as maple, elm, willow, birch, and beech a good well-drained humus is sufficient.

The successful cutting is shown in **8–26** one year later, transferred to a large container. The maple has been planted on top of a lava rock and then is allowed to grow unrestricted for two more years.

The same maple, seen in **8–27**, has been raised slowly over two years to start exposing both the rock and the roots around it. The rock planting is ready to be transplanted into its first bonsai container.

The heavy bushiness in the top of the tree is a good example of the apical dominance of this plant (see **8–28**). A large lower branch can be used as a new top. The maple will not only have a more interesting trunk line, but the new top will grow quite quickly.

Presumably I can get this maple, along with its rock, into the green bonsai container shown in **8–29**. I remove the tree and rock from the plastic pot and, work-

8–22

8–23

8–24

8–25

8–26

8–27

8–28

8–29

8–30

8–31

8–32

is now extended, will increase in girth dramatically the coming spring. The exposed roots will cling ever closer to the rock.

The finished height of this trident maple is only eighteen inches (see **8–32**). This planting promises to give back years of viewing pleasure, and it is only four years old.

BONSAI BY EARTH LAYERING

This is a method of choice for sprawling-type plants such as low rhododendrons and creeping juniper. These plants will root themselves quite easily when a portion of stem comes in contact with the ground. Cut into the bark at the point where the branch will be buried, and roots will appear more quickly and be stronger. When the branch has plenty of new roots to support its foliage, detach it from the parent plant; care for it like a one-year-old transplanted seedling. Do not begin bonsai training for one year.

BONSAI BY AIR LAYERING

This is an excellent way to get good bonsai material from existing larger trees. Some good examples are crab apple, pyracantha, cotoneaster, cryptomeria, cypress, flowering apricot, cherry, and plum. Choose a branch that has a "miniature bonsai" already formed. Pay attention to where branches are located so that you don't have to do much pruning after the selected area strikes roots. Make a cut one inch wide all the way around the branch where you want new roots to form. Make sure that the cut is deep; cut to the cambium layer and a bit beyond. Cover the cut area with rooting hormone and wet sphagnum moss, and hold it in place with clear plastic sheeting. Cover this with black plastic to keep the light out and the heat in. Check occasionally to make sure the moss remains wet. In a few weeks new roots should be sprouting from the top edge of the cut area. When sufficient roots have sprouted, the inside of the clear plastic will be partially covered with visible white root hairs. Now you simply sever the "new plant" from its parent branch below the cut you previously made. Trim off any excess stub you don't need, and plant in the

ing with plenty of water, I choose large artistically placed roots to show off. The other roots are removed.

The roots have been separated out as much as is feasible without excess damage to the rock planting (see **8–30**). Some roots will be trimmed away since there are plenty present to support new top growth. Then fresh bonsai soil is added by working it around with chopsticks.

The maple has an excellent future (see **8–31**). Its rootage is diverse and well distributed. The apex, which ground or a suitable container. Wait one year for your new plant to stabilize before beginning to train as a bonsai.

With pine, it works better to use wire as a "tourniquet" instead of cutting into the bark. Wind some copper wire around a branch as tight as you can, and coat with rooting hormone. Wrap as in the method above, and wait. This method may take as long as two years, but it is especially suitable for slow-rooting species such as pine, hemlock, spruce, fir, and larch.

BONSAI BY GRAFTING

For a more complete description of grafting techniques, I refer the reader to a specialized text. I include this very brief mention so that the beginning bonsai student is introduced to as complete a presentation of methods for creating bonsai as possible.

Grafting can be the only way to make some varieties of plants thrive. Often unusual sports or mutations are not strong enough to live without a powerful root stock driving them along. A good example is the contorted filbert. Seeds from this plant are often sterile. Those that do sprout will perform poorly and will usually die within two years. The same can be said about most Japanese laceleaf maples. Nursery workers graft these trees in order to combine the vitality of a wild root stock with the rare growth form found on the top of the plant. By completing the graft in very early spring, the sap is not under a great deal of pressure yet, and the corresponding cambium layers can be matched and secured. When the new union warms up in the spring, sap is transferred between the two plants; if the connection is good, a new plant begins. As with all bonsai material, wait until the new plant is stabilized before training.

BONSAI FROM NURSERY STOCK

The most popular way to acquire bonsai material is shopping at a local nursery; so I will discuss this method of creating bonsai at some length. The key to finding promising specimens with little effort is to be selective.

Look for unusual plants in and among ordinary ones. With permission from the manager or owner, remove the container and inspect the root ball. Look for signs of burlap; these trees usually are difficult to use. Avoid trees with dark, flabby, or evil-smelling roots. Select plants that have small leaves or needles. Favor those with short internodes and low branches. Make sure, if there are no needles in close to the trunk, that it is a variety which will bud back so that you don't have large bare areas that will remain without foliage. If possible, shop for fruiting trees while the fruit is still visible; the same with flowers. This will give you a better idea of their size and scale than a typically faded photograph on a plant tag. If possible, investigate with your fingers at the base of the trunk. Look for a prominent root buttress and evenly spread roots.

Plants that are one-sided are difficult to correct, even in several years. Separate the branches carefully with your hands and look at the trunk in the middle of the plant. Good bonsai material will have a regular decrease in trunk diameter from the bottom to the top. Trees without trunk taper are difficult to style. Try to find plants where you can remove major branches towards the rear of the trunk. These plants will not only have hidden scars, but will possess increased taper on the trunk.

Look carefully for a possible apex. If there is no way to successfully terminate your trunk while shortening it, you will end up with an abrupt, artificial-looking top which will require years to hide or correct. Most of all, be patient and yet spontaneous. Good material is almost instantly obvious; but typically you may have to pass over thousands of ordinary plants to find the one unusual plant that will be suitable as bonsai material. When in doubt, keep looking!

A DECIDUOUS BONSAI FROM NURSERY STOCK

The English oak, *Quercus robur*, shown in **8–33** was found among a group of shade trees that had not sold the previous spring. It had been field-grown for most of its life, propagated from seed. It is approximately ten years old. The tree was originally sixteen feet tall, and it has been shortened drastically just to get it into the studio! It is planted in a pulp pot that is sixteen inches high and twenty inches in diameter.

This oak was bare-rooted two years earlier and planted in potting soil; many fine root hairs should be present. If this tree were in a burlap bag, there would be a great deal of mud, and the fine roots instead would be located far from the base of the trunk. Because there should be many fine root hairs, one of the two bonsai containers shown should be feasible. A smaller bonsai pot will show off the bonsai trunk size much better than something big and deep. However, often a compromise must be reached to make sure the tree survives the transplant.

The peat pot was removed with a small hatchet to preserve the root ball as much as possible (see **8–34**). Note the white root tips, a sign of spring. The oak tree is usually the best indicator that winter is over. As a species, the oak is the most reluctant to display new foliage. When the oak tree leafs out, it's time to plant your spring garden.

The root surface and the buttress of the trunk have been more or less established (see **8–35**). Note the grey mouldy appearance in the potting soil. Oak trees thrive in this mould and you should retain a portion of this existing soil for the purpose of "reinfecting" the new bonsai soil.

With a hatchet, lopper, and a bonsai scythe, the lower two thirds of the roots have been removed (see **8–36**). This is all the root removal necessary at this time. The upper part of the tree can now be pruned. The reddish color of the roots and base of the trunk will go away as they are exposed to sunlight.

A close-up of the right side of this tree is shown in **8–37**. I cannot emphasize enough that the reason this oak is viable bonsai material is because an alternate apex has formed around the strong existing apex. The main trunk, which continues upwards to the full height of sixteen feet, has an opportune smaller apex just beside it, to the right. The larger trunk can be removed, the scar placed towards the back of the tree, and the smaller apex will take its place visually.

The trunk diameter at the level shown in **8–38** is too large to cut with traditional concave cutters. A small folding saw is more appropriate. It is not necessary to make a perfect cut with the saw. Come as close as you can, and then the finishing touches can be done with a large spherical knob cutter.

The large trunk is carved away with the purpose of tapering the area as smoothly and gradually as possible (see **8–39**). The size of the scar can be ignored; in time, the area will heal over, and it will look better year after year. A scar of this size may take ten years to disappear; but fortunately, the design can ensure that the scar is not visible from the front.

The area has been carved away slowly, making sure that all nearby branches have connecting bark left intact

(see **8–40**). Once inside the cambium, or living area, as much wood can be removed as desired. Continue carving until the contours are smooth and the trunk taper is as natural-looking as you can make it.

As with all wounds this size, it is helpful to utilize some kind of protection (see **8–41**). In this case, a light coating of mud was mixed with white carpenter's glue. You can see, it is not the size of the wound that is important, but the shape that remains after carving.

The same area of the tree shown in **8–41** is shown in **8–42** except that the photograph is taken from where the viewer would normally look. Notice that there is no visible sign of a scar. This is an excellent example of good bonsai design. Even a judge in a bonsai show is instructed to ignore the back of the tree.

At this point, unfortunately, a small compromise must be reached (see **8–43**). If the tree is turned so that the large trunk scar is invisible, a medium-sized root protrudes directly towards the front. Bonsai design is replete with compromises. The medium-sized root scar is still more desirable than viewing the relatively large branch scar; so the root is removed.

Actually, the removal of the root uncovered some very nice looking roots that were hidden (see **8–44**). This rootage spread is quite superior to having tried to retain the large forward-facing root. These roots are well balanced and placed around the trunk to provide nutrition and visual support. Remember to keep the roots wet.

The existing branches still go clear up to the ceiling, so major pruning is in store for this tree (see **8–45**). Try to make as few cuts as possible, keeping them hidden from view. If you are unable to do so, make the cuts so that the scars face to the right or the left.

The same view of the branch structure as shown in **8–45** is shown in **8–46**. The tree height has been reduced by another two and a half feet.

The tree is ready to be potted (see **8–47**). The traditional broom style has been chosen because of the dense branch placement and general existing twigginess— sometimes called secondary ramification.

Carefully identify those large roots on the underside of the root ball that will prevent the tree from going into the bonsai pot you have selected (see **8–48**). It is extremely important to recognize the value to the tree of every root you remove. In this case, the total root mass is large, well divided, and productive; so the removal of a few large protruding roots will not be of great concern. If this tree lacked active white roots close in to the trunk, it would be unwise to remove too many large roots. For such a tree, it would be far wiser to overpot the bonsai in its first year.

In preparation for potting, you will use screens to cover the large drain holes found in commercially available bonsai containers (see **8–49**). One-inch soffit screen is a readily available and appropriately sized screen. Bonsai nurseries sell a popular plastic screening for this same purpose. For this pot, I'll bend six-inch-long pieces of sixteen-gauge copper wire into staples that will secure the screen in place.

First, make two loops in the wire (see **8–50**). One loop passes above and the other passes below. Make sure that the distance between the two parallel portions is approximately the diameter of the drain hole you are covering.

Next, bend each long section against the wire until it forms a right angle (see **8–51**). The two long sections point in opposite directions.

Grasp each loop between thumb and forefinger without grasping any other part of the staple (see **8–52**). Twist the middle section like a barber pole so that the two long sections are pointing in the same direction. The result is a highly useful bonsai pot screen staple.

Insert the two long ends through the screen and flare them out on the underside of the pot (see **8–53**). This staple is especially useful against sowbugs, slugs, snails, and beetles, which can push away a screen that is placed over the drain hole without being secured. An added advantage is that the copper near the drain hole slightly inhibits root formation, allowing increased drainage.

Working quickly, I remove the remaining roots that interfere with potting into the bonsai container (see **8–54**). The roots are kept wet at all times. The object is to present to the viewer a surface that looks balanced, stable, and well distributed.

The tree is temporarily placed in the pot to determine not only where it fits, but also to adjust the height in the pot by removing lower roots (see **8–55**). Two surface roots were removed to balance the surface appearance.

The potting as shown in **8–56** is finished. The container was borderline too small. Fortunately, fine root ramification in this tree made it possible to safely transplant into a container this size. While this oak is without leaves, a dormant spray of lime sulfur will eliminate any overwintering insects and disease. At the same time, I can get rid of the greenish hue of the trunk caused by high winter humidity. An applied spray of 3 tablespoons of lime sulfur per quart of water should whiten up the bark considerably overnight.

The finished bonsai is shown in **8–57**. Certainly the shallow container helps to show off the large, stately trunk. The finished height of the tree is twenty-six inches; the trunk is three inches in diameter. It is placed in a green oval bonsai container from Japan that measures sixteen inches by ten inches at a height of two and one quarter inches. Notice that the lime sulfur spray has generally whitened the bark and evened out the color in much the same way sunlight would eventually do. The soil mixture is 35 percent rotted compost mixed with oak leaves and steer manure. The remainder of the soil is volcanic pumice to ensure excellent drainage. The roots were treated by soaking them, pot and all, in a mild Vitamin B_1 solution, which included 5 percent phosphorus, 5 percent 1-naphthalenealetic acid to induce root formation.

The same oak tree is shown in **8–58** one month later. Spring has arrived. When an oak tree finally leafs out like this one is one of the most accurate ways to tell that the soil is warm enough to plant your vegetable garden. In another month, it will need thinning out to avoid congestion. Water oak bonsai as you would pine or juniper; the roots do not like to be wet all the time. Look for surface dryness, then wait three more days before watering again. When you do water, water well. Apply three good drenchings at least fifteen minutes apart for best results. Here in Oregon, the leaves will mildew if kept too damp; water only the pot to avoid this problem. If rain lasts for several days, bring the oak bonsai into the house until the dampness goes away.

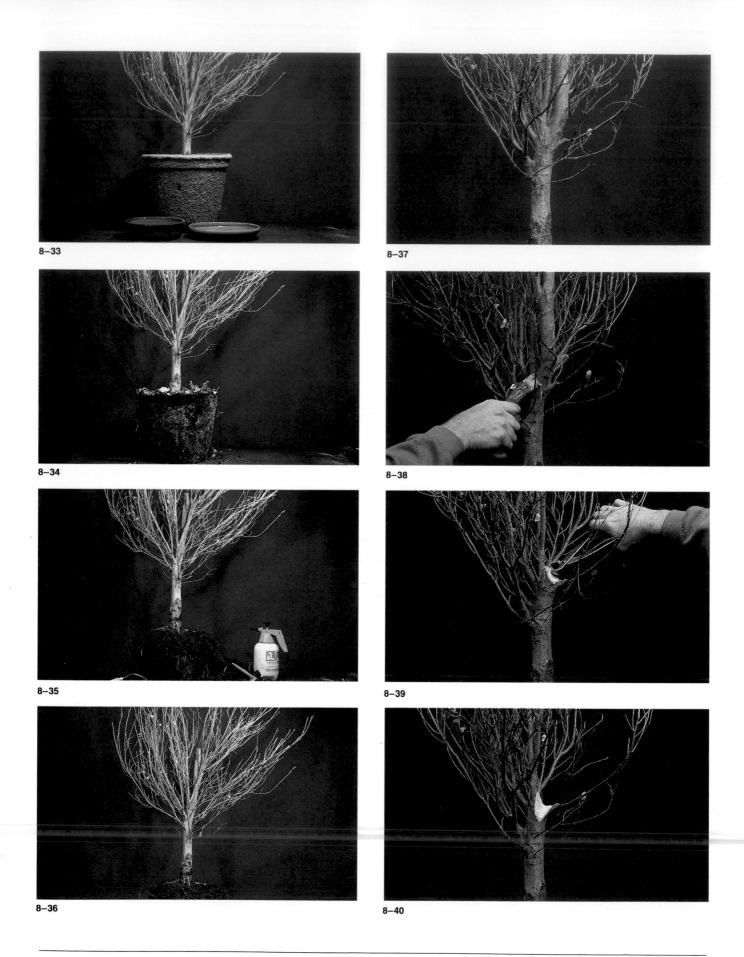

8–33

8–34

8–35

8–36

8–37

8–38

8–39

8–40

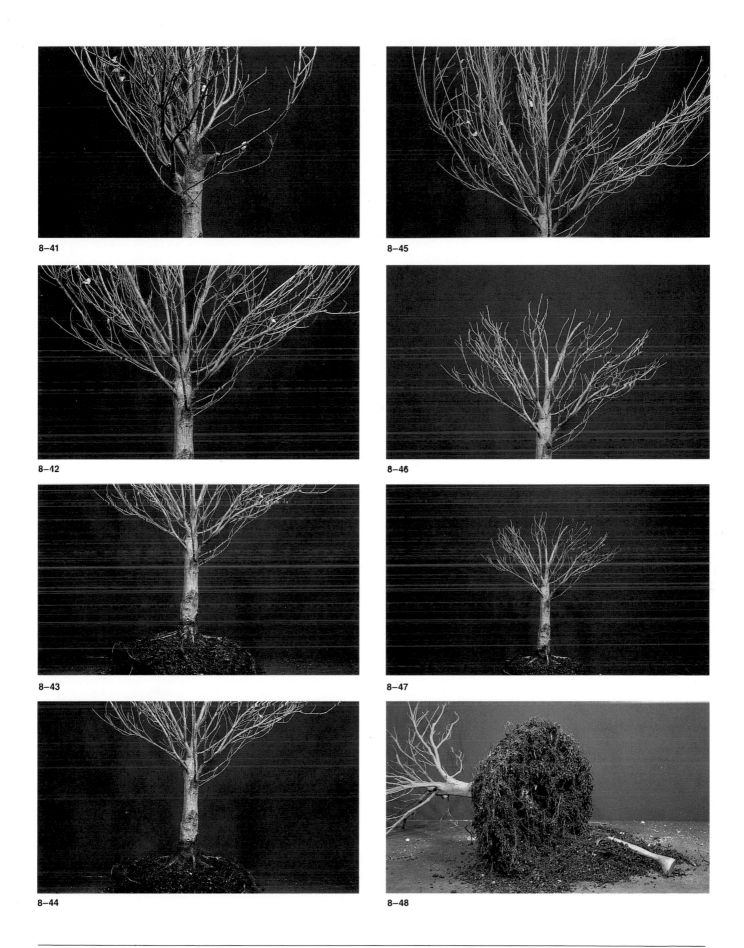

8-41

8-45

8-42

8-46

8-43

8-47

8-44

8-48

CREATING A BONSAI

137

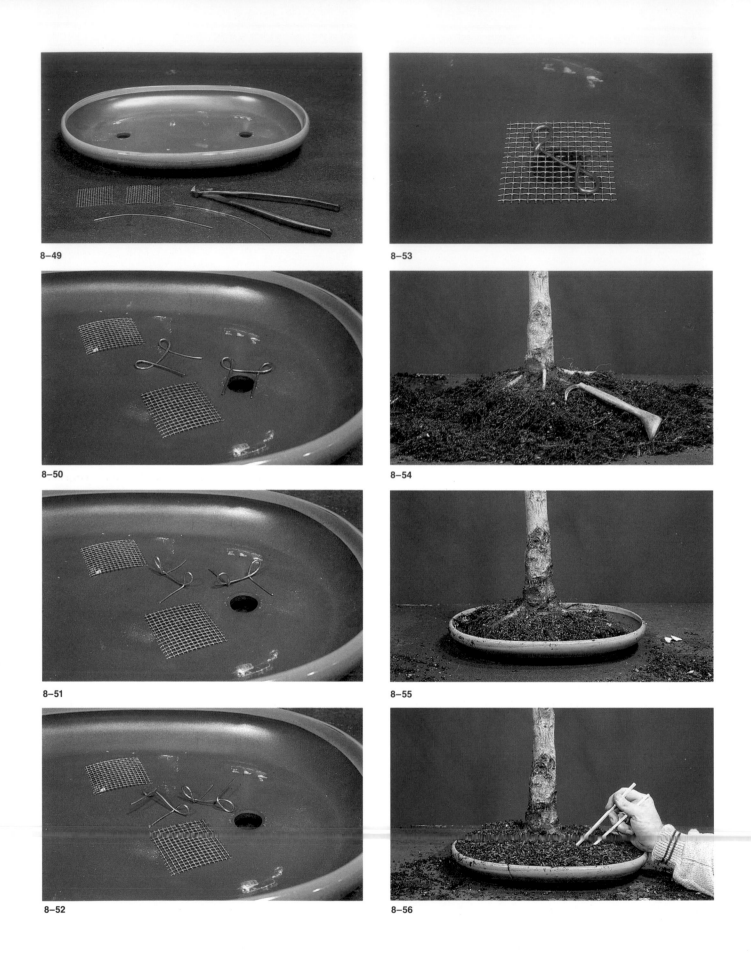

8–49

8–53

8–50

8–54

8–51

8–55

8–52

8–56

8–57

8–58

A PINE BONSAI FROM NURSERY STOCK

A bristlecone pine, *Pinus aristata*, obtained from a local nursery is shown in **8–59**. It has been field-grown for a number of years as evidenced by the burlap bag that contains the roots. Judging from the condition of the burlap, this tree was probably dug two years ago; the bag is neither rotting away nor new and intact. The pulp container that surrounds the burlap bag measures sixteen inches tall by eighteen inches in diameter. The pine is approximately eight years old and was likely grown from seed, given the degree of difficulty in growing this species from cuttings.

The three bonsai containers shown are possible candidates into which the tree will go after its first root pruning and styling. The season is early spring and is ideal for drastic work on most species. This tree was selected because of its many branches and relatively thick trunk. At this point, there is no way to tell what the final bonsai will look like.

The peat container has been removed as shown in **8–60**, exposing myriad fine, white root tips. This is a

sign that this tree is healthy and starting to actively grow.

The burlap bag is removed carefully because the fine root hairs are predominantly growing in the outside potting soil rather than continuing to grow in the thick muddy soil from the field in which it was growing previously (see **8–61**).

With a root hook or other dull instrument, carefully comb down the surface roots until a pleasant level is reached (see **8–62**). The real soil surface level will be at the maximum diameter of the trunk and will display many nicely shaped roots spreading out in all directions.

The bottom half of the root ball is cut off flat using a small hatchet or a sharp sickle as shown in **8–63**. Moisten the roots well with a fine mist of clear water from a spray bottle. I have become very fond of the compressed air pump–type spray bottles. It is important from this moment on that the roots remain moist at all times. There will be no further root work until the top foliage has been trimmed and styled; so it is a great help to place the tree on a small turntable for ease in studying and for reaching all the branches without further disturbing the root ball.

With small snippers, scissors, and bonsai concave cutters, remove all the dead twigs, needles, and leaf debris from the foliage (see **8–64**). Because pine wood is very soft, do not attempt to create *jin*, *shari*, or *sabamiki* on a pine tree; it will rot away in just a few years. Prune away all branches flush or slightly concave for best healing results.

This tree has three main trunks (see **8–65**). I cannot style this as a three-trunk bonsai, however, because the branches occur too high up on the tree. As it is, I have no choice but to remove two and retain only one large dominant trunk. If I remove the two on the left, the abrupt angle to the right does not leave a pleasant taper to the remaining trunk. If I remove the two trunks on the right, the remaining trunk line leans far to the left, tapers very little, and, as a result, a new and convincing apex would have to be positioned too far away from the base of the tree. The remaining choice seems best: removing the two outside trunks. The resulting trunk line is curved in an interesting way—sort of an informal upright or *Moyogi* style. A new apex is possible fairly close in and a compact form begins to take shape.

Cut off a large branch with an appropriately sized tool (see **8–66**). Do not attempt to cut through a branch that is too large for your concave cutter. It is better to first use a saw, and then trim the area with several small cuts. It is not necessary to cut accurately with the first bite of the cutting tool. In fact, it is very easy to cut off too much this way.

After the first cut, you can trim up the area nicely by using a small spherical knob cutter (see **8–67 and 8–68**). If you make the cut slightly concave, healing will be very fast, and new bark will completely cover the scar in just a few years. If you leave a small stub end remaining, healing will never be complete and the scar will remain an entry area for insects and disease.

The trunk line in the bottom half of the tree as shown in **8–69** is now quite defined. A most interesting shape is emerging. As it turns out, quite by accident, I chose the correct front of the tree right from the beginning. All other angles show off the new scars too much. Remember, I can move the small branches around quite easily with wire so they will not obstruct the trunk. I now have some decision-making to do. I will have to define the trunk line in the top half of the tree.

A close-up look at the top third of this tree as shown in **8–70** reveals that there are four possible trunk lines. Three come towards the front, and a fourth projects towards the rear. I certainly do not want this tree to look as though it is falling down backwards, so I'll eliminate the fourth choice from consideration.

Perhaps it is just because I have styled many bonsai before, or perhaps it is just the nature of interesting bonsai to be a bit twisted and bent (see **8–71**), but I would automatically eliminate the middle of the three trunk lines just because it is "boring."

Now I have another difficult decision to make (see **8–72**). Does the trunk line go the left or to the right?

Looking at this tree from a little farther away may help (see **8–73**). After looking at these two possibilities for over an hour, I came to the conclusion that most bonsai enthusiasts would select the apex on the left. For the purposes of this workshop, it is perhaps the most appropriate.

Before removing the branch on the right (see **8–74**), I want you to see what an interesting, yet unconventional, bonsai I would have if I were to utilize the apex on the right.

Once the apex has been established, the basic form of the bonsai becomes quite evident (see **8–75**). This will be a *Moyogi*-style tree with horizontal branches set out at various levels. The top third of the trunk, since it is still relatively supple due to its youth, will be heavily wired to exaggerate the trunk's existing bends.

Excess branch length has been removed as well as all needles that are two or three years old (see **8–76**). Ev-ergreens are deciduous trees with three-year-old foliage, and their annual shedding is equivalent to the leaf drop that we are accustomed to seeing in the fall. Two-year-old needles are removed for ease in wiring. It is much more difficult to wire over and around needles than bare stems. The recently transplanted tree also has a greater chance of success if there are more roots than foliage.

The basic bonsai shape has now been established as shown in **8–77**. Every branch has been wired, and then carefully bent into the best position. This tree normally grows in harsh conditions in nature; bringing the branches down at a sharp angle from the trunk gives the tree the alpine appearance often associated with annual heavy snow load and frost. The bristlecone pine, limber pine, and Murrayana pine tend to have a "memory." When the wire is cut off in late June, some branches will start to creep back to their former positions. For this reason, wind the wire quite loosely and remove it after the second spring instead of after the first, as is the norm. Also, you can exaggerate the bends a little to allow for the minor straightening out when the wire is removed.

It is time to pot this tree (see **8–78**). Whenever possible, try to clean out all the muddy soil with medium pressure from a garden hose. The roots are wet all the time compared with the slow "pick-it-away" method.

The roots are now washed clean of mud and silt, allowing me to examine the entire root structure (see **8–79**). Remove any large unproductive roots that interfere with potting into the bonsai container you have chosen. Remove all dark-colored or slippery roots; they are usually dead or diseased. Locate the ideal soil surface level for your tree; then remove all tiny roots above that level. The best root buttress is found where the trunk is at its greatest diameter and where a number of pencil-sized roots originate from the trunk.

Add soil one handful at a time, and work it into and among the rootage with a chopstick (see **8–80**). For best results, use a variety of motions with your hand, sometimes thrusting, sometimes using a gently rocking or circular motion. Occasionally, place the chopstick deep in the soil, and vibrate it back and forth quickly to help settle the dry granules into and around air pockets below the roots. Take your time; it is an important step and should take at least fifteen minutes. When you cannot get any more soil into the pot, smooth the surface with a small brush; then water well. A mild solution of Vitamin B_1 will help the tree recover from this fairly shocking experience.

The bonsai is almost complete (see **8–81**). I can now refine the branch placement and do some more careful pruning. New pine shoots grow on young branches that receive sunlight, so I can promote new budding and, especially, back budding, by thinning the needles a little. Removing needles from the lower parts of branch tips helps let in more sunlight and looks tidy. If we retain too much foliage at this stage of development, there may not be enough rootage to support all of the foliage; some random dieback of branches would be observed in about three weeks.

The completed bonsai measures only seventeen inches high and sports a three-and-one-half-inch trunk diameter (see **8–82**). The container used was the smallest of the three pots found in the very first photograph (refer to **8–59**). This tree will spend six weeks in partial shade, receiving no direct afternoon sun at all. The new shoots this year will not be pruned away, but kept in their entirety. The soil mix was 90 percent lava cinders and 10 percent rotten hardwood chips mixed with aged steer manure. Like all newly created bonsai, this tree will never be completely "finished." With careful maintenance, however, it has the potential to develop into a fine bonsai, a work of art; it could have been just another shrubby tree in someone's yard.

8–60

8–61

8–59

8–62

8–63

8–64

8–65

8–66

8–67

8–68

8–69

8–70

8–71

8–72

8–73

8–74

8–75

8–76

8–77

8–78

8–79

8—80

8—81

8—82

A MAPLE GROVE BONSAI

This technique for creating a maple grove bonsai applies equally well to all deciduous bonsai species—elm, birch, beech, alder, and hornbeam in particular. First, select a good variety of sizes from one species. Seven plants of red maple, *Acer rubrum*, ranging from two to six years of age are shown in **8—83**. These trees have been grown for bonsai purposes and, therefore, have some trunk development in spite of their small size.

I find it helpful to arrange the potential grove of trees in order of size (see **8—84**). In the back row are trees number one, two, and three going from left to right; in the front row, trees number four, five, six, and seven. A successful grove uses this size disparity to achieve the illusion of depth. In other words, tree number seven should look as old as tree number one. The reason it is smaller is because it is "farther away." I can trim these trees later to exaggerate this effect after they are potted.

When arranging a forest or grove planting, don't be bound by a fixed arrangement. Rather, study each tree carefully in sequence, starting with the tallest, and let "the tree itself" determine where it will look the best. The front of tree number one is shown in **8—85**. It is the front because no other view of this tree is better. Studied from this view, the tree is mostly bare in the bottom two thirds. Foliage has not been allowed to grow; therefore, there must have been another tree growing very close to it, restricting new foliage. In addition, this tree is relatively tall and straight compared to the others; so it must have had a sheltered life. This tree's shape can make sense in the grove by nestling another tree close to it.

Tree number two is not the best candidate, because it, too, is rather tall and lanky (see **8—86**). If numbers one and two were side by side in a grove, they would both have more lower branches. Instead, let us look for a bushier tree.

Tree number three is a likely candidate (see **8—87**). Not only is it bushy—which would account for the lack of lower branches on tree number one—but it also has a pleasing similar curve to the trunk. To prepare them for the future grove I'll take them out of their containers and try to fit them tightly together.

First, I more or less equalize their heights (see **8—88**). The number-one tree should not only be the tallest tree in the grove, but it should have the tallest root system as well—its root buttress should be the most predominant.

The root buttress plays an important role in the presentation of the tree (see **8—89**). When this feature is exposed on these two trees, it becomes immediately obvious that they can not be planted close together. The strong root buttress on tree number three is too strong on the right side, and this tree must be planted on the other side.

The relationship shown in **8—90** is better for two reasons. The roots fit together tighter, and the two trunks form a complementary line.

The large amount of rootage on the right side of tree number two makes it prohibitive to get very close to tree number one (see **8—91**). If tree number two is placed to the right of the pair of trees, the trunks lean too much towards each other. This would not happen in nature. I will plant tree number two on the left, therefore, and tuck it in as close as possible without damage to the main roots. This is my basic trio of maples. The rather unpleasant straight branch on tree number two may be removed later if it can be replaced by one of the smaller trees.

Now, to put these three in the oval blue glazed pot. Since the planting seems to move so nicely from right to left, I will plant the maples off center on the right side (see **8—92**). This will provide more room to slant tree number two.

The remaining four trees for our seven-tree grove are shown in **8—93**. They are from left to right numbers four, five, six, and seven. Six and seven will be exchanged; six is a good prospect for the smallest tree because its foliage is at a lower level.

I'll trim it, then rearrange the trees (see **8—94**).

Now I have all the trees in order from left to right (see **8—95**). I'll place them in the blue container one at a time, starting with tree number four.

Tree number four complements the inside trunk line of tree number two quite well (see **8—96**).

This makes the straight and ugly branch on tree number two unnecessary, so it can be removed (see **8—97**).

With that branch removed, the trunk lines are readily visible, and the grove appearance starts to show quite well (see **8—98**).

How to place tree number five? It is long and lanky and a bit similar in shape to tree number two. I try slanting it to the outside and see if the trunk lines harmonize. That seems to work out all right (see **8—99**).

Tree number six is now in place (see **8—100**). Note how effectively a smaller tree behind a larger one gives an added degree of depth to the planting. It is becoming difficult to keep these slanted trees upright without the weight of additional bonsai soil; so I will add some.

The almost completed seven-tree grove is shown in **8—101**. I think that anyone looking at this planting would be thinking that there must be water on the left side. Maple trees tip towards water in nature. On the left side of the pot, it would be nice to include a narrow crescent of gravel to give the illusion that we are looking at a high point on the inside curve of a stream bed. The maples grow, not only towards the water, but also the light. The light comes from the stream clearing and also is reflected from the water.

The finished grove is shown in **8—102**. A bit of moss here and there adds some stability to the scene, and the addition of pea gravel to the left side of the pot gives the illusion of water. The new leaves come out as a coppery-green color, then turn to bright green in the summer. The bright autumn color is almost an iridescent red. This planting will require water every day for the next three weeks to let new roots become established. Full shade is best for two weeks and then only dappled sunlight as it goes into its first summer. Next year, it can tolerate full sun when the temperature stays below 90 degrees F (32.2 degrees C). The tallest tree is sixteen inches high and the container is an eighteen-inch oval.

8—83

8—84

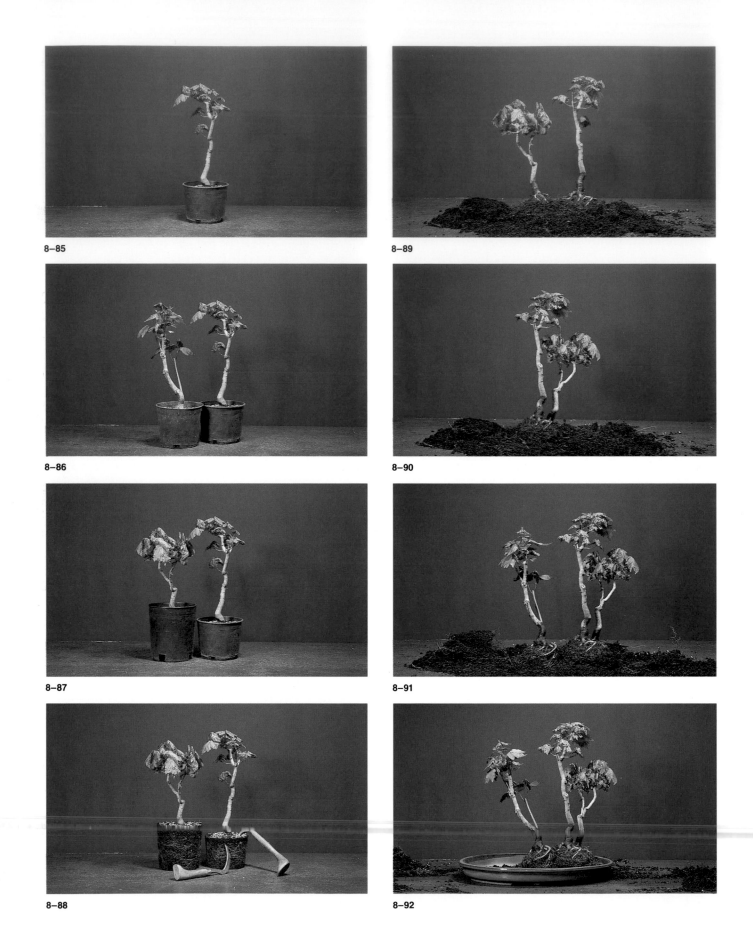

8–85

8–86

8–87

8–88

8–89

8–90

8–91

8–92

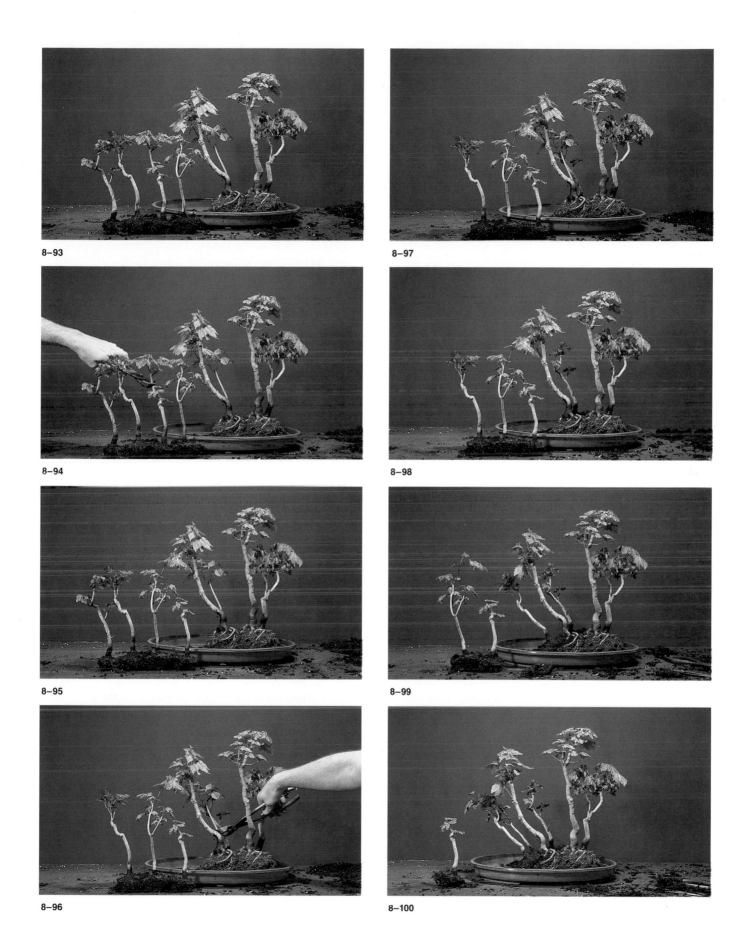

8-93

8-94

8-95

8-96

8-97

8-98

8-99

8-100

8–101

8–102

A BROADLEAF EVERGREEN BONSAI FROM NURSERY STOCK

The plant shown in **8–103** is a rhododendron, variety "Creeping Jenny," obtained from a local garden center. It is planted in a pulp container measuring sixteen inches across and nine inches tall. Total height of the planting as it is now is twenty-seven inches. I selected this plant because it had some trunk curvature, reasonably small foliage, and, by poking around with my finger in the soil, I came across some interesting surface roots. The relatively small, blue bonsai pot shown is my best guess as to the most appropriate container after the foliage is pruned back and the basic bonsai shape is revealed.

The peat pot has been removed (see **8–104**). The rhododendron was field-grown previous to being potted, and the bottom six inches of soil around the root ball simply fell away. Using a root scythe, a root hook, and chopsticks, the soil surface was taken down about one inch around the trunk and three inches around the outside edge. Don't ever bare-root a tree for longer than three minutes; the fine root hairs need protection and

moisture at all times. This root ball will be left intact while design decisions are made to the upper half of the tree.

Grub worms were found in the soil as it was being combed away (see **8–105**). They are inactive in colder weather, but begin to feed on the plant at night as spring temperatures rise. As this rhododendron is potted, most of the root ball will be carefully examined for overwintering pests; these are removed with tweezers.

Three major branches have been removed from the base of the trunk (see **8–106**). Rhododendrons do not form trunks for many years. This specimen is only six years old; but an illusion of age can be created by removing these large lower limbs now. By rotating the planting slowly, it is easier to select the front of the tree. Dead twigs have been removed and the soil surface debris cleaned up. There are only three major branches that have the potential for forming the top portion of the trunk. The task now is to visualize their removal one by one to decide which of the three forms is the most natural, yet interesting trunk line.

Pruning decisions are not always easy to make (see **8–107**). The large branch to the right was removed, and the outermost section of the back branch was actually torn off in order to save the close-in leaves it was supporting. Most of the potential bonsai is now evident.

It is time to turn the tree around again, and consider all angles as the final style is developed (see **8–108**). From this side, the lower branches contribute more to the overall design.

A large upper branch coming towards the viewer from this angle contributes nothing (see **8–109**). The same branch, when viewed from the opposite side is still too large and bulky compared to others at the same level; so it is removed.

This side was supposed to be the front (see **8–110**); however, the lower branches look even lower when viewed from this side. The pruning scars are more visible, and the trunk lines are not as clear. When this happens, there is no need to fret; the creative process allows for adjustment along the way. The other side turns out to be the best front.

Some extra branch length was removed as well as all the flower buds (see **8–111**). When a tree is struggling for survival after severe pruning, the last thing it needs is to push out spring flowers as well! Do your bonsai a big favor in their first year, and remove all fruits, flowers, nuts, and berries. They will come back even stronger the next year.

It is now time to pot the tree (see **8–112**). Make sure

the drain holes in the pot are covered with soffit screen and secured with wire staples to keep pests out. Check your supply of bonsai soil to see that there is enough on hand. Formulate the soil to suit the species; rhododendrons thrive on mostly organic mulch. Take the tree outside and remove most of the old soil with the gentle pressure from a garden hose. Work especially to wash away all mud and heavy clay. Keep the plant moist at all times, even the foliage.

Compare the root mass with the pot in which it will be planted (see **8–113**). Remove all fine, hairy roots that are too close to the surface.

Trim away large roots that will not fit into the container, and gently bend smaller productive roots into the pot (see **8–114**). Mist the roots often while working; this should take no more than five minutes.

Once the roots are in the pot, begin immediately to cover them with fresh bonsai soil (see **8–115**). Tamp the soil between the roots gently with a chopstick to remove air pockets. Keep packing in more soil until no more can be added. This should take about fifteen minutes. Check the position of the tree in the pot constantly. Make sure that it is upright in the container when viewed from the side. When the soil is all secure, and the tree is in the position desired, water well immediately by soaking it in a shallow tub of water or mist it repeatedly with a fine-spray hose nozzle.

When looking at this tree, visualize a venerable old rhododendron that clings to life on a faraway island in the Sea of Japan (see **8–116**). The foliage is still too sprawled—especially on the right side. The obvious wounds need dressing, and a tiny branch on the upper left needs to be wired down so that it will start forming an important role in the large space it occupies.

The final touches have been made (see **8–117**). The new bonsai has been watered well, wounds sealed, and leaves gently scrubbed clean. This tree has good potential because of its strong rootage, clean trunk line, and interesting curves. Its finished height is only sixteen inches, including the pot, and it sports a four-and-one-half-inch trunk; not bad for a bonsai only two hours old! With time, the foliage will thicken on each branch, the leaf size will reduce to less than half its present size, and the bright red blooms will be spectacular.

8–103

8–104

8–105

8–106

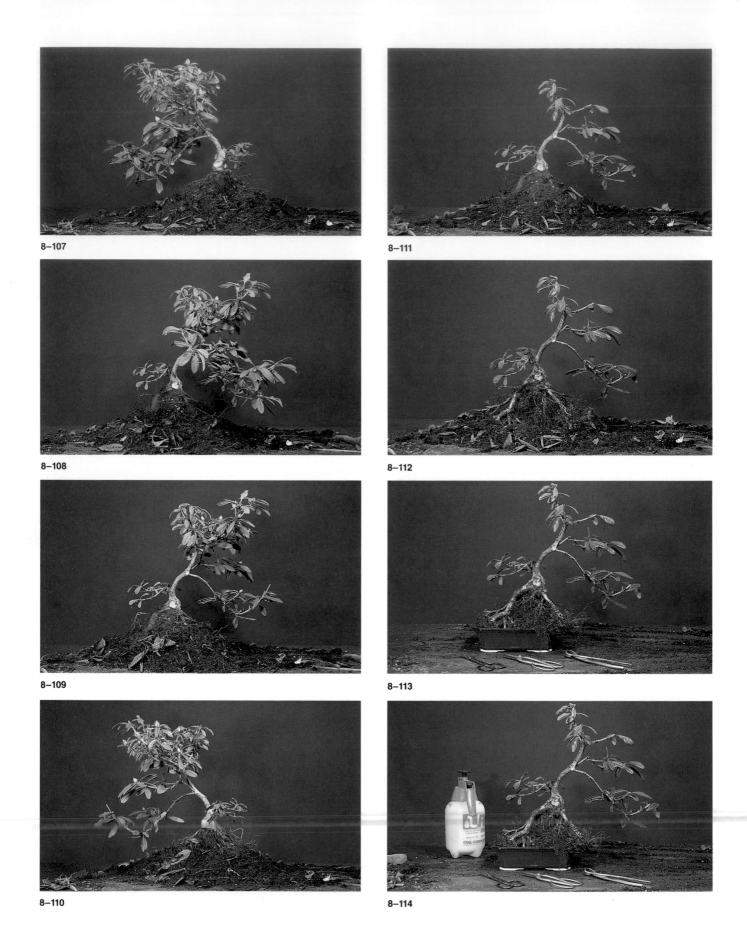

8–107

8–111

8–108

8–112

8–109

8–113

8–110

8–114

8–115

0–116

8–117

8–118

MAINTAINING A SPRUCE BONSAI

The bonsai shown in **8–118** has been in training for one year. It was styled at a bonsai club workshop and is now ready for refinement. The tree is an Alberta spruce, *Picea glauca conica*, obtained from three-gallon nursery stock. It is approximately nine years old, measures twenty-six inches high, and has a two-inch-diameter trunk.

With tweezers, all surface debris is removed from the soil (see **8–119**). Pick and choose colors, types, and sizes of moss starting to grow; favor those mosses that are slow-growing, compact, and tolerant of full sun. Remove weeds, making sure their long tap roots are pulled up along with the tops. Needle drop, while natural, contributes little to the health of the bonsai; It is better to remove it entirely. Replace washed-out areas with fresh bonsai soil to maintain a good root buttress.

Scrub the container with a coarse rag with a bit of detergent in it (see **8–120**). If there is an excessive accumulation of moss on the sides of the pot, a little bleach will easily remove it. For tough stains and white mineral deposits, vinegar dissolves them away. Do not use abrasive cleansers or steel wool for they will damage the finish on the pot. After a thorough cleaning with soap and water, the pot is rinsed well and a light coat of mineral oil is applied to restore its polished appearance.

The pot is clean and polished, the roots are groomed and trimmed (see **8–121**). Fresh soil has been added and only the best moss has been retained. It's time to refine the branch structure.

The existing branches are all in good locations due to last year's thinning, pruning, and styling (see **8–122**). Probably, most viewers would guess this tree is from ten to twenty years old. I should be able to do a bit better than that by achieving a greater illusion of age. This tree actually looks reasonably young due to the angle of its branches. A spruce tree starts out its life with branches aimed up at a 45-degree angle above the horizontal. As the tree ages, the branches slowly are brought down due to their weight and the pressures from frost, ice, and snow load. On a very old spruce near timberline, the branches are aimed considerably below the horizontal. With the use of guy wires, this condition can be mimicked to make conifers look older than they actually are.

I use the guy-wire method for bringing down these branches for several reasons (see **8–123**). There are many branches, and, wired in the conventional manner, the trunk of this tree would be entirely covered with copper. The guy-wire method works well when only a downward pull is required, which is true in this case. Last, it is a good opportunity to introduce you to yet another training technique. Start by wrapping the pot with four horizontal wires passing close to the trunk. Twist them to tighten them up, and trim off the excess.

The lowest three branches will be removed (see **8–124**). When all the foliage is being lowered, it makes little sense to retain branches that will be so low that they will approach touching the soil.

With these branches removed, I can start lowering the remaining foliage (see **8–125**). I begin by wiring the lowest branch first and working up to the top of the tree. Wrap the wire first around the branch, then slowly pull down. Do not attach the wire first to the base, and then attempt to fasten the other end to the branch.

Determine the one point on the branch where you will achieve the best results (see **8–126**). You will find that if you choose a point too far out, a weeping effect is achieved; this is sometimes desired, but not for this tree. If you choose a point too close to the trunk, too much force is required to pull the branch into position.

Protect the branch with a few winds of floral tape or similar cushioning material (see **8–127**). Aim the wire down to the base wires in the most appropriate direction. Sometimes this is straight down, but often it is on the other side of the trunk. It is not necessary to make the loops tight and snug; a few turns of the wire around a loose loop are sufficient.

The first branch is shown in **8–128** down and in place. I will prune, trim, and refine their shapes after all the foliage has been lowered. Next spring, as new buds are coming out, the branch will increase in diameter and back-bud considerably due to increased light; the branch tips will curve slightly up towards the sun, giving the tree an overall graceful appearance.

Eight of the lowest branches are now down (see **8–129**). You can begin to visualize the appearance of the tree already. The remaining branches are lighter, and can be wired to each other instead of the base.

The spruce has "aged" quite a bit in about an hour; of course, some refinement will be necessary (see **8–130**). Small branchlets poking straight up or straight down from the main branches should be removed. The branches should conform quite strictly to only one angle below the horizontal. Minor adjustments can be made easily by bending the wires slightly with a pair of pliers. Three branch wounds need to be sealed.

The great quantity of copper wire is distracting as well. I find it useful to coat the bright copper with a light touch of lime sulfur. The bright color immediately disappears, changing to an almost black hue. The creative eye can then focus more easily on the trunk, branches, and foliage, giving an idea of what it will look like after the wire is removed next spring.

The finished spruce is twenty-four inches high with a trunk diameter of two and a half inches (see **8–131**). The Japanese rectangular tray is eighteen inches by thirteen inches with a height of two and a half inches. With the illusion of age given to it, I hope you agree that most viewers would now guess its age between thirty and forty years, maybe more.

8-119

8-120

0-121

8-122

8-123

8-124

8–125

8–126

8–127

8–128

8–129

8–130

8–131

A JUNIPER BONSAI FROM NURSERY STOCK

The pathetic-looking San Jose juniper shown in **8–132** was obtained from a local nursery. It has had a hard life so far. It was trimmed back last year to try to compact the plant and, at the same time, promote some budding back. On some branches, this method was successful; but other branches did nothing. There are scars from past insect damage, from handling, from past pruning, and even from sun scalding due to lack of water. It is overgrown with weeds and needs lots of care; it is very nearly perfect for bonsai!

One of the two bonsai containers shown in **8–133** will be its future home. The reddish brown container is the ideal size, while the brown oval one on the right will be reserved just in case the tree needs a little more room.

As with all bonsai styling, begin first to locate the root buttress (see **8–134**). Most bonsai stylists do not spend enough time at this important step. Good root presentation contributes greatly to the illusion of age; spend a little more time studying this aspect of the new tree.

A tremendous infestation of grub worms, millipedes, and sow bugs have created a vast network of chambers, tunnels, and nests in this soil (see **8–135**). This may be the reason for the poor performance of this juniper. Fortunately, all of this soil will be removed during repotting; there is no need for insecticides or panic. Insects of this sort only consume decaying humus, not live roots.

The juniper is all cleaned of weeds, debris, and things that move around (see **8–136**). It has been placed on a turntable for easy access during trimming and styling. This appears to be the back of the tree.

A better view of the juniper is shown in **8–137**. There are no forward-facing branches, the rootage is nicely spread out, and the trunk has a subtle curve in it that moves towards the viewer.

Wrap the exposed rootage with a moist towel while styling the top (see **8–138**). The towel can be misted occasionally with a spray bottle to ensure that the roots stay wet at all times. This removes the necessity of hurrying through the design stage—one of the most creative and satisfying aspects of the art of bonsai.

As you can see in **8–139**, some twigs budded back nicely; others grew new growth only on the tips, and still others completely died. So much damage suggests a windswept style to make sense. Assuming then that the wind is coming from right to left, I will shorten the branches on the right because they would not survive here against the "wind."

If I nick the branches slightly with a concave cutter, I can then break them off in a predictable fashion (see **8–140**). It is scary to just grab a brittle branch and yank at it to break it off. Sometimes, a bit too much comes off all at once.

With a pair of pliers, I can start breaking branches off and peeling bark at the same time (see **8–141**). On dead branches, the textured jaws found on some pliers are useful to remove stubborn bark.

On live wood, compress the bark several times from every angle you can reach, and the cambium will easily split apart (see **8–142**).

A pocketknife is useful to get into the smaller crevices and to help peel away stubborn dead bark (see **8–143**). Attention to detail is important; take your time. Do not cut away small bumps and protruding twigs from dead areas. A successful *shari* or *jin* contains these minute details.

The trunk has been completely peeled away on the right side and on most of the front side (see **8–144**). About half of this *shari* was dead already, so the tree will not suffer any considerable setback.

A view of the *jin*, *shari*, and *sabamiki* is shown in **8–145** from a distance. This design feature certainly dominates the tree. The extra-long branches can be pulled down with wire and layered out away from the windy side. I know of no other style than *Fukinagashi* that is able to utilize thin, attenuated branches that have hardly any growth on them. All other styles favor thick, compact branches.

I will use the pull-down method to secure the branches in a lower position (see **8–146**). If conventional wiring is used, it would have to wrap around the *sabamiki* first and then out to the branch. I would prefer to keep these areas clear for lime sulfur treatment. Protect the live bark when securing a wire; damage will occur within days on unprotected branches.

The Number One branch has been wired down to a bundle of strong roots below (see **8–147**). Notice that the point of attachment to the branch is fairly close to the trunk. An attachment farther out would create a weeping branch—an undesirable sight on a windswept tree.

The second branch is brought down to the rear (see **8–148**). This conserves green foliage on an otherwise sparse tree as well as contributes to the feeling of depth. The branches will be pruned later.

The back branch is in place and the long superattenuated third branch now has room to come down (see **8–149**). If you lack a point of attachment to the roots below, circle the pot with a loop of wire; then attach the branch wire to the pot wire at a convenient location.

The third branch is down and in place (see **8–150**). It is not necessary to wind and unwind the wire to secure the branch at the perfect height. If the branch needs to be adjusted downward slightly, make a few kinks in the wire with a pair of needlenose pliers.

By bringing down the apex, we also bring down with it a number of smaller branches (see **8–151**). These can be refined by wiring in the conventional manner. Bending down the trunk also closes up a large space between the third branch and the apex. It also makes the tree look more windswept.

By thinning and pruning the branches, I can start to see the layered branch structure (see **8–152**). The remaining branches are wired and pulled back to avoid competing with the other existing branch lines. Prune carefully after wiring. Remove upward- and downward-facing growth to promote a compact layered appearance.

After some pruning and wiring details, this tree is ready for lime sulfur on the *sabamiki* (see **8–153**). If the dead area was freshly peeled, it would require some time to dry out; otherwise the lime sulfur has trouble adhering. This area was mostly dead already, so one application will produce results by the next morning.

The lime sulfur produced a nice natural-looking grey overnight (see **8–154**). The dead areas are now looking good while being protected from insects and disease. The tree has been trimmed carefully, and the wires given a final adjustment; the wires can come off in about a year. This is most certainly a windswept style; the basic design is established. A tree growing like this in the wild would have to be growing on an exposed rocky bluff perhaps overlooking a windy gorge to display this much stress. Average winds of thirty to forty miles (48 to 64 kilometres) an hour would be necessary. The foliage can be thickened up, but all it requires is regular maintenance. Pinch back new errant shoots as they appear, and watch the tree develop into something to be proud of.

8–132

8–133

8–134

8–135

8–136

8–137

8–138

8–139

8–140

8–141

8–142

8–143

8–144

8–145

8–146

8–147

8–148

8–149

8–150

8–151

8-152

8-153

8-154

BONSAI FROM THE GARDEN

I have described salvaging juniper shrubs from the dump pile. Look carefully around your yard; there may be an overgrown foundation planting that has a nice trunk on it. A sprouting stump might be suitable material to shape into a broom-style bonsai. Woody plants that have been mowed down, nicked, or damaged are prime candidates for bonsai. You could spend three years nurturing a seedling; so why not invest a few years working with material in your yard? You can gradually reduce the size of arborvitae, prune back an old boxwood hedge, or open up a congested Alberta spruce while each is still in the ground. Root-prune these later on by digging them up; then put them back in the same hole. This encourages new roots to form closer to the trunk and will increase your chances of success when potting this tree a year or two later.

A CASCADING BONSAI

The plant shown in **8–155** is a silver fir, *Abies amabilis*. It is doing quite well as evidenced by deep green needles as well as the heavy profusion of new growth. Back budding is profuse, and there are no areas of bare wood that do not have new growth sprouting out. When this plant was dug from the garden, numerous white, healthy roots were evident. The cascade style is strongly suggested by the shape of this tree. Hugging low to the ground due to snow, wind, and frost conditions, the sprawling mass of foliage is well suited to being stretched out in a more or less vertical form.

From the other side, shown in **8–156**, you can see that a large root has failed. This may present a design difficulty because most *jin* and *shari* are branches or trunk sections that have died. If this angle is chosen as the front of the tree, the *jin* element would have to be carved from a root. Simply cutting the dead root off would be unsatisfactory because the resulting scar would last for twenty years. In any case, the root can be shortened for ease in potting the plant.

Heavy, dense roots such as those shown in **8–157** are easy tasks for a coarse pruning saw. Make sure that the surrounding bark is free of pumice or sand; wash the area with water to ensure a quick, clean cut without damage to the saw blade. Under no circumstances should you try to cut large items like this with loppers or large concave cutters; they will bend or break.

After removing the root, I can polish the cut end with oil and use a magnifying glass to count the rings. Perhaps you can make out in **8–158** that the rings are far too numerous to count with the naked eye. It's no wonder; the root is about eighty-five years old.

It is extremely difficult, if not impossible, to style a cascading bonsai while the plant is lying down on a table (see **8–159**). In most cases, whether you are working with wild stock or nursery stock, it is preferable to pot the tree first. Fortunately, the pot is usually round, octagon- , or hexagon-shaped; so it does not matter where the "front" of the tree is.

The dull, glazed brownish black pot shown in **8–160** has a light-colored clay area at its base where the glaze is absent. I find this bright area distracting to the eye; so I try to find an indelible felt pen that matches the color of the glaze and paint the offending bright clay until it is no longer visually distracting.

It's time to pot (see **8–161**). Prepare your container, as usual, with soffit green and wire staples covering the drain hole. Work quickly, keeping the roots moist at all times.

The critical part of this step is to get the tree into the container and secured firmly (see **8–162**). It does not matter whether the tree is perfectly positioned; minor adjustments can be made later. Just do not make this step a fatal one; take two hours fiddling with the roots just to get it into the pot, and your plant will be suffering indeed!

The plant is in the container (see **8–163**). It may or may not be planted at the right angle, and the front of the tree hasn't been determined yet. The container has been placed on a turntable for styling. The plant has been thoroughly watered with a dilute solution of Vitamin B$_1$. There were sufficient roots present so that any additional treatments were unnecessary. From this view, the large dead root scar is highly visible, and it presents a considerable design problem. The area will have to be carefully carved to make it look natural and weathered. From this side, however, there are two definite attributes. The apex of the tree twists and turns beautifully towards the viewer, and so does the long Number One branch that forms the cascading section.

By contrast, the other side shown in **8–164** has only one plus; the trunk is not interrupted by the large scar. Notice that the trunk from this angle is actually smaller than a bit farther up; this would be a considerable design defect in itself. The apex faces the rear as does the lowermost extension of the cascading branch. For these reasons, the other side makes the better front.

An important word, however, for the beginner: Choosing a front is for design purposes. If in the end, the other side happens to look better, so be it. Always prune away branches in such a way that you leave many options open to you. In other words, *jin* the branches even when they are in the rear and not visible. You may find later that you are glad that you did.

This bonsai has enormous potential, but it is hard to visualize because of all the foliage (see **8–165**). The best design for this tree makes it necessary to incorporate a great deal of *jin* and *shari*. It is helpful, at this point, to eliminate the unwanted branches by "stubbing" them off. The stubs can then be carved into *jin* or *shari*. Some of the scraggly top section can be removed first.

It is already easier in **8–166** to see the trunk line. The idea now is to connect the recently removed branches and the large dead root area; but first some more unneeded branches can be removed.

The branches seen in **8–167** conflict with the furthermost extension of the apex. They not only clutter the appearance of the tree, but they also confuse the viewer as to where to locate the top of the tree.

I hope you can start to see the apex in **8–168**. Some branches still in the background confuse the view. These will be stripped of bark and used as part of the design. Those dead branches that clutter the overall appearance will be almost totally removed.

I really do not know how long a stub to leave when I cut branches off like this (see **8–169**). Not until after these areas are stripped of their bark and linked to one another with dead *sabamiki* will I know whether or not they need further carving.

The major trunk development is shown in **8–170**. The tallest branch is not the apex; but because of its location and suppleness, it will be bent around to be a back branch. The branches that have been removed were too high on the trunk and too large to be bent down.

From the front of the tree, the apex can be seen quite well (see **8–171**). Notice how this apex compares to the other branches that were cut away. I hope you agree that this was the best choice. It helps to exaggerate the slant of the trunk and initiates the lean into a cascade style.

To peel the bark off freshly pruned branches, squeeze them gently with a common pair of pliers (see **8–172**). Use expandable pliers for larger branches and needlenose pliers for tiny branches. A handy tool for this purpose is a Japanese *jin*-making pliers. There is an additional feature built into them; they have a sharp shovel-faced jaw that helps scrape away tough areas and delineates stripped areas from barked areas.

The bark comes off quite easily after this treatment (see **8–173**). Be sure to delineate with a pocketknife or *jin* maker all the areas you do not want to strip. Stripping branches that have been dead for some time is a far more difficult task. The bark adheres tenaciously to the underlying wood, and it must be carefully cut away with carving tools.

Some of the branches have been stripped as seen in **8–174**. Notice that the cut ends are too obviously cut with a pruning tool. These ends have to be torn with a pair of pliers to give them a more natural-looking appearance. Over an hour of carving time is represented between **8–173** and **8–174**. Proceed slowly to avoid injury and be sure to leave as many small twigs intact as possible. *Jin* that contains knot holes, texture, and numerous smaller projections looks properly rugged. Extra time spent carving these details will show in the final product.

The top section of *jin* shown in **8–175** is complete. The large dead root wound is going to be a formidable task. The root is so old that the wood is extremely hard; it is difficult to break off in natural-looking patterns.

Remember to water your tree. It has been recently transplanted and watering several times a day is necessary. Misting the foliage helps also.

Some of my favorite carving tools are shown in **8–176**. From left to right, they are an X-Acto knife, Japanese *jin*-making pliers, three bamboo-bound carving instruments, a small pair of channel-expanding pliers, and finally, a folding pocketknife with replaceable, disposable blades.

Most of the *jin* and *shari* have been carved (see **8–177**). There are refinements to be made, but the next obvious stage of the plant's styling is the wiring of the three most important elements: the apex, the back branch, and the outermost extension of the cascading first branch. The back branch is first.

Start wiring with at least two turns around a stable section of branch or trunk, then continue in barberpole fashion until the branch has been wound its entire length (see **8–178**). Refer to Chapter Six on bonsai training for wiring instructions.

The back branch is in place in **8–179**. This tree is so old that two winds of wire were required where normally one is adequate. Once the wire is attached, bend the branch gradually and with steady pressure into the desired position. An even force will make sure that the live cambium layer is not damaged more than absolutely necessary. The apex is next.

When wiring, try to protect new buds as much as possible (see **8–180**). Do not wire over small branches or twigs. Gently tease new growth out of the way while slowly winding the wire. Make sure that the wire is loose enough so that new growth can arrive without damage.

The new apex is up and in place in **8–181**. The tip should lean in the same direction as the cascading branch and the main trunk; otherwise the planting would be internally inconsistent. Strive for a theme or main idea and stick with it throughout the tree. Be consistent.

The cascading portion of the Number One branch can now be wired (see **8–182**). This is perhaps the most important element of this tree; so study the style carefully before bending any branches. I find it helpful to draw the tree first—just accurately enough to develop the design without actually moving branches around needlessly.

The basic bonsai shape has been established in **8–183**. The apex is highly visible as are the trunk line and the tip of the Number One branch. This is a formal cascade, *Kengai*, because it has a viable apex. The Number One branch is responsible for the cascade, rather than the trunk. The foliage triangle is well defined—or more accurately, it *will* be well defined, for that is the next step in styling.

First of all, I might as well show off the *jin* I so carefully carved (see **8–184**). This not only thins out the cascading branch, but it also lets the viewer know that the outermost extension of the trunk is dead. This is an important concept because it explains why this tree is a cascading tree—namely the trunk failed to thrive in a horizontal fashion. The lower branch was better protected from the natural elements, and therefore, the tree took on this unusual shape.

I think just a bit of refinement in the large root *jin* and this tree will be ready for lime sulfur (see **8–185**). It was extremely difficult to try to hide such a large scar; but I feel that if I visually connect the two major *jin* areas by stripping bark between them, the huge round appearance the wound has now will be diminished.

By visually connecting the two areas, the bull's eye appearance of the large root *jin* is reduced (see **8–186**). This tree is now ready for lime sulfur. It should be noted that the lime sulfur is going to have different color effects on different *jin* areas. The branches that were already dead will whiten considerably while those *jin* areas recently stripped of both foliage and bark will repel the lime sulfur somewhat and, therefore, will come out a slightly different shade of grey. In a few months, after a second coat, the colors will even out considerably.

Apply the full-strength lime sulfur just as it comes from the bottle without diluting it (see **8–187**). Pour a small amount into a small container. Paint the lime sulfur on the *jin*, *shari*, or *sabamiki* carefully, yet generously, with a small artist's brush. Apply two coats where the liquid seems to be repelled. Allow at least two days for the full white color to appear. Hot days and full sun seem to accelerate the bleaching effect; however, do not subject a freshly transplanted tree to full sun. Do not water immediately afterwards; some diluted lime sulfur may leach into your bonsai soil.

The finished cascade bonsai is shown in **8–188**.

8–157

8–158

8–155

8–159

8–156

8–160

8–161

8–162

8–163

8–164

8–165

8–166

8–167

8–168

8–169

8–170

8–171

8–172

8–173

8–174

8–175

8–176

8-177

8-178

8-179

8-180

8-181

8-182

8-183

8-184

8–185

8–186

BONSAI FROM COLLECTED MATERIAL

Located where I am in the Willamette Valley, within a couple of hours I can be at the beach or in the mountains. Not much farther there is high desert, canyons, and rain forest. Each of these natural landscapes offers its own varieties of native plants, most of them suitable for bonsai. Every year, my bonsai club goes out on a "dig." We come back exhausted and sore but with great satisfaction and mental relaxation from getting out in nature.

Advance planning can help minimize your physical effort. Familiarize yourself with the soil conditions where you are going to dig and bring tools that are appropriate for the job. In sandy soil, you will need to bring containers for the freshly dug plants, because the soil will fall away from the roots too easily. When digging in average forest soils, the root ball will stay sufficiently together with burlap or plastic wrapping. When digging in rocky areas, a shovel is inappropriate. Far more useful are a pick and a hammer. Use safety goggles at all times when hammering on rock or when striking other metal objects such as wedges, bars, or chisels. Spray the foliage with an anti-desiccant before digging. Bring plenty of water for yourself and the tree, and dress for changes in weather. Be sure to obtain any necessary permissions or permits. Ranger stations will let you know where and what species you can dig. On private land, oral permission is sufficient.

Trim away portions of the tree you know you will not need and pack the plant carefully for travel when it is finally dug. Take as much soil and rootage as you can. You can always trim off excess later. When you get back home, make sure your tree is still wet, especially the root ball. Plant immediately in the ground and forget about it for a year. Water and fertilize it only lightly throughout the next growing season. Nothing will doom a native plant faster than too much water and fertilizer. Provide your recent transplant with good, well-drained soil and ideal light conditions, adequate water, and it will thrive. For best results, make sure that some of the old soil remains on the roots.

8–188

BONSAI FROM COLLECTED PLANT MATERIAL

The plant shown in **8–189** is a mountain hemlock, *Tsuga Mertensiana*, gathered from the rocky slopes of an alpine lake one year ago. It has not been pruned in any way except that some of the dead branches were shortened in order to get it into a plastic bag. The container is a traditional Japanese training pot. Some of the original soil was saved and run through a sieve to remove the silt and smaller needle debris. The hemlock was then bare-rooted with the pressure from a garden hose and placed immediately in this container. The original soil was amended with pumice and packed tightly around the bare roots.

Some new growth appeared last fall and the foliage has lost some of its native yellow-green color in favor of a bright grassy-green hue. This species is very difficult to transplant; with special care, the chances of success are improved. Its age can only be estimated. It grew one-half inch this year. The growing tip is now thirty-eight inches from the base of the trunk; making an assumption of steady growth, it at least seventy-six years old. The rings in the cut ends of dead branches are twenty-two to the inch. This tree has a three-and-a-half-inch trunk which converts to seventy-seven years.

The roots will not be disturbed for another three years, but I can begin styling this natural bonsai.

With the trunk leaning off to the right, the three main branches come more or less towards the viewer. One of the three should become the new apex, another wired down to look more like a branch, and the third removed. The apex will be best if it is consistent with the trunk's lean to the right.

From the side shown in **8–190**, the only usable apex is the presently dead top. While *jin* may be a desirable apex in some cases, a live apex seems better when it is available. The other side becomes preferable as the front.

The odd-looking growth seen in **8–191** is often mistaken for an adventitious bud or new shoot. Actually, it is a dwarf form of mistletoe, a parasite, that attaches to certain conifers in the Northwest forests. Physical removal is the only known effective cure, but it may continue to grow underneath the bark if it is simply plucked off.

Cut away a small portion of the bark around the area, making sure to go deeper than the cambium in order to assure that it will not regrow (see **8–192**). If the cut area is longer along the grain of the wood, there is a better chance of removing the parasite, and the cut takes less time to heal. It also looks more natural and cuts across fewer vascular bundles carrying water and nutrients.

The Number One branch has been formed by bringing down one of the three main branches (see **8–193**). The branch was very tough to move because of its age; so the "cheat" method was utilized to wire it in position. Avoid using these wire turnbuckles because strength is gained at the expense of proper positioning. Fortunately, from only two points I can correctly position this branch.

The pressure points have been padded with several layers of floral tape (see **8–194**).

By repositioning this branch (see **8–195**), I can see that the apex needs to be tilted up a bit farther. I have established the Number One branch and the trunk line. It is clear only at this point that the remaining large branch is superfluous and should be removed.

The question still remains whether or not the top *jin* is important enough to remain or whether it should be removed entirely (see **8–196**). I'll take off the unneeded branch a bit short of the *jin*. I can then work on wiring the remainder of the apex and take another look at it later.

This bonsai is starting to look more like a tree and less like a shrub that has had a hard life (see **8–197**). The internal consistency of the bonsai, however, is a design consideration. It is time to question the validity of such a prominent apex, considering the past history of this plant. In nature, how often a strong apex has been thwarted is evidenced by the dead material near its base. A shorter apex will make the tree compact and consistent with the *shari* on the trunk.

The apex, as seen in **8–198**, has been lowered by bringing up a new top with wire and by lowering the surrounding branches a little more. It looks to me as if the *jin* only clutters the line of the trunk, and, therefore, it should be removed. Unfortunately, I lose a valuable point of attachment for my Number One branch turnbuckle; so I have to position the branch in another way.

The clean, simple line of the trunk in **8–199** is now uninterrupted. The eye easily follows the extreme slant from left to right. The Number One branch is wired in the conventional manner with an assist from one turnbuckle below. Its heaviness of foliage is distracting when compared to the upper section of the tree. It needs to be thinned.

The foliage triangle, as seen in **8–200**, is now well defined—from the apex to the tip of the Number One branch to the tip of the Number Two branch.

It is time to refine the *shari* (see **8–201**). The cut ends of the dead branches are obvious and abrupt. There is a lack of gradual taper from the root buttress to the slanting trunk as it passes over the *shari*. Heavy bark covers the dead areas, inviting insects and disease. Reducing this area is easy; reducing the *shari* so that it looks natural is very difficult. It requires time, patience, and attention to detail.

After four hours of carving, the *shari* has been reduced in height two and one half inches (see **8–202 and 8–203**). Carving away this area strongly reinforced my concern for the health of the tree. Many types, sizes, and manner of insects, grubs, nests, eggs, and odd-looking fungi were uncovered in the process.

The *shari* has been coated heavily with lime sulfur dormant spray in **8–204**. It was applied full strength with a small artist's brush. Freshly scraped wood has to dry for several weeks before the lime sulfur will adhere. This *shari* was already dead and dried out; so the application was made immediately after carving.

Eight hours later, the *shari* is quite well bleached out (see **8–205**). The somewhat bright white appearance will fade into a natural driftwood hue after several waterings. Lime sulfur should be reapplied any time there is evidence of rot beginning, such as a regional blackening, orange spots, or a spongy appearance to the wood.

From a distance, the *shari* still appears too dominant (see **8–206**). It's not just the bright color; it comes from the suggestion that this tree is just a branch of what used to be a larger tree. That is actually true; but it defeats the illusion that this is a miniature tree. If the *shari* were to taper more quickly from the base towards the living trunk, the bonsai might regain dominance over the *shari*. The dead tips that point towards the left, if reduced, would increase the flow from left to right, presenting a more consistent style.

A close-up of the shari remodel in **8–207** shows how the left side has been curved to accentuate the trunk line. The newly cut areas were retreated with lime sulfur.

For this year, the styling is finished; the rest takes time. The pot now seems too large for the planting (see **8–208**). This extreme slanting style is almost *bunjin* in appearance. Eventually, it would look best in a round or oval *bunjin*-type container with tall legs. The height of the pot should be very close to the diameter of the trunk and the width should be about one inch smaller than the existing pot; but remember, this is a training pot. This large container will help develop the rest of the bonsai.

Mountain hemlock is somewhat apically dominant, so the upper branches will thicken quickly as compared to the lower Number One branch. Since this is a recent transplant from the wild, the planting should not be placed in its ideal-sized pot too soon; the existing roots need three more years to establish themselves.

8–189

8–190

8–191

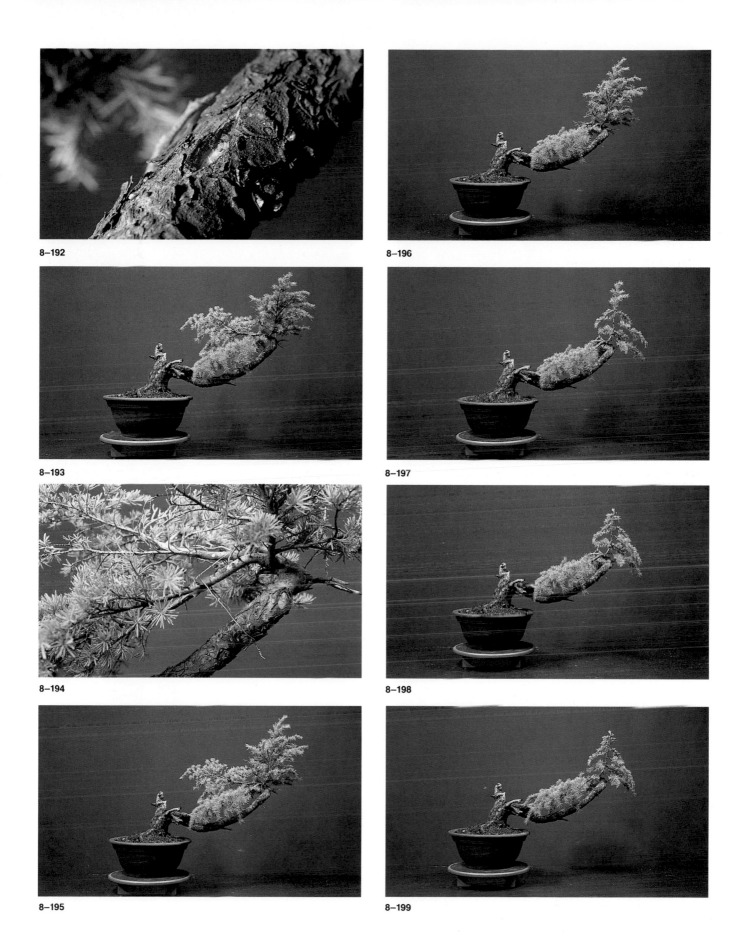

8–192

8–196

8–193

8–197

8–194

8–198

8–195

8–199

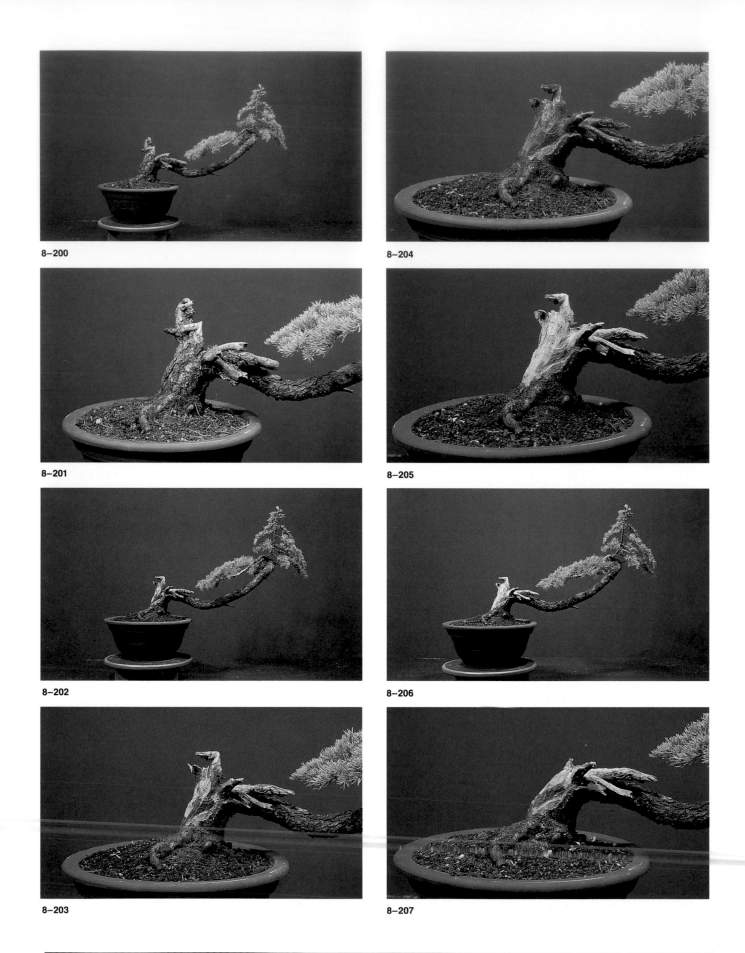

8–200

8–201

8–202

8–203

8–204

8–205

8–206

8–207

8–208

DECIDUOUS BONSAI FROM COLLECTED MATERIAL

This method of obtaining material has particular advantages. You can obtain native species that are well suited to growing in your local climate. With careful scouting and selectivity, you can find specimens that are older than typical nursery stock. In addition, plants that grow in the wild tend to be more interesting subjects due to their twisting and weathering.

The plant shown in **8–209** is a native vine maple, *Acer circinatum*, dug from the side of a mountain stream at 3000 feet in altitude. The pruning and styling techniques demonstrated here with this specimen are appropriate for all deciduous species, particularly elm, alder, hornbeam, maple, birch, beech, and wild fruit trees.

This tree has many possibilities (see **8–210**). It was dug the previous fall just as the leaves were turning red and yellow. This spring a large profusion of new foliage indicates that this specimen is ready for its first styling. Last winter, the tree was heeled into a raised bed of rotted sawdust shavings. The root system has more than doubled in size already. When collecting trees from the woods, an appropriate heeling-in period is necessary before any training. If this tree did not look as healthy as it does, the best course of action would be to wait one more year before styling it.

As with all bonsai projects, begin by exposing the root buttress (see **8–211**). It is impossible to determine the front of the tree without first locating the significant surface roots that will contribute to the design.

Gently remove the soil with a root hook, chopsticks, or scythe to expose these most important roots (see **8–212**).

It is hard to avoid getting excited about a plant when you can uncover major roots such as these shown in **8–213**. The rootage is going to be exposed a bit more later on as the bonsai is being potted; but for now, the front of the tree has been firmly established.

The tree is then temporarily wrapped with a moist towel while the branches are being trimmed (see **8–214**). Indoors is best for this operation because outdoor air is especially drying. (With nursery stock, the outdoor air is not as critical because the roots and their potting soil stay intact during pruning.)

Using simple nails, secure a towel around the tree while working on it (see **8–215**). Do not pound the nails into the rootball, but rather perforate the towel and gently insert the nails between the roots.

I cannot stress enough that moisture must be on the roots at all times (see **8–216**). Students may inadvertently kill a tree because they get involved in pruning and styling and forget to mist the rootball.

The use of the turntable is especially desirable when working on collected specimens (see **8–217**). The turntable allows free movement during styling without endangering the tree.

It's time to shape the basic trunk line by removing unwanted large branches (see **8–218**). This superfluous backward-facing branch can be removed with medium-sized pruning loppers. Do not worry about cutting the branch off perfectly with the first cut; lop off the branch fairly close to the trunk. When the foliage is removed, you can see better what you are doing.

With this large branch removed, the basic trunk line is becoming established (see **8–219**). Don't be mistaken by retaining large branches for fear of making a big scar. A large trunk with small branches tends to enhance the illusion of age. Large branches detract from the trunk line and make the tree look younger than it actually is.

The scar formed when the large back branch was removed is shown in **8–220**. Carve away the excess wood with carving tools or a spherical knob cutter, as shown. Don't hesitate carving deeply into the heartwood. This area is all nonliving material; as the living cambium grows out, the scar will be reduced or eliminated altogether. Where scars are going to be visible on the front of the tree, break the branch off rather than cut it off so that the tree remains natural-looking.

Partway through the carving process, you can see how effective the spherical knob cutter is (see **8–221**). The concave cutter, by contrast, seems to have difficulty cutting and recutting the same area.

The completed cut area is shown in **8–222**. A wound this size needs a wound sealer. One of my favorites is a bit of mud mixed with white carpenter's glue. It helps hide the scar and protects the area from insects and diseases.

The same area after treatment with the wound sealer is shown in **8–223**. This wound is on the back side of the tree, and it will not show as you view the bonsai from the front. This is an important concept; always hide large scars whenever possible.

Continue shaping the trunk as shown in **8–224**. This large lower branch should be removed because it starts too low on the trunk, is too large in diameter to be retained, confuses the viewer as to where the trunk line is going, and it has a straight, uninteresting shape.

The second branch is removed and the scar covered up with wound sealer (see **8–225**). The trunk shape is now quite clear. This tree is not just losing mass quantities of foliage, but the tree is beginning to look more like an older tree instead of just a bushy shrub. If you can visualize that transformation, you can create bonsai.

The large branch on the left in **8–226** is showing poor growth. Most of it was removed during the digging process, and it has not recovered well. Since it is near the front of the tree, it is better to break the branch off. A vise-grip pliers gives a predictable and controlled break. If the branch is very big, a slight notch with a saw will guarantee that the break will be at the proper place.

The break occurred in just the right place as seen in **8–227**. A slight notch, made by a large concave cutter, was necessary on the top of the branch. Then by pulling down and to the right with the vise grips, a natural-looking break was formed.

The finished break is natural-looking and becomes part of the natural design (see **8–228**). With that branch removed, it is time to give attention to the tall top of the tree.

A rule of thumb for good proportion says that the lowest foliage on a tree be located about one third of the way up the trunk (see **8–229**). Lowering the top is a better option than stripping off the lower branches.

Fortunately, this tree has an excellent location for reducing its height (see **8–230**). The scar will be hidden to the left side, and a new top will be formed to the right side, balancing the undulations of the trunk.

With the apex of the tree so severely shortened, the eye is drawn to the long, dead branches on the upper left (see **8–231**). I feel they should be retained because of all the other deadwood on that side of the tree. Their length is a bit overpowering, however.

By reducing the length of the dead branches, I can balance the total appearance of the tree (see **8–232**).

The viewer can imagine, perhaps, that some natural calamity happened to the upper left of this maple which accounts for the curvature of the trunk as well as the location of a new top on the upper right side, creating a classical *Moyogi* style.

It is time to pot this tree (see **8–233**). The basic style has been established, the trunk line is defined, and, except for some possible wiring, the foliage triangle is quite visible.

Three possible containers are shown in **8–234**, all just about the right size and shape. Match the diameter of the trunk with the height of the pot. In younger trees, this is just not feasible; but it gives a good proportional rule of thumb to work towards for future development.

After some careful consideration, the blue-green Japanese container on the left seems to best complement the tree (see **8–235**). The *Moyogi* style is curved and angular like the pot. The cloud feet on the bottom of the container seem to mimic the circular dead areas of the tree's bark. Moving quickly, strip the tree of its unneeded bulky roots, and at the same time try to protect the smaller viable roots.

The tree fits quite well into the pot (see **8–236**). Some pruning of the major roots was necessary, but many smaller roots were retained. There are still some surface roots that are too small and too high; they should be removed. One major visual impact of this bonsai is going to be its grand rootage.

As with all potting and repotting, once the roots are in place and protected with a light layer of mist, take the time to make sure all air pockets are removed as you add fresh bonsai soil (see **8–237**). Make sure your drain holes are covered with soffit screen and are secured in place with copper wire staples before potting the tree.

The finished maple bonsai is shown in **8–238**. It must be understood that deciduous trees bud back more readily than conifers in general. While this may seem an extreme pruning episode for a tree, it is important to know that this much foliage removal might be inappropriate for a hemlock or spruce. It is now only a matter of time before this relatively sparse first styling explodes into a show-worthy tree with just three more years of training.

The finished height is just twelve inches and the trunk is four inches across, which harmonizes well with the height of the container. The age of the maple is estimated to be eighty years.

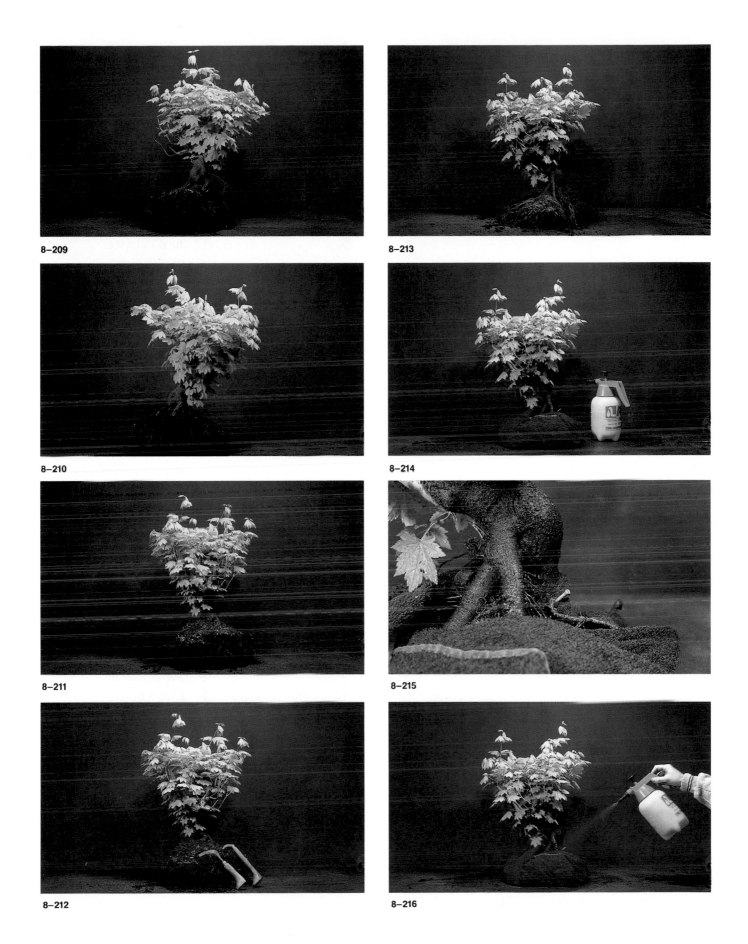

8-209

8-213

8-210

8-214

8-211

8-215

8-212

8-216

8-217

8-218

8-219

8-220

8-221

8-222

8–223

8–224

8–225

8–226

8–227

8–228

8–229

8–230

8–231

8–232

8–233

8–234

8–235

8–236

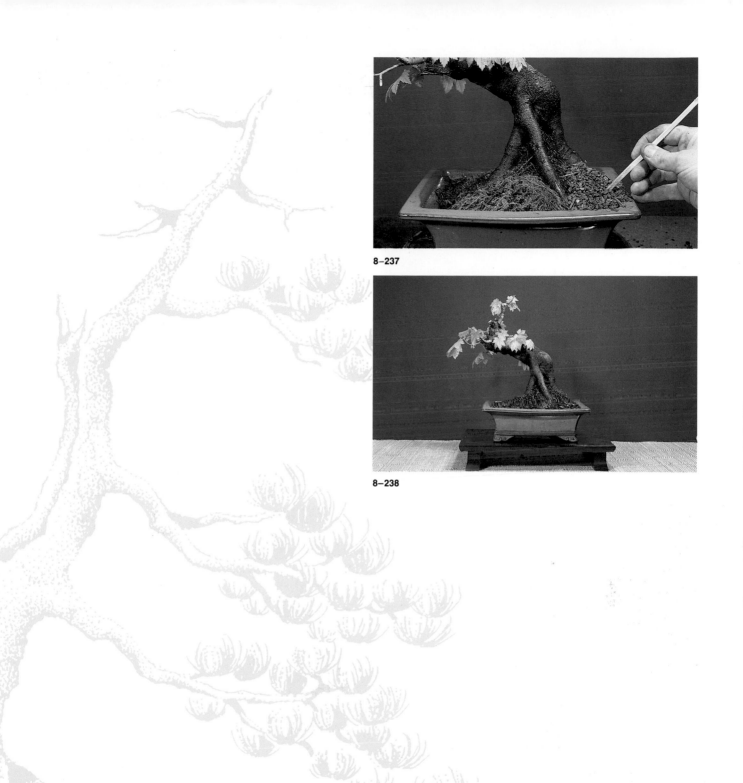

8-237

8-238

9

CARE AND MAINTENANCE

THERE ARE MANY REASONS WHY BONSAI FAIL to thrive, but I think it is surprising that the majority of bonsai failures could have been easily prevented. Probably nine out of ten deaths can be attributed to lack of water in August. The remaining ten percent can be equally divided between freezing in winter, overwatering, overfertilizing, trying to grow an indoor plant outdoors, trying to grow an outdoor plant indoors, and repotting incorrectly. The number of bonsai lost to insects and disease is actually quite few.

My intention is to make sure you know how to identify a sick plant. Follow good bonsai horticulture and take just a few seconds each day to check for signs of trouble. I usually do this as I water. Approaching each tree individually, I make a quick assessment. These are things to look for:

1. The tree is staying wet too long. For instance, it usually requires water every three days, but this time it's been almost a week and it still feels damp when a fingertip is plunged into the soil.

2. When you water, the excess water doesn't pass through the soil rapidly; it stays for a few seconds on the surface of the soil. A slight scum is starting to form on the soil surface.

3. The plant is usually a strong grower, yet a few weeks have gone by and new growth is weak and spindly. Buds have formed on the branches, but they are not opening up.

4. There appears to be enough moisture in the container yet the tree is wilting—not a lot, but the new growth is pointed down instead of slightly up as it usually does.

5. The tree usually has a bright green color and now it looks a bit dusty; almost like looking at it through a haze or smog. The plant feels a bit on the dry side when the foliage is lightly touched.

6. Spring has come and all your other trees are coming out quite nicely, but this one tree seems a bit slow. Its growth looks pale and slightly curly. Some of the leaves do not look true to form.

7. The growth that is coming out makes you think the tree is root-bound. Needles are too short; leaves are too small. Flower buds are not forming at all. But when you check the roots, they look healthy and uncrowded.

If any of these conditions exists for your bonsai, you have probably spotted a potential problem early enough to save the tree. Do not let conditions such as these lull you into a "wait and see" attitude. Act immediately and the bonsai can be saved.

Pull the plant out of its pot and inspect the roots. Feel them with your hands. If they are slippery or slimy, hose them off until the rinse water is clear. Gently grasp one pencil-sized root and pull on it. If the outer covering pulls off, leaving a whitish inner core, you have root rot and you need to treat with a fungicide. If you see bumps or nodules on some of the roots, squeeze them gently and if they pop or smash flat, you have nematodes. Cut away the infected area and spray lightly with a systemic nematocide. Most of the time, when you pull your tree out of the pot, you will see nothing unusual. Other times, you will find a snail's nest, thousands of sow bugs, earwigs, or perhaps even just a broken pot!

After this initial inspection, and after the obvious problems have been taken care of, plant this tree on the ground. Tease the roots apart slightly and lay the root ball on the soil surface, then mound some well-draining mulch over the roots; don't actually dig a hole. Some suitable materials to cover your roots with are rotted sawdust, sand, perlite, decomposed granite, leaf mould, or vermiculite. Do not fertilize or cover with rich manure soils. Do not cover with bark chips or fresh sawdust either. These products will rob nutrition from your plant. Water your tree well, making sure it is soaked clear through, then begin misting it lightly every so often. Try to keep the soil moist but not soggy. Check the plant's roots after a few weeks; you should be able to lightly dust off some mulch and see the beginnings of white root hairs where before there were none. If in doubt, leave the bonsai planted; even if it takes a year or two. It is better to have a live bonsai in your yard than a dead one in a pot. You can always repot later.

ANNUAL EARLY SPRING CARE FOR DECIDUOUS BONSAI

The tree shown in **9–1** is a cork bark Chinese elm, *Ulmus parvifolia cortica*, twenty-two inches high with a three-inch-diameter trunk. It is potted in an antique Japanese container. Let's go through its early spring care step-by-step to see how to care for an established deciduous bonsai.

There is a profusion of mushrooms that developed during warmer fall rains (see **9–2**). Their presence indicates that the organic component of the bonsai soil is rotting into compost and should be replaced. They also suggest that, last fall, nitrogen was applied too late or perhaps the plant was watered inadequately.

The mushrooms themselves do not pose a risk to the bonsai (see **9–3**). In fact, I usually leave a few of them just because they are so darned cute!

Just as with your lawn, fallen leaves do not allow sunlight to reach the plants below them (see **9–4**). Remove this debris from your moss on a regular basis throughout the season, but particularly in winter after all the leaves have fallen.

Remove weeds while they are still small (see **9–5**). Once their tap roots descend to the bottom of the pot, they are so intermingled with the tree's dense root system that they are difficult to remove completely.

A close-up of the fruiting bodies of a mature clump of moss are shown in **9–6**. The type of moss from which they grow determines their treatment. These particular flowers originate from a desirable moss that is slow-growing, silvery grey, and grows well in full sun. Left untouched, this type of moss will soon spread as new spores are distributed by wind, rain, or insects. If these stalks originated from a less desirable, clumpy, or woolly type of moss, they could be cut off with a small pair of scissors.

The same treatment would be appropriate if no more moss was desired due to overcrowding (see **9–7**). Moss should cover no more than one third of the soil surface.

The undesirable type of moss shown in **9–8** is starting to spread onto the trunk. This growth hides an important aspect of the illusion of age in a bonsai, the root buttress.

Remove this moss carefully and thoroughly (see **9–9**). Note that the trunk bark is darker because sunlight was unable to bleach it grey as in the area immediately above.

The presence of moss on the trunks of your bonsai could be an indication that you are overwatering (see **9–10**). Get into the good habit of watering your trees individually as they show signs of need, not because you happen to be working in the backyard. If persistent moss grows back immediately, a very light dilution of lime sulfur will prevent its resurgence.

Remove all moss from the edge of the pot (see **9–11**). It is unsightly and interferes with water penetration and respiratory exchange in the root system.

Replace heavily dug-out areas with fresh bonsai soil (see **9–12**). Be sure to tamp down adjacent moss clumps or they will dry out.

The root seen in **9–13** is distracting to the overall harmony and consistency of the surrounding roots. It should be removed.

This is better (see **9–14**). Notice how the remaining rootage is better defined, more even, and closer to the same size.

The two roots shown in **9–15** are growing parallel to one another, one on top of the other. Only the bottom root is needed. The upper one is a bit high compared to the surrounding roots and, with it removed, the soil surface is more even.

This is much better (see **9–16**). The bottom root is closer in size and level with the surrounding roots.

The two roots in **9–17** are too high and too exposed. The soil under them has been washed away this winter and must be replaced. If there were some roots directly under them, it would look much better to simply remove both of them. No such replacement roots exist this year, but perhaps next year.

A compromise is reached, however (see **9–18**). I can remove the thinner and higher root of the two, retaining the larger one in front of it. By stuffing fresh soil under the remaining root, I can possibly stimulate a new root to grow there.

Good surface rootage has all of the following features: well distributed around the trunk, similarity in size, pencil-sized or larger, disappears into the soil before reaching the edge of the pot, and consistency in height, shape, and texture. The smaller secondary roots that are shown in **9–19** are found only on this side of the trunk. They should be removed to balance the overall appearance.

Small roots are not found in nature because they do not spontaneously sprout from primary exposed roots. They become visible sometimes after flooding or erosion, but that is not an appropriate style for the elm tree (see **9–20**). Most bonsai should represent stability and harmony rather than change and destruction.

Working on deciduous bonsai while the leaves are absent affords the owner an excellent overall view of the health of the tree. While working on this elm, I discovered an unpleasant, although fairly predictable surprise (see **9–21**). A small colony of woolly aphis was trying to overwinter between two corky plates of bark. By applying a small artist's brush or cotton swab that has been soaked in mineral oil, you can suffocate the pests easily.

Let's begin branch pruning. Start with the most obvious defects and progress to the smaller details. It is difficult to tell when to stop pruning; unless you show some restraint, after a couple of hours you may have very little tree left! Improve your tree, but try to make these improvements as subtle as you can. Get into the good habit of taking a break every 15 minutes. Get away from your tree for a while. When you return to look at what you have accomplished, you may discover that you have pruned away more than you had intended.

The cork bark elm sometimes produces excess cork near recent pruning scars (see **9–22**). The largest defect on this tree is a cork swelling where a major branch was removed last year.

By trimming away the bark only, I can prevent its return next year (see **9–23**). If I prune too deeply and reirritate the cambium layer, the cork knob will return.

The resulting wound, since it is fairly large, has been covered with one of my favorite wound sealers, which is mud mixed with white carpenter's glue (see **9–24**). It provides protection as well as some immediate aesthetic improvement due to its dark color.

One of the most appealing aspects of deciduous trees in winter is their twiggy quality (see **9–25**). A large number of branches that divide and redivide create an overall effect that is lacy and highly detailed. Thus, it is important to force these divisions wherever possible. Trim long, boring branches short, and make them sprout into smaller branches.

The first branch seen in **9–26** is more interesting without the long tube-shaped branch section. The wound has been sealed and new sprouts will appear as the spring growth appears.

Remove all twigs that grow straight up or straight down, layering out the branches so that the sun can reach all the inner branches and keep them healthy (see **9–27**). A tree that remains thick and dense all over will die from the inside, similar to what we can observe on the inside of hedges.

After pruning, the new buds are pointing in the right direction (see **9–28**). New growth will be horizontal. Prune away tangled and congested branches. Try to make all secondary twigs short and interesting rather than long and boring. Always prune with the new growth in mind. In early spring, you can direct the new growth even before it starts.

The elm seen in **9–29** is now all trimmed and ready for spring. The new growth will appear in a few weeks. Buds will grow particularly fast towards the ends of the branches and will extend rather quickly as the tree draws its first energy from the sun. These new shoots should be kept short by trimming often—which promotes more side shoots as well. Your pruning efforts all year long will be evident the following spring.

Six weeks later (see **9–30**), the elm is leafing out nicely.

9–1

9–2

9–3

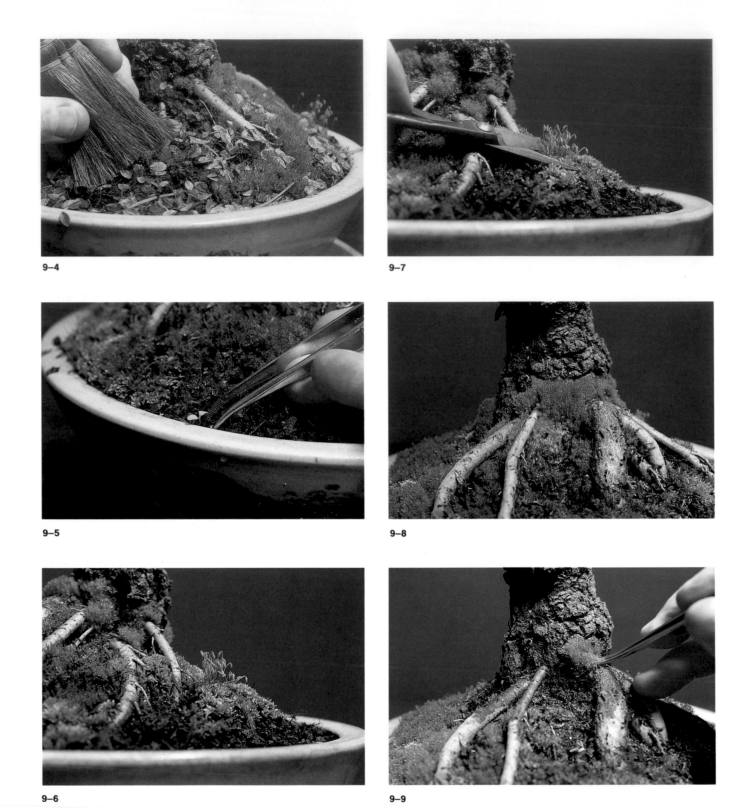

9–4

9–5

9–6

9–7

9–8

9–9

9–10

9–11

9–12

9–13

9–14

9–15

9–16

9–17

9–18

9–19

9–20

9–21

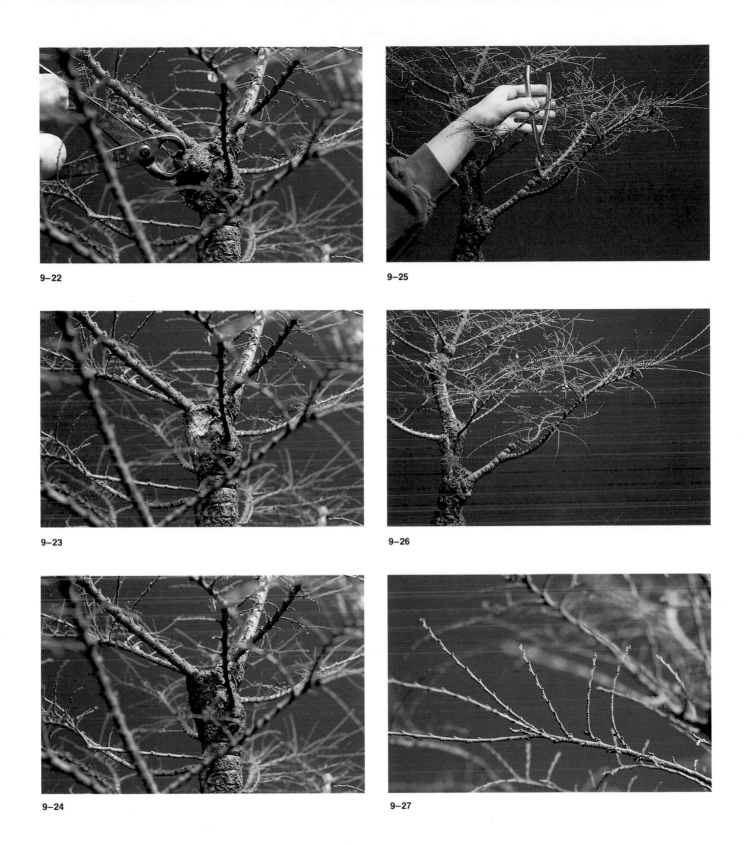

9–22

9–23

9–24

9–25

9–26

9–27

9–28

9–29

9–30

MAINTAINING A BLOOMING BONSAI

A deciduous rhododendron variety called "Pioneer" is shown in **9–31**. It is in full bloom at the end of February before the leaves come out, similar to the Mollis or Exbury azaleas. With most species of flowering plants, the best time to prune is just as the flowers wilt and fade. This would not be true with any of the fruit-bearing plants obviously, because you would be harvesting the fruit along with the flowers. For plants such as crab apple, you have to prune away every other branch every other year to maintain shape and apples.

The blossoms seen in **9–32** are just at the proper stage for removal. The flowers are wilted, brown, and the seed pods behind each of them are starting to expand. Seed removal at this stage is quite beneficial to the plant because the growth demand on the bonsai is reduced.

A close-up of the rhododendron shown in **9–33** makes it easier to see the tiny, tender young leaves that are just starting to sprout. By removing these leaves now, I am able to force latent buds into use. If this plant were not pruned back severely now, the outside growth would prosper, leaving the inside buds to wither away. A new blossom bud forms for next spring at the end of each new branch. By pruning now, we avoid the awful situation later of pruning for shape or bloom when we cannot accomplish both.

After pruning, the bonsai looks a little bleak, but rest assured, new leaf buds will break open where formerly there were none (see **9–34**). Even on old wood, the plant "remembers" where leaves used to be attached years ago. These latent meristematic areas are stimulated into becoming adventitious buds when the branch tips are removed. Instead of this bonsai getting bigger and wider every year, it can easily be kept the same size by annual trimming in this manner.

Six weeks later (see **9–35**), this rhododendron has profuse new, green compact growth. The flower buds for next year will be forming in about a month, but they will still be too small to notice until late summer. If thinning or refinements are necessary, minor trimming can be accomplished now without damage to next year's blossoms.

9–31

9–33

9–34

9–32

9–35

WATERING BONSAI

As a bonsai student in Japan, I first was only allowed the honor of weeding the master's bonsai. Then I got promoted to moss removal. After a few months, I was permitted to prune off a few errant new twigs! What surprised me was that the last thing I would learn how to do—the final compliment—was learn how to water. The late Zeko Nakamura said, "Pruning a tree badly is no more serious than getting a bad haircut, it always grows back. But when you pick up the watering can, you hold in your hands the power of life or death." When I was finally handed a watering can, I knew it was my diploma; I had graduated.

Properly screened bonsai soil minimizes the chances of watering-related problems. Excess water passes immediately through the soil particles and on through the drain holes. The flushing action prevents the buildup of minerals and salts and also helps remove dust, dirt, and excess fertilizer. The particles themselves cling to just the right amount of moisture so that healthy white root hairs can thrive. Most watering-related problems can be eliminated with good bonsai soil.

Know your water source. If it's municipal water, does it contain too much salt, chlorine, or calcium? Water from slightly polluted sources can be made safe for human consumption by various laws and agencies, but this is usually accomplished by putting things into it rather than taking the problems out. Your trees do not need fluoride for strong, healthy teeth. I have previously recommended trying to grow a potted radish. This is an excellent way to test your container growing skills, but it doubles as a way that you can test your water. If a large band of sediment accumulates on the inside rim of your pot, you have a high mineral content in your water!

I suggest that you store your bonsai water in a large barrel or vat and draw from it as necessary to water your bonsai. By storing water like this, you allow chlorine and fluoride to escape into the air and heavier minerals and impurities will sink to the bottom.

When you do water, whether from a bonsai watering can or by fine mist from a hose, water at first from a distance, then allow a bit of time—five minutes is sufficient—before watering again. On the second watering, move in closer, and try to rinse off the leaves, stems, twigs, and branches. They "enjoy" the shower and it helps wash off dust and moss spores. By now your bonsai should be fairly wet, but water it a third time anyway. It often takes three waterings to totally wet all the soil particles on all sides. Drench the area directly under the trunk and flush excess impurities from inside the rootball.

Try always to water in the morning before the sun is hot. If additional water is needed that same day, water early enough so that the bonsai does not spend the night dripping wet. Insects, slugs, snails, and disease are encouraged when a bonsai is left wet at night. Observe how the water drains as you apply it to the soil surface. Remember, a plant that does not drain well needs further attention. It may be root-bound or the soil may be compacting itself over time. In either case, it's time to repot.

Regulate the light conditions of your plant by observing the length of time needed between waterings. If a small bonsai is regularly requiring water three times per day, you might consider giving it more shade. Or perhaps a pine tree is requiring water only once a week; the pine would thrive better if it had more sun. Its roots would stay warmer and its branches would tend to thicken and bud back better.

Water your bonsai in the rain whenever possible. Your neighbors will think you are strange, but actually, even in a downpour, not much rainwater will get into a bonsai pot. The foliage canopy tends to shed water much like an umbrella. Once the rain has moistened the foliage and the soil surface, why not add just a bit more water and make it meaningful even for the plant. Shallow watering is always ineffective and essentially meaningless.

Beware of underwatering. Young, vigorous, and fast-growing species require a great deal of moisture. Let the plant and the pot determine its watering schedule. It may be necessary to overpot these plants or move them to a shady location; but do not constantly wilt your bonsai. A certain amount of wilting will decrease leaf internodes, but if wilting occurs every week, the plant becomes too stressed. Take some corrective action.

Beware of overwatering and do not overwater a sick tree. When a tree is suffering from or recovering from insect damage or disease, its water demands will be diminished. Do not give too much water to a deciduous tree in fall color. The leaves or needles are dormant and there is a decreased uptake of moisture from the roots. Too much water at this time tends to make the fall season very short; the beautiful leaves turn quickly brown and fall off. By the same token, do not overwater a defoliated tree. When the leaves are off, whether by pruning or by nature, the bonsai requires less moisture.

Shallow pots drain less easily than deep pots. Make sure that flat *saikei* trays and forests on slabs are not overwatered. Also, beware of keeping foliage too wet. Pines, juniper, and alpine conifers look best when their needles and bark are sun-dried and shiny. Too much moisture slows down their growth and makes them look soggy and pampered. Avoid moistening the foliage of plants that get mildew easily. This includes roses, peaches, apricots, and plums. It is better to prevent mildew than have to treat it with fungicides.

INSECT CONTROL

A good rule of thumb is to follow good horticultural practice in providing thorough preventative maintenance; then, when insects do attack your bonsai, they are found early, are few and far between, and can be picked off by hand. Only when these efforts have failed do you resort to insecticides, and even then, try the least toxic ones first.

Good horticultural practice means that you pay close attention to a number of things. When you water, make sure that the tree is flushed out well; a good hard spray to the foliage will knock off most aphids. Make sure you move the pot aside and direct a solid spray on the bench directly where the pot was resting. Wash off the underside of the container and check that there is nothing hiding in the drain holes. At least once a year, remove all the bonsai from your bench and scrub it with a mild bleach solution, then apply an oil-based wood preservative. This will discourage the bench from harboring pests and disease. Use shelf material that does not promote decay; metal, cedar, redwood, or treated wood is best. Clean up fallen leaves, old stumps, and rotten boards around the yard. They offer hiding places for insects. Where possible, drive a large spike straight into the bottom of the legs of your bench; then set each leg into an empty soup can. Water will, of course, accumulate in the can and keep crawling things from getting up onto your bench from the ground. The spike keeps the wooden leg out of the water. This is a very easy way to prevent damage from slugs, snails, caterpillars, sow bugs, and beetles. You can even put a bit of beer in each can as "bait."

For most insects, a simple insecticide can be made by mixing a teaspoon of liquid dish detergent into a quart of water in a common household misting spray bottle. Do not shake vigorously; just rock the spray bottle to and fro until the detergent is diluted by the water. Several applications may be necessary, but this mix is not harmful to the bonsai. However, do avoid getting large amounts of it into the soil. Another good insecticide is diluted sticker spreader that you can purchase at most garden centers. It is simply an emulsifier that is usually used in conjunction with other insecticides; but, by itself, it is good for controlling soft-bodied and sucking insects. For all other insects, I recommend dipping a cotton swab into the diluted insecticide and applying it directly to the affected area. For example, a systemic insecticide such as Orthene™ is recommended for controlling the coolly spruce gall aphid. The aphid hides itself inside new growth on spruce trees, deforming them into a grotesque gall. By dipping the cotton swab into the diluted insecticide and applying it directly to the distorted growth, I am avoiding spraying the whole tree to control just a few aphids.

When possible, try to get a positive identification of the pest. Capture a few of them or bring damaged branches to a garden center or extension service agent. Get a recommended insecticide, but apply it only to affected areas—carefully. Follow the dilution directions on the label in general, but cut the concentration in half for bonsai just to be on the safe side—even if it means applying it more than once. Wait three days between applications when one application doesn't seem to be enough.

When you notice ants crawling around on your bonsai, they are there because you didn't notice the aphids. They are attracted to the sticky sweet residues that aphids excrete as they suck on your tree. Don't kill the ants, just use the dish detergent to get rid of the aphids, and the ants will eventually go away. Spittle bugs will protect themselves from the spray by enveloping themselves with their bubbly secretions. Just hose them off your tree; they are quite harmless. Scale insects protect themselves with a hard coating. They look just like adventitious buds at first glance, but on closer inspection, they appear gathered together and concentrated in small colonies on the protected surfaces of branches. Just dab a little Diazinon™ mixed with sticker spreader on each of their shields with a cotton swab. Check them a few days later. If they are powdery and fall off easily, they are gone.

Make sure that the insect that you see is actually doing the damage that you are observing. Sometimes we overreact. Just because there is a beetle near our damaged bonsai that doesn't mean it's guilty. It may be "just passing through," or it could be feeding on the pests that are actually doing the damage. Go out at night with a flashlight, and you will probably catch the real pest in the act.

DISEASES OF BONSAI

With all pests, prevention is the best cure; this is particularly true for many diseases. Good garden cleanup will eliminate most disease organisms. Remove all debris from around your tree: fallen leaves, soggy moss, bird droppings, twigs, shedding bark, and any rotting humus. Keep your trees as light and airy as possible. A windy location is better than a damp, still area. As mentioned, water in the morning only. Drill holes in your bench if water stands around on it.

On some fungus- or blight-susceptible trees, it may be necessary to treat with a fungicide on a regular preventative basis. I find that because of the high humidity in the Northwest, I have to spray my stone fruit trees before the mildew attacks their leaves. Powdery mildew is not a big problem as far as being a threat to the life of the tree; it is just disappointing to have to live with the unsightly leaves until new ones grow out. Similarly, twig dieback on filbert, cotoneaster, and dogwood seems to be so common in my region that I pretreat these trees with fungicide before the damage occurs.

Know the problems of species, and if possible, avoid infection by preventative spray application. My neighbors' birch tree has aphids and black spot on it every year, so I am alerted to those pests in particular. In your own area, watch to see what problems are common, and try to keep your bonsai protected.

If you notice unusual growth on your tree, cut it out immediately; it is probably a virus. Virus infections cannot be cured, only physically removed. They usually look like sudden, unpredictably odd growth. They can make a branch look bright pink when the normal color is red. They can cause whole branches to be all coiled instead of straight. They can cause a maple tree to suddenly have one branch come out with variegated edges, or two colors of stems, or tiny leaves. In general, any sudden change in one portion of a tree may indicate virus infection. Cut that isolated area off, dispose of the trimmings, and sterilize your tools.

FERTILIZER FOR BONSAI

Fertilizers are necessary for good plant growth. A well-balanced fertilizer contains equal portions of nitrogen (N), phosphorus (P), and potassium (K)—or NPK. These three elements, in that order, are always found on a bag or bottle of fertilizer; look for them.

Plants grow in spurts. For outside bonsai in my general longitude, most of the year's growth is concentrated in the spring. The best way to control the growth of bonsai is to limit the amount of nitrogen they get in the spring. I recommend a low-nitrogen fertilizer such as 5–10–5 for most of the active growing season from March until July. During hot weather, limit the use of fertilizer to cool days, and apply 16–16–16 sparingly. As the tree is settling down for winter, a bit of bone meal and 0–10–10 will help it form new branch and flower buds for next year. While it is extremely cold, apply nothing. Anticipate your spring growth by another single application of 16–16–16 again in February.

Vary your sources of fertilizer. They don't contain the same amounts or numbers of trace minerals and micro-nutrients. You will get better results by giving your trees a varied and, therefore, complete diet. Utilize organic sources as much as possible.

Apply fertilizer to your bonsai only after watering them, and always on a cool day. Excess nutrient remaining on the soil surface will promote algae and fungus. Time-release fertilizers should be inserted into the bonsai soil directly before potting or repotting. If these pellets are allowed to remain on the soil surface, a darkish green scum will soon appear, and within a few weeks, an unwelcome growth called liverwort will infest the container. Both of these conditions interfere with watering and drainage. To help prevent their buildup, always apply a well-diluted solution of liquid fertilizer, wait a few minutes, and then rinse the bonsai with clear water. Bonsai require small amounts of nutrition only, so the plant does not become too vigorous and bushy. By keeping the fertilizer weak and by applying it often, you are assured that the plant is receiving all it needs, but also preventing excess buildup. Granular fertilizers that are not designed for dilution should not be used. There are numerous powders and liquids available on the market that are meant to be diluted in water. Remember that a 10–20–10 fertilizer becomes a 5–10–5 if the amount of water is doubled.

WINTER CARE

Most bonsai are lost due to lack of water in the summer. Probably the second most common cause of death is failure to protect the plant in winter. All plants have varying resistance to cold temperatures. The best winter care for your tree is to give it *almost* as much cold as it would receive in its native habitat. Most native trees from the lower United States will take frost, but not freezing. Those from the mountains or the Northern extremes of the United States and Canada will tolerate freezing provided the roots are covered with snow.

No plants enjoy being in a container outside when it

is fifteen degrees. When it becomes clear and cold and the thermometer drops below freezing, protect your bonsai by bringing them into an *unheated* room of your house. If you live in an area where severe cold temperatures regularly extend beyond just a few days, you will have to resort to more elaborate winter protection. In the spring and early summer, I use a greenhouse to help propagate seedlings and cuttings. I find this same shelter quite helpful for winter protection. The greenhouse has electricity, and the thermostat is set for 30 degrees. This allows deciduous trees to lose their leaves, and pine trees to get adequate winter dormancy. The greenhouse, however, must be opened during sunny weather during the day to prevent the trees from overheating.

The following summary should be helpful in establishing a winter "cold priority" for your bonsai collection:

1. When the temperature drops to 40 degrees F (4.4 degrees C), protect citrus, jade, cerissa, and tropicals.

2. When the temperature drops to 30 degrees F (−1 degree C), protect fuchsia, Chinese elm, bald cypress, Canary Island pine, Monterey cypress, and other warm-weather plants from semitropical areas.

3. When the thermometer drops to 25 degrees F (−4 degrees C), protect most bonsai. This includes all deciduous, fruit, nut, and berry trees, all lower-elevation pines, and similar conifers. The only exceptions are the hardy high-desert juniper, alpine conifers, and subarctic plants, which will tolerate 20 degrees F (−6.6 degrees C) even in a small pot. Plants do not need to be this cold in order to be healthy.

There are numerous methods used around the home for winter bonsai protection. In an area where freezing temperatures are few and far between, the easiest method is to simply bring them into an unheated room of the house, such as the garage, utility room, or unused storage area. Where freezing periods are extended to weeks or months at a time, the tropicals and semitropicals can just become house plants, and the hardy species can remain outside in a protected area.

To protect bonsai outside, take them off their benches, and set them on the ground near the foundation of the house. There, they are out of the direct blast of winter winds and are in an area where slight heat leakage from inside the house warms the surrounding air and soil a few degrees. For additional protection, mound fallen leaves over the pots and trunks of the bonsai. For deciduous material, it doesn't hurt to even cover some lower branches a bit, but always leave evergreen trees uncovered. For added protection, a little granular slow-release nitrogen can be added to the leaf mulch. This will initiate the decay process and heat up the pile ever so slightly.

For extreme areas where winter comes early and stays late, I know of no better method to store bonsai than in a cold frame. Construct a base two or three feet below ground level, and cover with glass or plastic. Apply heat with a shielded light bulb on a thermostat; direct light from a 100-watt bulb at night interferes slightly with the dormancy of conifers. When the sun comes out during the day, be sure to raise the lid because the "greenhouse effect" will cause temperatures in the cold frame to soar to more than 80 degrees F (27 degrees C).

Keep your bonsai a little on the dry side, and do not water just before dusk. Ice crystals expanding inside a pot can make it explode apart. For your peace of mind, I suggest removing trees from their valuable containers each winter. You can make temporary winter quarters for these trees with cedar slats or inexpensive plastic pots.

Keep a good thermometer outside the kitchen window, and look at it often. Another thermometer is a must in your cold frame or greenhouse. If you are temporarily storing bonsai in your garage, monitor the temperature in there as well. Apply heat if necessary. I prefer the thermometers that register last night's low point. They have a small metal sliding piece that is advanced by the mercury inside. When the temperature goes back up the next morning the metal indicator is left behind showing last night's low temperature; this is a useful guide to what to expect the following night.

Watch the weather reports, and don't get caught surprised by a sudden winter ice storm. Make plans in advance so that you can protect your bonsai quickly. After a few years, you will become expert on winter care; there is no stronger learning experience than losing a valued bonsai. Ask around among other bonsai enthusiasts in your area. If possible, visit their homes, and look at what successful growers do for their trees. Above all, do not wait for the first storm to come to make winter care arrangements. Plan ahead and this season will be just one more enjoyable bonsai experience.

10

BONSAI DISPLAY

WITH ALL DISPLAY, THE PRIMARY CONSIDERA- tion is to place the middle of the trunk at eye level. Halfway up the trunk in the front of the tree should be an imaginary dot—indelible in your mind at all times while training and styling your tree. This point is always positioned at eye level. Even bonsai show judges are trained to position themselves at this level for judging purposes even when the display table is far too low.

Bonsai always look best with a plain, neutral back- ground which shows off the artist's intent; it brings out the branch structure and the trunk line. Lighting should be focused on the tree but modest in intensity for the sake of both the tree and the viewer. A harsh spot- light can curl leaves on a maple and distract the viewer's eye towards the foliage rather than the trunk line.

DISPLAY IN THE GARDEN

Nothing welcomes a garden visitor more than a special stand at the entrance (see **10–1**). This stand should be about 42 inches from the ground and have a neutral backdrop for viewing a bonsai. This welcoming tree may be changed often so that the season can be well represented to your guests.

The bulk of the bonsai garden usually consists of a "growing shelf" that is situated where the trees get protection from the sun at 2:00 P.M. in the summer (see **10–2**). This can be accomplished by placing the bench on the west side of the lot under a canopy of shade trees or by utilizing a more artificial method such as seasonal

10–1

10—2

shade cloth, lath strips, or lattice. Again, 42 inches high is best for full enjoyment of the display. This height brings the trees into easy reach for watering, weeding, and general maintenance pruning.

A properly elevated bench makes it easy to do routine work on your bonsai with a minimum of bending, reaching, or lifting (see **10—3**).

For growing purposes, it is best to group similar bonsai together. This is not the best display for show purposes, where variety takes precedence. Gather all your smallest bonsai together for ease in watering. Group your sensitive-leaved plants in one shady spot to avoid a disappointing August leaf burn. Let all the hardy conifers enjoy the sunshine together on the warmest part of the bench. By grouping trees together like this, problems can be spotted earlier.

10—3

BONSAI DISPLAY IN THE HOME

The Japanese have maintained a delightful tradition, the *Tokonoma*, a display area just inside the main entrance. There is a recessed area, or display that is rather boxlike, that hides the lighting fixtures above. The display alcove itself is typically lined with fine woven reeds or bamboo matting. A prominent shelf supports a bonsai on its intricate wooden stand. Lower and higher shelves display accompaniment plantings, mud figures, or viewing stones. The back wall is interrupted only by a hanging scroll displayed off to one side so that it does not interfere with the bonsai background. Because most Japanese households entertain their guests while seated on the floor, the display is designed to be appreciated at that eye level. In Western homes, the display level can be adjusted to accommodate the higher eye level due to sitting in chairs.

Japanese plants symbolize wishes. For example, a black pine wishes the guest long life; the bamboo, perseverance; and nandina, prosperity. The display in the *Tokonoma* offers an excellent opportunity for the homeowner to be artistic, creative, and yet traditional. Even the simplest display shelf allows the bonsai artist to bring bonsai into the home. You can rotate trees from the outdoor bench through the home in this manner. It is a satisfying way for you to assess progress on your bonsai and welcome your guests as well.

BONSAI DISPLAY AT A SHOW

Perhaps the most difficult aspect of the bonsai show is getting the benches or tables high enough. One successful way is to place additional wooden shelves or boxes on top of the tables. A tablecloth can then be draped over both the box and the table surface. Additional drapes can be placed at the front edge of the table to hide its legs.

Another method that works quite well is to cut small lengths of pipe to fit over the existing table legs. Measure the length of pipe needed to raise the tables to 42 inches for best display. Most hardware stores can cut galvanized pipe to a uniform length with an electric cutter.

One of the nicest shows I've seen utilized freestanding painted wooden structures that usually are used to display artwork, jewelry, or small sculptures. Each bonsai was displayed at its own ideal height, and the total effect leaned more towards an art gallery appearance instead of the customary horticultural club.

Plain backgrounds are a must. Bonsai displayed in the center of a room are ineffective; not only can the backs of the trees be seen, but the public cannot discern the difference between the back, front, and sides, giving the new viewer a confusing idea of what bonsai is all about.

Form the display so that a natural traffic flow is established from the entrance clear on through to the exit. During the show, minimize the number of exits to help secure the bonsai. Trees should not be allowed to leave for any reason during the exhibit!

The bonsai should be arranged so that there is an interesting variety of colors, shapes, styles, and sizes. Be generous with accompaniment plantings, viewing stones, and multiple stands. Avoid grouping similar trees, such as two cascades, together. Utilize murals, Shoji screens, and scrolls. If possible, create an entryway *Tokonoma*. Soft music adds an extra dimension of pleasure to the whole show. Make brief labels for each tree, and try to provide the public with basic bonsai information, such as local club meetings, other shows, and some bonsai horticultural principles.

Staff your show with people who can answer questions and provide additional sources of literature, supplies, and classes where people can follow up on their newfound interest. Supply chairs or benches for resting and viewing. Visitors should not be rushed through. Allow for photographs, and provide refreshment where feasible.

SHOPPING FOR BONSAI

It is possible to come into contact with some aspect of bonsai in nearly every shopping mall, nursery, and major department store. Unfortunately, most of the time we see small, uncut dwarf junipers that have been hurriedly stuck into a plastic bonsai pot without regard to artistic merit. These so-called bonsai give the public a distorted sense of the essence of growing these special trees.

Bonsai, above all, is half horticulture and half art; special attention must be given to the artistic merit of a potential bonsai before it can satisfy that requirement. It is true that, in time, even these production trees could become legitimate bonsai if given the necessary attention, but beginners are often better off choosing good plant material from a nursery and potting it themselves.

Good bonsai is characterized by the amount of care the artist has put into the arrangement; the pot harmonizes with the plant, and the plant has been styled to the extent that it is recognizably different than the average twig or cutting from the parent plant. Fine bonsai have some actual and perceived age. Purchasing bonsai material that has pencil-sized trunks tends to frustrate the grower; it is years before they will grow sufficiently to be satisfying.

Purchase from a reputable dealer. Avoid county fair sales and inexpensive mail-order houses. I don't recommend buying bonsai from a grocery store or variety five-and-ten-cent store. Be cautious with purchases from nurseries or garden centers. If possible, talk with the person who makes them; this is most often not the nursery owner. A good bonsai nursery is, of course, your best source. Unfortunately, there are few of them around; be prepared to travel a bit.

Ask for recommendations from local clubs and societies, and get several opinions. A good bonsai investment is something you can enjoy for many years to come. Don't rush out and buy the first one you see. Take your time, make your decision based on your own personal preferences and desires, and you can't go wrong. Enjoy!

Bonsai Glossary

Acerifolius Maple-like leaf form

Accompaniment plantings A landscape in nature with plants and trees that would normally grow in the same environment; particular attention paid to compatible scale, color, variety, species

Adpressus Pressing against; hugging plant form

Air layering The process in which roots are developed on a stem or branch which is above the ground

Albus White color

Altus Tall plant form

Angustifolius Narrow leaf form

Apex The culminating extension of the trunk

Aquifolius Spiny leaf form

Arboreus Tree-like plant form

Argenteus Silvery color

Armatus Armed

Aureus Golden color

Australis Of Australia

Azureus Azure, sky-blue color

Baccatus Berried or berry-like

Ball shape *Tama-zukuri*; in the shape of a ball

Bankan Coiled style; a spiralled trunk

Barbatus Barbed or bearded

Bilobate Divided into two lobes, as of a leaf

Bipinnate Doubly pinnate, as of a leaf consisting of a central axis and lateral axes to which leaflets are attached

Bolt The growth of a plant too quickly to flowering at the expense of good overall development

Bonkei A landscape created with sand, gravel, boats, huts, figurines, and lanterns in a large, flat tray-shaped pot with no living plants

Bonseki A landscape created with mini figurines, nonliving foliage, and the appearance of water created with a mirror

Borealis Of the north

Bract Leaf-like appendage at the base of a flower; sometimes brightly colored as in poinsettia

Broadleaf Foliage which is not a needle shape or scale-like

Broom style *Hoki-dachi, Hoki-zukuri, Hokidachi*; a style intended to resemble the shape of a broom; best suited to twiggy deciduous trees

Bulb style *Shitakusa*; perennials

Bunjin, Bunjinji Literati style; free-form style that is unexplainable, personal, knowledgeable; irrespective of rules of style, design, and growth

Buxifolius Leaves like boxwood

Caesius Blue-grey color

Cambium A thin formative layer consisting of xylem and phloem in all woody plants that gives rise to new cells, responsible for secondary growth, and transmits nutrients

Campanulatus Bell- or cup-shaped

Campestris Of the field or plains

Canadensis Of Canada

Canariensis Of the Canary Islands

Candidus Pure white color; shiny

Candle flame shape *Rosoku-zukuri*; in the shape of candle flame; arborvitae, for example

Canus Ashy grey color

Capensis Of the Cape of Good Hope

Capitatus Head-like

Carneus "Flesh"-colored, pinkish-beige

Catkin String of single-sex flowers, without petals, often pendulous; found on trees such as alder, birch, and willow

Cereus Waxy

Chilensis Of Chile

Chinensis Of China

Chlorosis A diseased condition in plants characterized by yellowing; frequently caused by a lack of iron

Chokkan Formal upright style; straight, vertical trunk

Ciliaris Fringed

Citrinus Yellow color

Clustered style *Tsukami-yose*; clustered group with multiple trunks springing from one tree

Coccineus Scarlet color

Coeruleus Dark blue color

Coiled style *Bankan*; a spiralled trunk

Compactus Compact, dense plant shape

Compound leaf A leaf, consisting of two or more leaflets

Concolor One color

Cone Fruit of a conifer consisting of wood scales enclosing naked multiple ovules or seeds

Conifer Cone-bearing plant; may be deciduous

Confertus Crowded, pressed-together plant shape

Cordatus Cordate; heart-shaped

Cornutus Horned

Crassus Thick, fleshy

Croceus Yellow color

Cruentus Bloody color

Culm The hollow-jointed stems of grasses, especially bamboo

Cultivar Cultivated variety

Cultural dwarf Manipulation of growth characteristics, which results in dwarfing

Cutting Any plant fragment cut off for the purpose of rooting a new plant

Damping off Fungus disease usually attacking cuttings or seedlings

Deciduous Referring to plants that drop their leaves or needles at the end of the growing season

Decumbens Lying-down plant shape

Decurrens Running down the stem

Defoliate The early removal of leaves; a common artificial technique in bonsai training

-dendron Tree

Dentate Sharply toothed leaf margins

Depressus Pressed-down plant shape

Desiccate To dry up or cause to dry up

Dieback A progressive plant condition characterized by stem failure, starting from the tips of leaves and branches. Could be disease, insect, or environmental damage

Discolor Two colors, separate colors

Dissected Usually a highly intricate natural cutting of a leaf, as in *Acer palmatum dissectum*, also called lace leaf

Diversi Varying

Double-trunk style *Sokan*; two trunks attached to each other in the bottom quarter of the tree; the larger of the two trunks is displayed slightly forward of the smaller

Driftwood style *Sarimiki, Sharimiki*; large areas of deadwood; desert, beach or high-altitude appearance

Drip line A circle directly under a tree that corresponds to where water drips on the ground, usually just inside the tips of the lower branches

Earth layering Creating roots on a stem or branch by burying a section in the ground

Edulis Edible

Elegans Elegant; slender, willowy plant shape

Elongated style *Goza-kake*; exaggerated first branch balanced by a special wide pot; sometimes found over water

Epiphyte A plant that grows on another for support; not to be confused with parasite

Eye An undeveloped growth bud

Exposed-root style *Ne-agari*; air space under roots that suggests erosion

Fallen-cone style *Yama-yori*, hundred-tree style; hundreds of sprouts from one vicinity

Fastigiatus Branches erect and close together

Five-tree style *Gohon-yose*; a group planting of five trees

Floridus Free-flowering

Formal Regular, rigid, and geometric, as in formal upright design

Formal cascade style *Kengai*; first branch extends below the bottom edge of the pot; pot sits on a stand

Formal upright style *Chokkan*; straight, vertical trunk

Fruticosus Shrubby

Fukunigashi Windswept style, the slant of the tree indicates wind direction, as though the tree were growing on a mountain or near a beach; slant may be extreme or gentle

Fulgens Shiny

Genetic dwarf Small size and other characteristics are genetically determined

Genus A classification of related plants; the first word in a botanical name

Glaucus Covered with grey bloom

Gohon-yose Five-tree style; a group planting of five trees

Goza-kake Elongated style, exaggerated first branch balanced by a special wide pot; sometimes found over water

Gracilis Slender, thin, small plant shape

Grandis Large, showy plant shape

Grass plantings *Kusamomo*, including bamboo

Group planting style *Yose-uye*, *Yose-ue*; more than nine trees or any larger prime number; a grove or group planting rather than a forest

Han-kengai Semi-cascade style; foliage of first branch must extend below the top edge of the pot. *Dai-kengai*: vertical cascade; *Gaito-kengai*: mountain-top cascade; *Taki-kengai*: waterfall cascade; *Ito-kengai*: string cascade; *Takan-kengai*: two-trunk cascade

Harden off The progressive adaptation of a tender plant to the full brunt of harsh outdoor conditions

Hardy A plant that can resist cold; usually expressed as hardy to −15°F (−26°C), for example

Heavy soil A term which is commonly used to describe clay or compacted soils

Herbaceous Nonwoody

Hokidachi, Hoki-dachi, Hoki-zukuri Broom style; a style intended to resemble the shape of a broom; best suited to twiggy deciduous trees

Hollow-trunk style *Sabakan*; as the heartwood rots away in some species, a hollowed-out trunk is formed; live oak, coast redwood

Honeydew Any secretion caused by sucking insects on a plant, usually attracting ants

Hortensis Of gardens

Humisusis Sprawling-on-the-ground plant form

Humilis Low small, humble plant form

Humus The late stages of rotting organic material

Hundred-tree style *Yama-yori*, fallen-cone style; hundreds of sprouts from one vicinity

Hybrid Plant created by crossing two species of the same genus or two varieties of the same species

Informal upright style *Moyogi*, *Ta-chiki*; curving upright trunk; apex is over rootage

Internode A section of a stem between two successive nodes

Insularis Of the island

-ifer, -iferus Bearing or having

Ikadabuki Raft style; single tree on its side with branches trained upright as though they were all individual trees; visually creates a forest

Ilicifolius Holly-like leaves

Impressus Impressed upon

Incanus Grey color

Ishizuke, Ishitsuke, Ishitzuki Rock-garden style; characterized by entire tree planted on a rock, but no soil in the pot; possibly water, sand, or bare glaze in the bottom of the pot

Jin The dead apex of a tree, usually found only on hardwood trees; literally means "God" and is symbolic of the Supreme Being's influence on nature

Kabudachi Sprout style, *Miyama-kirishima*; characterized by sprouts which have developed on an old stump, a section of fallen tree, or part of a rotten log; sprouts arranged like flowers to contrast new life with old tree

Kasa-zukuri Umbrella shape; in the shape of an umbrella

Kengai Formal cascade style; first branch extends below the bottom edge of the pot; pot sits on a stand

Knobby-trunk style *Kobukan*; healed-over sprouts; often caused by stress in nature

Kusamomo Grass plantings, including bamboo

Kyuhon-hose Nine-trunk style; a group planting of nine trees

Laciniatus Fringed or with torn edges

Laevigatus Smooth

Lanceolate Lance-shaped

Lateral Positioned at the side; an extension of a branch or a shoot

Lath Usually refers to a series of wooden boards erected above plants to provide artificial shade

Laurifolius Laurel-like leaves

Leaching The removal of substances from the soil by excess watering

Leader The dominant upward single central growth of a plant

Leaf mould Partially decomposed leaves; not yet humus

Leaf scar The slight indentation left on a twig that remains after a leaf stalk is removed

Leaflet Division of a leaf, either palmate (fan-shaped) or pinnate (feather-shaped)

Legume Pod or seed vessel of the pea family, splitting lengthwise to release seeds

Light soil Commonly referred to as sandy soil; more precisely, well-aerated soil

Linear Long and narrow, with parallel sides

Literati style see *Bunjin*, *Bunjinji*

Littoralis Of the seashore

Lobatus Lobed; projection or division of a leaf or petal

Luteus Reddish yellow color

Maculatus Spotted

Matsu-zukuri Pine-tree shape; in the shape of a pine tree; may also be used for deciduous trees

Meristem A formative plant tissue usually made up of small cells capable of dividing indefinitely and giving rise to similar cells or to cells that differentiate to produce the definitive tissues and organs

Miyama-kirishima Sprout style, *Kabudachi*; characterized by sprouts which have developed on an old stump, a section of fallen tree, or part of a rotten log; sprouts arranged like flowers to contrast new life with old tree

Mollis Soft, soft hairy

Montanus Of the mountains

Moyogi *Tachiki*, informal upright style; curving upright trunk; apex is over rootage

Mucronatus Pointed; terminating in a point

Mulch A loose, organic covering over soil or to describe the process of applying such a layer

Nanahon-yose Seven-trunk style; a group planting of seven trees

Nanus Dwarf

Natural dwarf A plant which is dwarfed by the forces of nature

Natural style *Yomayori*, *Yomayose*; natural, informal grouping

Ne-agari Exposed-root style; air space under roots that suggests erosion

Nejikan Twisted style; trunk spirals upward with growth

Netsunari Root-connected style; trees sprout from long surface roots of more than one rootstock; occurs naturally in willow, quince, Chinese raintree, vine maple, wild cherry

Nine-trunk style *Kyuhon-yose*; a group planting of nine trees

Nutans Nodding, swaying

Node Joints occurring at intervals along the stem of a plant from which a leaf or bud develops

Obtusus Blunt or flattened

Octopus style *Tako-zukuri*, *Takozukuri*; overexaggeration of informal upright style with many zigs and zags, including rootage and branches

Officinalis Medicinal

-oides Like or resembling

Opposite Leaf arrangements in pairs along an axis, one opposite the other

Organic matter Any material that was alive at some point; for example, peat, bark, and manure

Ovate Egg-shaped, with the larger part towards the base

Palmate With leaflets or lobes radiating like outstretched fingers from a central point

Parasite A plant growing on another and using up nutrients from the host plant

Parvifolius Small leaves

Patens Open spreading

Peeled-bark style *Sharikan*; damage to bark as the result of lightning or other trauma; not driftwood

P'en Tsai The Chinese word for bonsai, an art form which predates the Japanese art

Perennial A nonwoody plant that lives for three years or more

Perlite Natural minerals expanded by heat to form a light, porous granule for use in propagating or lightening soils

Petiole Leaf stalk

Phloem A complex tissue in the vascular system of higher plants consisting mainly of sieve tubes and elongated cells. Its fibres function in translocation, support, and storage

Pinching back Nipping of tips of branches by hand

Pine-tree shape *Matsu-zukuri*; in the shape of a pine tree; may also be used for deciduous trees

Pinnate, pinnatus A compound leaf with leaflets, usually paired on either side of the stalk like a feather

Plenus Double, full

Plumosus Feathery

Populifolius Poplar-like leaves

Praecox Precocious

Procumbens Trailing plant shape

Prostratus Prostrate plant shape

Pumilus Dwarfish, small plant shape

Pungens Piercing

Purpureus Purple color

Radicans Rooting, especially along the stem

Raft style *Ikadabuki*; single tree on its side with branches trained upright as though they were all individual trees; visually creates a forest

Repens, reptans Creeping plant shape

Reticulatus Net-veined

Retusus Notched at blunt apex

Rhizome Modified stem which develops horizontally underground

Riparius Of river banks

Rivalis, rivularis Of brooks

Rock-garden style see *Ishizuke, Ishitsuke, Ishitzuki*

Root-over-rock style *Sekijoju*; tree roots placed over and trained to grow on one or more rocks; trees may be planted immediately in this manner or developed gradually

Root-connected style *Netsunari*; trees sprout from long surface roots of more than one rootstock; occurs naturally in willow, quince, Chinese raintree, vine maple, wild cherry

Rootstock Part of a grafted plant which supplies the roots; same as understock

Roso-zukuri Candle flame shape; in the shape of a candle flame; arborvitae

Rubens, ruber Red, ruddy color

Rufus Ruddy color

Rugosus Wrinkled, rough

Sabakan Hollow-trunk style; as the heartwood rots away, in some species a hollowed-out trunk is formed; live oak, coast redwood

Sabamiki, Shaba-miki A bonsai design element that copies natural hollowing and decay of the trunks of hardwood trees; may include the characteristic twisting of the juniper species, the hollowing-out of oak, or the vertical stripping of the trunk as branches are stripped off as in timberline trees

Saccharatus Sweet, sugary

Sagittalis Arrow-like

Saikei A "living landscape" of trees planted on rocks, with streams, cliffs, valleys, and caves; contained in a large, flat tray-shaped pot

Saikei forest planting Characterized by particular emphasis placed upon a detail, such as trunks, foliage, number of trees, or landscape feature

Saikei one tree Placement of one tree next to other elements, such as rock(s), mountain, stream, bush, ridge, mountaintop, cave, natural bridge, etc.

Saikei two tree Characterized by harmony, balance, interest, and stability of trees and landscape features; similarities in shape, front and back, direction, profile, spacing, position, interval. Also, three-tree, five-tree, group planting

Salicifolius Willow-like leaves

Sambon-yose Three-tree style; relationship between height, width, branches, and depth is symbolic of sun, moon, and earth; or heaven, earth, and man; or father, mother, and child

Saramiki *Sharimiki*, driftwood style; large areas of deadwood; desert, beach or high-altitude appearance

Saxatilis Inhabiting rocks

Scabrus Rough feeling

Scandens Climbing plant shape

Scoparius Broom-like

Sekijoju Root over rock; tree roots placed over and trained to grow on one or more rocks; trees may be planted immediately in this manner or developed gradually

Semi-cascade style *Han-kengai*; foliage of first branch must extend below top edge of the pot

Seven-trunk style *Nanahon-yose*; a group planting of seven trees

Shakan Slanting style; straight or curved trunk; slant is not forward or backwards; apex is not over roots. *Sho-shakan*: minimum slant; *Chu-shakan*: medium slant; *Dai-shakan*: maximum slant

Shari A dead branch or fragment of a dead branch found on hardwood species; found as a horizontal design motif

Sharikan Peeled-bark style; damage to bark as the result of lightning or other trauma; not driftwood

Sharimiki Saramiki, driftwood style; large areas of deadwood; desert, beach, or high-altitude appearance

Shidare-zukuri Weeping style; fashioned after the weeping willow tree

Shitakusa Bulb style; perennials

Slanting style *Shakan*; straight or curved trunk; slant is not forward or backwards; apex is not over roots

Soju, So-ju Two-tree style; relationship between tree heights, widths, lowest branches creates illusion of tree in the distance

Sokan Double-trunk style; two trunks, preferably in the bottom quarter of the tree and one in front of the other

Species The word in a botanical name following the genus

Sphagnum Bog mosses that are collected as a source of organic soil amendment

Split-trunk style *Sabamiki*; the trunk of the tree has split due to trauma; one side may be dead

Spore A simple cell for reproduction in some primitive plants, such as ferns, algae, and moss

Sport Genetic mutation

Sprout style *Miyama-kirishima, Kabudachi*; characterized by sprouts which have developed on an old stump, a section of fallen tree, or part of a rotten log; sprouts arranged like flowers to contrast new life with old tree

Spur Specialized short branch on a fruit tree which produces the blossom

Stomata Microscopically small openings in the epidermis of the green parts of a tree or other plant through which gases pass out of and into the plant from the air

Stratification The plant and seed requirement for certain minimum cold periods before successful seed germination or flowering

Stress Any plant condition that threatens its health, such as too much water or too little water

Subspecies The word in a botanical name following the species, expressed in lower-case letters

Sucker Plant growth on a grafted plant that originates on the rootstock; also improper term for watersprout on fruit trees

Suiseki A viewing rock or stone placed on a custom-made, carved, and footed wooden stand. The stone is viewed from a specific perspective

Symbiotic Describes relationship between two plants in which mutual benefit is derived

Systemic Any chemical product which is transported into the sap of the plant by absorption; the pest at which it is directed is poisoned as it eats its plant "host."

Tachiki *Moyogi*, informal upright style; curving upright trunk; apex is over rootage

Takozukuri, Tako-zukuri Octopus style; overexaggeration of informal upright style with many zigs and zags, including roots and branches

Tama-zukuri Ball-shaped

Tap root A large, central root that grows fast and straight down for the purpose of reaching a deep water table

Tender Not hardy; usually genetic, but could be used to refer to plants that need to be hardened off

Thinning out Pruning to achieve a more open structure in the plant

Three-tree style *Sambon-yose*; relationship between height, width, branches, and depth is symbolic of sun, moon, and earth; or heaven, earth, and man; or father, mother, and child

Top dress To add material, such as mulch or fertilizer, to the surface of the soil

Topiary The art of shaping bushes and trees into unnatural shapes, such as animals or mazes

Tosho Triple-trunk style; similar to three-trunk style except that all three trunks come from the same tree

Truss A terminal cluster of flowers, such as in the rhododendron species

Tsukami-yose Clustered style; a group style with multiple trunks springing from one tree

Twisted style *Nejikan*; trunk spirals upwards with growth

Two-tree style *Soju, So-ju*; relationship between tree heights, widths, lowest branches creates illusion of tree in the distance

Umbrella shape *Kasa-zukuri*; in the shape of an umbrella

Underplanting Planting a low plant under a larger one, such as a ground cover under a tall shrub

Variety Any capitalized name with quotation marks around it when included in a botanical name, such as *Juniperus chinensis sargentii* "Shimpaku"

Vermiculite Heat-puffed mica, a soil-lightening amendment

Watersprout Unchecked, sudden upward growth as the result of severe pruning

Weeping style *Shidare-zukuri*; fashioned after the weeping willow tree

Wettable powder A pesticide that can be applied by first mixing with water

Whorl Three or more leaves, branches, or stems growing out from one location on a branch; best known as a problem in pine bonsai design

Windswept style *Fukunigashi*; the slant of the tree indicates wind direction, as though the tree were growing on a mountain or near a beach; slant may be extreme or gentle

Yama-yori Fallen-cone style, hundred-tree style; hundreds of sprouts from one vicinity

Yomayori, Yomayose Natural style; natural, informal grouping

Yose-ue, Yose-uye Group planting style; more than nine trees or any larger prime number; a grove or group planting rather than a forest

Suggested Reading List

Adams, Peter D. *Successful Bonsai Gardening*; London: Ward Lock, 1978.

——— *The Art of Bonsai*; London: Ward Lock, 1981.

——— *Bonsai Design: Japanese Maples*; New York: Sterling Publishing, 1988.

Ainsworth, John. *The Art of Indoor Bonsai*; London: Ward Lock, 1988.

Behme, Robert Lee. *Bonsai, Saikei and Bonkei: Japanese Dwarf Trees and Tray Landscapes*; New York: W. Morrow, 1969.

Bollman, Willi E. *Kamuti: A New Way in Bonsai*; London: Faber, 1974.

Brooklyn Botanic Gardens. *Handbook on Dwarfed Potted Trees: The Bonsai of Japan*; Brooklyn, NY: 1974.

——— *Handbook on Bonsai: Special Techniques*; Brooklyn, NY: 1977.

Chan, Peter. *Bonsai Masterclass*; New York: Sterling Publishing, 1988.

——— *Create Your Own Bonsai with Everyday Garden Plants*; Vancouver, B.C.: Cavendish Books, Inc., 1989.

Chidamian, Claude. *Bonsai: Miniature Trees*; Princeton, NJ: Van Nostrand, 1955.

Clark, Randy T. *Outstanding American Bonsai*; Portland, OR: Timber Press, 1989.

Derderian, C. T. *Bonsai for Indoors*; Brooklyn, NY: Brooklyn Botanic Gardens, 1976.

Engel, David H. *Creating a Chinese Garden*; London: Croom Helm, 1986.

Giorgi, Gianfranco. *Guide to Bonsai*; New York: Simon and Schuster, 1990.

Gustafson, Herb L. *Miniature Living Bonsai Landscapes: The Art of Saikei*; New York: Sterling Publishing Co., 1994.

Hall, George Frederick. *Bonsai for Americans: A Practical Guide to the Creation and Care of Miniature Potted Trees*; Garden City, NY: Doubleday, 1964.

Hirota, Jozan. *Bonkei: Tray Landscapes*; Tokyo: Kodansha International, 1970.

Ishimoto, Tatsuo. *The Art of Growing Miniature Plants and Landscapes: Japanese Bonsai and Bonkei Adapted to American Conditions*; New York: Crown Publishing, 1956.

Katayama, Teiichi. *The Mini-Bonsai Hobby*; Tokyo: Japan Publications: Distributed by Japan Publications Trading Co., 1974.

Kawamoto, Toshio. *Saikei: Living Landscapes in Miniature*; Tokyo: Kodansha International, 1967.

Kawasumi, Masakuni. *Bonsai with American Trees*; Tokyo: Kodansha International, 1975.

Koide, Nobukichi, Saburo Kato, and Fusza Takeyama. *The Masters' Book of Bonsai*; Tokyo: Kodansha International, 1967.

Larkin, H. J. *Bonsai for Beginners: The Art of Growing Miniature Trees*; New York: Arco Publishing Co., 1969.

Lesniewicz, Paul. *Bonsai: The Complete Guide to Art and Technique*; Dorset, England: Blandford Press; Distributed in US by Sterling Publishing Co., 1984.

——— *Indoor Bonsai*; Dorset, England: Blandford Press; Distributed in US by Sterling Publishing Co., 1985.

——— *The World of Bonsai*; New York: Sterling Publishing Co., 1990.

Lifang, Chen. *The Garden Art of China*; Portland, OR: Timber Press, 1986.

Murata, Kenji. *Practical Bonsai for Beginners*; Tokyo: Japan Publications Trading Co., 1964.

Murata, Kyuzo. *Bonsai, Miniature Potted Trees*; Tokyo: Shufunotomo Co., Ltd., 1964.

——— *Introductory Bonsai and the Care and Use of Bonsai Tools*; Tokyo: Japan Publications, 1971.

Naka, John Yoshio. *Bonsai Techniques*; Santa Monica, CA: Dennis-Landman Publishers, 1975.

——— and Others. *Bonsai Techniques for Satsuki*; Tokyo Ota Bonsai Nursery, 1979.

Nakamura, Zeko. *Bonsai Miniatures: Quick and Easy*; Tokyo: Shufunotomo Co., 1973.

Nippon Bonsai Association. *Classic Bonsai of Japan*; Translated by Jon Bestor; New York: Kodansha International/USA, 1989.

Ohashi, Haruzo. *Japanese Courtyard Gardens*; Tokyo: Graphic-Sha Publishing, 1988.

Perl, Philip. *Miniatures and Bonsai*; Alexandria, VA: Time-Life Books, 1979.

Pike, David. *Bonsai, Step by Step to Growing Success*; Ramsbury, England: The Crowood Press, 1989.

Roger, Alan. *Bonsai*; London: The Royal Horticultural Society, 1989.

Samson, Isabelle and Rémy. *The Creative Art of Bonsai*; London: Ward Lock, Ltd., 1986.

Stewart, Christine. *Bonsai*; London: Orbis, 1981.

Stowell, Jerald P. *Bonsai, Indoors and Out: How to Grow Decorative Trees from Hardy and Tender Plants*; Princeton, NJ: Van Nostrand, 1966.

——— *The Beginner's Guide to American Bonsai*; Tokyo and New York: Kodansha International, 1978.

Sunset Books and Magazines. *Bonsai: Culture and Care of Miniature Trees*; Menlo Park, CA: Lane Publishing Co., 1976.

Valavanis, William N. *Bonsai Creation and Design Using Propagation Techniques*; Atlanta, GA: Symmes Systems, 1975.

——— *The Japanese Five-Needled Pine: Nature, Gardens, Bonsai Taxonomy*; Atlanta, GA: Symmes Systems, 1976.

Van Gelderen, D. M., and J. R. P. Van Hoey Smith. *Conifers*; Portland, OR: Timber Press, 1986.

Vertrees, J. D. *Japanese Maples*; Portland, OR: Timber Press, 1987.

Webber, Leonard. *Bonsai for the Home and Garden*; North Ryde, NSW, Australia: Agus and Robertson/Salem House, 1985.

Yashiroda, Kan. *Bonsai, Japanese Miniature Trees: Their Style, Cultivation and Training*; Newton, MA: C. T. Branford Co., 1960.

Yonhua, Ho. *Chinese Penjing, Miniature Trees and Landscapes*; Portland, OR: Timber Press, 1987.

Yoshimura, Yuji. *The Japanese Art of Miniature Trees and Landscapes: Their Creation, Care and Enjoyment*; Rutland, VA: C. E. Tuttle, 1957.

Index